# The Invention of the Modern Hospital

The University of Chicago Press
Chicago and London

MORRIS J. VOGEL

# The Invention of the Modern Hospital BOSTON 1870–1930

The University of Chicago Press,
Chicago 60637
The University of Chicago Press, Ltd.,
London

**Library of Congress Cataloging in Publication Data**

Vogel, Morris J
   The invention of the modern hospital, Boston,
1870-1930.

   Bibliography: p.
   Includes index.
   1. Boston—Hospitals—History—19th century.
2. Boston—Hospitals—History—20th century.
3. Hospitals—United States—History—19th century.
4. Hospitals—United States—History—20th century.
I. Title.
RA982.B7V63        362.1'1'0974461        79-26052
ISBN 0-226-86240-2

Title page illustration: Boston City Hospital
ca. 1865, artist's conception. Courtesy of
Countway Library

MORRIS J. VOGEL is associate professor of
history at Temple University.

For My Mother and Father

# Contents

# Acknowledgments

At most hospitals, old records are regarded less as revealing historical documents than as difficult storage problems. Hospitals tend not to have procedures for keeping track of their outdated materials, let alone for coping with inquiring historians. Because of this, the hospital people upon whom I prevailed—at Beth Israel, Boston City, Children's, Massachusetts General, and Peter Bent Brigham—all had to go out of their ways to respond to my research needs. I am grateful to them, and to the sisters of St. Margaret's, who opened their convent records so that I might find something of a hospital that has long since disappeared.

Richard Wolfe, curator of rare books, introduced me to the rich collections of the Countway Library and was unfailingly helpful. Mark Haller and Linda Auwers, my colleagues at Temple University, read and commented on early drafts of the manuscript, as did Lester King, Barbara Rosenkrantz, and James Cassedy. For several months, Perry Duis entered the catacombs under the Center for Research Libraries with me, sharing conversation and his portable copying machine as we read Boston newspapers. My greatest intellectual debts are to Neil Harris, whose encouragement and questions continued beyond the dissertation that he guided, and to Charles Rosenberg, who has helped me explore an area of historical inquiry that he has done so much to shape.

Parts of chapter 1 appeared, in a different form, as "Patrons, Practitioners, and Patients," in the *American Quarterly* volume *Victorian America* (University of Pennsylvania Press, 1976), copyright 1976 by the Trustees of the University of Pennsylvania. A portion of chapter 2 appeared, in a different form, as "Machine Politics in Medical Care: The City Hospital at the Turn of the Century," in Morris J. Vogel and Charles E. Rosenberg, eds., *The Therapeutic Revolution* (University of Pennsylvania Press, 1979), reprinted by permission of the publisher.

I hope that I have let Ruth know how much I owe her. Her emotional support made the book possible; her intelligent and honest criticism improved it.

# Introduction

The general hospital of the immediate post-Civil War period was larger than its colonial and early-nineteenth-century predecessor, but differed little in other respects. It was a primitive institution treating the same socially marginal constituency that American hospitals had always served. Its patients were overwhelmingly the poor and those without roots in the community; dependence, as much as disease, distinguished them from the public at large. The patient class furnished little of the money that built and operated these institutions. Government, too, was only minimally involved in their funding. The majority were voluntary organizations, supported by the philanthropy of the wealthy.

Most Americans who sought the care of a doctor did not consider hospitalization. Physicians kept track of their seriously ill patients with frequent home visits, and surgeons might perform even the most difficult operations on kitchen tables or ironing boards stretched between tables. City dwellers too poor to afford medical fees might secure, in their own homes, the gratuitous services of a dispensary physician or surgeon. Only a minority of physicians practiced in hospitals in the 1870s; even they devoted only a minority of their time to such work. The hospital was not central to the practice of medicine. Good treatment was home treatment; sickness was endured, for the most part, in its traditional setting in the home and among family.

When Boston's first general hospital opened in 1821, there were only two other such institutions in the United States. Although a survey for the United States Bureau of Education identified 120 hospitals in 1873,[1] it was the next half century that saw the hospital come of age and assume the role and significance it has today. By the 1920s there were over six thousand hospitals in the country,[2] and the hospital had emerged as the center of advanced medical practice. Although it was not—and is not—a classless institution, it had evolved into a primary instrument in the health care of all social classes, and depended for financial support on a wider base of the population. Originally an institution whose use stigmatized its patients, the hospital had become an emblem of its community.

In "An Outline of the Development of the Hospital," Henry E. Sigerist traced three stages in hospital evolution. He noted that institutional care of the sick originated in medieval Europe in the incidental medical facilities provided inmates by poorhouses, guesthouses, and jails. In the second stage,

1

dating from the thirteenth century, hospitals emerged as specifically medical institutions but limited their care to the indigent and dependent sick. The development of the modern hospital began in the second half of the nineteenth century. Although considerably telescoped, these three stages were duplicated in the United States. Sigerist stressed that the hospital, at any given time, was the product of the interplay of social and medical forces. But though he found social forces, primarily urbanization, the most significant in stages one and two, Sigerist attributed the modern hospital, providing health care for all classes, to "the progress of medicine and surgery."[3]

But the imperative of science and technology cannot, by itself, explain the increasing recourse to an institution historically associated with the dependent and, in the case of the plague-ridden or insane, the dangerous. Such an explanation neglects different patterns of hospital use in areas with the same available technologies. Urban and rural Americans, for example, even when they live equidistant from hospitals, have been found to enter them at different rates.[4] Medical advance opened alternative possibilities, but it did not mandate specific developments.

The nineteenth-century revolution in medical knowledge cannot be neglected. In certain ways, its effect was obvious and direct. Antisepsis and asepsis, for example, freed the hospital from its long history as a seedbed of infection. Without this measure of safety, hospital use would not have spread beyond the socially marginal. The expanding scientific content of medicine also contributed to the growth of diagnostic and therapeutic skills with obvious direct consequences for the institution, but with indirect effects as well. These new skills—and more importantly the scientific attitudes on which they depended—were closely identified with hospital physicians. The medical revolution reinforced the professional aspirations of this limited group of practitioners. This elite was also generally involved in teaching, in consultation-oriented practices and, by the end of the century, in medical specialties. These physicians, themselves in many ways the product of the modernization of medicine, reshaped the hospital to fit their needs.

But the modern hospital, insofar as it can be characterized by care for patients of all social classes, appeared in advance of any medical imperative. Hospital use spread beyond the marginal before the hospital became the source of the best care and rendered traditional sites of care obsolete. Patients decided to enter hospitals for a variety of nonmedical reasons.

One such reason was the changing social ecology of urban life. The spread of new living patterns deprived many city dwellers, more comfortably settled than the hospital patients of an earlier day, of familial care in illness. Even the affluent were reduced to dependence on institutions. E. H. L. Corwin and others have noted the close correlation between hospital use and urbanization in the twentieth century.[5]

Well-to-do urban dwellers were not, however, generally the first of their class to rely on nonfamilial institutions for treatment. Patients from the rural and small town hinterland had come to large cities such as Boston for medical treatment at least since the early nineteenth century. As physicians sought to centralize their practices in the closing decades of the century, such patients began to enter newly established, often medically primitive private hospitals. At such facilities charity was unavailable, and patients paid for board and attendance. Bostonians, responding both to their own social situations and to the needs of their physicians, joined patients from outside the city in entering these private facilities for care.

These more respectable patients not only altered the public perception of the institution in general, but the process of change worked both ways. The sick were also more likely to consider hospitalization as it became less identified with pauperism and dependency. The hospital's image was influenced by the kind of patient who used the institution; that image was influential in determining who chose hospitalization.

As important as the class of patient or the level of medical care within the institution was the attitude toward patients. In the nineteenth century, that attitude embodied the sentiments and outlook of the nonmedical elites who founded and controlled voluntary hospitals. Even in helping the dependent, the fortunate remained unconvinced of the worthiness of their charges. Intended as charities for the poor and dependent, hospitals generally were moralistic and authoritarian even as they were benevolent and humanitarian. Objects of paternalism, patients could easily feel patronized and degraded.

As variables, institutional attitude, patient class, and level of medical care all influenced each other, of course, as they shaped the perception of the hospital. Yet these variables nonetheless existed independently of one another. Municipal and ethnic hospitals, caring for immigrants and those forced to rely on the city government for assistance, provide a case in point. Because of their origin and purpose, such hospitals remained closely identified with the traditional hospital patient. But ethnic and religious affiliation and municipal democracy made their patients feel less the passive recipients of the benefactions of others and more the claimants to what was theirs by right. Such institutions were responsive to the self-image of their patients. Their patients were no less likely to fear sickness as a medical crisis beyond their own control. They were, however, less apt than patients in hospitals organized as charities by the upper classes to feel themselves in a hostile environment controlled by lay groups they perceived as unfriendly and judgmental.

Gradually, concern with the patient as a moral and social being diminished, as effective control of the general hospital passed from lay groups to medical men because of the financial inability of the traditional donor class to maintain the institution and the mounting assertiveness of physicians that accompanied medical professionalization. This shift in control mirrored—and was facilitated by—the emergence of "scientific" attitudes toward values and society. Together these institutional and attitudinal shifts fostered the emergence of the hospital more as a purely medical institution and less as an instrument of social policy or social control. The patient became a clinical entity.[6]

Initially, this was a liberating change. Insofar as the hospital had earlier been aimed solely at the socially marginal, it had been repressive. But it was clear to some hospital pioneers in the early twentieth century, as it is in retrospect, that social consideration could be humane and that a narrowly medical pathology was not necessarily an advance. Ultimately, medical expertise came to be perceived as being just as condescending and controlling as the social elitism it had replaced.[7] But this was not the case when the hospital was originally redefined as a medical institution. The affluent became more likely to enter the institution as it shed its concern for social manipulation. This change in the patient class, in turn, made the hospital more a medical and less a social tool. When the more comfortably settled came to rely on the hospital, the medical profession had to rework its economic relations to the institution.

Social and medical attitudes and practices reshaped the hospital; the hospital in turn influenced attitudes and practices without its walls as well as within. The emergence of the modern hospital reflected a change in the kind of care the middle and upper class family offered its members. Removing birth, death, and often pain itself from the home led to changes in their significance; basic elements of the human experience came to be redefined as medical events.

No reductionist argument can satisfactorally explain the transformation of the hospital. The march of scientific progress, once fashionable as an explanation for changes in medical practice and organization, is insufficient. So too are currently advanced theories that favor the market model, or that identify either professional dominance, social reform, or social control as motivating forces; nor does the transformation follow a single unifying timetable. Focusing on Boston from 1870 to 1930, this book isolates a period and examines the complex of interrelated decisions and forces—cultural, economic, and political, as well as social and scientific—that contributed to the evolution of the hospital.

Much of the analysis applies to Boston's general hospital experience as a whole. Portions apply only to specific types of general hospitals—private, voluntary, ethnic, or governmental. A central theme, however, emerges: widespread acceptance of the propriety of going, when ill, among strangers for treatment.

The evolution of the hospital should not be understood as yet another milestone on the "march of medical progress." Institutional changes were neither necessarily progressive nor inevitably mandated by the growth of science and the bettering of medical practice. The hospital is no more the perfect form of medical organization and treatment today than it was the ideal response to the poor and socially marginal in 1870.

# 1. The Traditional Institution
## Charity and Medical Care
## in the 1870s

On January 7, 1870, Thomas Ryan entered the Massachusetts General Hospital as a patient. Machinery in the Lawrence textile mill where he worked as a mechanic had mangled his hand sixteen days before. A Lawrence physician had treated Ryan and saved his hand, but feared that the circumstances in which he lived, housed in uncomfortable quarters and lacking food, impaired his recovery. Recommending Ryan as "a very good man," his physician asked that he be admitted to Massachusetts General as a charity patient. There he might receive the "pure air, good food, tonics, etc.," that would restore his health. Ryan arrived at the hospital weakened by hemorrhage and with his hand in "a sloughly unhealthy condition." His treatment consisted of dressings for his wound and an invigorating diet; the record notes that he was "to have steak, etc." Under this regimen, Ryan rallied, was discharged as "well" on January 20, and was presumably able to return to the mills.[1]

Thomas Ryan benefited from no medical treatment that might not have been performed outside the institution. Ryan's poverty rather than a narrowly defined medical crisis, social rather than medical necessity, called for his hospitalization. Ryan's Irish birth and industrial accident made him the archetypical Boston hospital patient of 1870.

Hospital records are unclear as to who treated Ryan. It may have been Algernon Coolidge or Samuel Cabot, both of whom were among the four visiting surgeons on duty in the ten-month period covered by the volume of patient records in which Ryan was recorded. Coolidge and Cabot were as typical of the hospital's practitioners as Ryan was of its patients. Both were members of old Boston families and related by ties of marriage to the hospital's cofounder and first visiting physician, James Jackson.[2] Had Ryan entered a medical ward, he would have been attended by James Jackson Putnam, grandson of the founder and house pupil on the medical wards in January 1870.[3] Whoever treated Ryan at Massachusetts General was a member of Boston's medical elite, a tightly knit group often united by ties of family. These practitioners served the hospital without charge and their hospital patients without fee. They served in order to expand their medical knowledge and to make their medical opinions more attractive to private, nonhospital, paying patients. Hospitals furnished the clinics upon which the best medical practice of the nineteenth century was based.

Thomas Ryan's physicians may also have been descendants of Patrick Tracy Jackson and Francis Cabot Lowell, cofounders with Nathan Appleton of the Boston Manufacturing Company and brother and brother-in-law, respectively, of Dr. James Jackson. Boston's medical elite was related to its social elite; donors shared family ties with doctors. The Bostonians who supported Massachusetts General belonged to a class to whom ties of family and a sense of family responsibility held extraordinary significance. By their contributions, they underwrote the work of their medical relations. And the charitable and intellectual activity of the latter served to legitimate the status of the larger Boston elite of which they were a part.

The case of Thomas Ryan illustrates yet another facet of the hospital experience of 1870. Like most people admitted to the Massachusetts General, Ryan was a charity patient and occupied what was termed a free bed.[4] Some patients were specifically nominated for free beds by hospital contributors; others were routinely authorized by the trustees. In either case, patient care was supported by the voluntary contributions of Boston's upper class. Because donors did not expect that they or members of their families would ever enter the general hospital as patients, donations were, in a sense, selfless—made in the tradition of Protestant stewardship. But hospitals did provide indirect benefits to their contributors. In 1871, several Appletons, a Lawrence, and a Lowell subscribed to the hospital's free bed fund.[5] All were members of the Boston Associates, investors in the textile mills of Waltham, Lowell, and Lawrence where the patient Ryan was injured. The Ryan case demonstrates how these beneficiaries of industrialism used the hospital to ease distress among the victims of the industrial process and promote the process as well.

Boston in 1870 was a city of one-quarter million people and the hub of a metropolitan area of over six hundred thousand. The city exercised economic hegemony over the New England region and was a nationally important center of commerce, industry, and finance. The China trade, source of some of its great fortunes, had languished, but the city countinued to profit from its interior and coasting trade and from its mercantile connections with India, Europe, and Latin America. By the Civil War, foreign trade had been eclipsed by domestic industry. Boston's ownership of the textile mills of the Merrimac Valley and northern New England was the most obvious manifestation of this shift, but within the city itself, industries such as clothing, footwear, foundries, and sugar refineries employed great numbers of workers. Investment banking competed with manufacturing as a source of economic well-being.[6]

Boston provided much of the capital that financed the great railroads of the American interior—the Union Pacific and the Santa Fè, for example—and railroads had an immediate and visible impact on the city as well. Their operations employed eight-hundred city residents. Railyards and terminals defined the northern and southern limits of the central business district, shaping the physical appearance of the city. The port, second only to that of New York, spread along the congested waterfront at the eastern edge of the business district and spilled into South and East Boston and Charlestown. The docks employed hundreds of stevedores and longshoremen; over three thousand teamsters and expressmen bound the wharves and rail terminals to the central business district. The central district itself lay to the east of the Common in 1870. An area of warehouses and workshops as well as markets and financial institutions, it had grown rapidly during the mid-nineteenth century to displace previously residential areas. The very process of urban growth furnished work for the city's unskilled laborers, more than thirteen thousand of whom were counted by the 1870 census.[7]

The central business district shared the original Boston peninsula with several sharply differentiated residential districts. In 1870, the warehouses and workshops of the business district—the old South End—were interspersed with tenements. On the northern edge of the peninsula were the North and the West End. The former, a once fashionable area, housed many of the laborers who performed the unsteady jobs of the commercial district. Both the North and the old South End were heavily Irish. The West End, which would become, in part, an immigrant tenement neighborhood in the 1880s, was largely working class and native born in 1870. South Boston, not on the original peninsula, was an industrial was well as port area and the site of the third major residential concentration of foreign born Bostonians.[8]

Boston spread beyond its original peninsula in the nineteenth century by filling in the bays and tidal flats surrounding the city, and by annexing suburban towns. Expansion led to an increasing differentiation of land use. As the growth of the business district changed the nature of established neighborhoods, new residential areas were developed for the comfortable classes. One such area was the new South End, which rose at mid-century in what had been the south cove. This early upper-middle-class suburban retreat beyond the peninsula enjoyed only temporary respectability. By the '70s and '80s it was being abandoned and on its way to becoming, along with part of the West End, a vast lodging house district. More durable as a home for proper Boston was Beacon Hill. Its elegant homes dated from the late eighteenth century. Together with the adjacent Back Bay, filled and peopled in the second half of the nineteenth century, this area was the city's most exclusive residential neighborhood. Here lived the prosperous Bostonians who did not migrate to the new fashionable suburbs. The Brahmin class, a closed elite by 1870, was heavily represented in these two neighborhoods. Here, too, in the attics of fine mansions, lived a sizable proportion of the city's more than fourteen thousand, predominantly Irish, domestics.[9]

The occupational structure and neighborhood geography of the city was related to its patterns of health, debility, and disease. Bostonians suffered the kinds of accidents that afflicted the inhabitants of other late-nineteenth-century commercial and industrial cities. Much of the physical labor of the city was inherently unsafe. The Massachusetts Bureau of Statistics of Labor noted the "large number of casualties" on the docks. Longshoremen fell off platforms or into ships' holds, teamsters were crushed by their loads, steam and street railroad workers were jammed between cars or run over by them. Laborers—constructing buildings, laying streets, or burying pipes—fell from scaffolds or were buried in crumbling excavations. The exposed belts, shafts, and gears of machinery, in the factories and mills of the city and the industrial suburbs, claimed their victims.[10]

Many of the fevers, fluxes, and disorders of the nineteenth century do not translate easily into modern diagnoses. What is clear about the pattern of sickness, however, is the widespread nature of infectious disease. The census reported consumption as the leading cause of death in Massachusetts in 1870, accounting for twenty percent of the statewide mortality of nearly twenty-six thousand. Pneumonia and cholera infantum followed, each with 6.5 percent. The spread of these diseases was abetted by congestion and primitive sanitation. The poor and immigrant neighborhoods of Boston suffered disproportionately, but no neighborhood escaped. Contemporaries were not unaware of the relation between poverty and disease. The State Labor Bureau pointed to the homes of unskilled laborers, and even of "the better orders of workingmen," as the cause of "disease of various types." Commenting on the prevalence of pneumonia during one "unusually severe" winter, the chairman of Boston's Board of Health noted: "The present mortality is confined almost entirely to the laboring people, and the well-to-do part of the community escape almost altogether. The truckmen and street laborers are the chief sufferers."[11]

The nature of the hospital as an institution for the poor in the nineteenth century no doubt reflected, in part, the epidemiology of certain diseases and accidents. But the incidence of sickness and injury is insufficient as an explanation of hospital use. Tuberculosis, for example, a very much class-oriented disease and the greatest killer in the late-nineteenth-century city, generally disqualified its victims from hospital admission when it was diagnosed as a lung disease.[12] Further, a significant proportion of ill health and of hospitalizations resulted from conditions that were much less the respectors of class than cholera infantum and tuberculosis. There is no indication that the diseases of childhood, as opposed to those of infancy, were more likely to strike one neighborhood than other. Taken together, measles, diphtheria, whooping cough, scarlet fever, and croup accounted for nine percent of the mortality in Massachusetts in 1870. Sprains, dislocations, and fractures, with abcesses and superficial tumors, the staples of mid-nineteenth-century surgical practice, were not uniformly the result of occupational hazards. Street railways were both unsafe and democratic, running down citizens of all classes. Complaints diagnosed symptomatically as coughs, heart ailments, stomach disorders, and seizures covered numerous disease processes and were endemic throughout the population.[13] All these accounted for hospital admission among the poor and socially marginal—but did not result significantly in hospital admissions among the comfortably settled who had similar medical needs. The pattern of ill health in Boston in

1870 does not account for the relative absence of the fortunate classes from hospitals.

The home was the primary site of medical care in Boston in 1870.[14] Accident victims, for example, though they might be injured outside the home were likely to be brought home and cared for there. Speaking in 1864 at the dedication of the Boston City Hospital, its president, Thomas C. Amory, acknowledged that it was unlikely that hospitalization would replace the ideal of home care. Amory gave an example of what he regarded as a futile attempt to remove the prejudice against hospital care.

> One of our former governors, who had held the highest federal offices at home and abroad, who gave to the University its largest bequest, meeting with an accident in the street from which he narrowly escaped with his life, insisted, in order to remove this prejudice, upon being carried to the [Massachusetts General] Hospital. His example may have had its effect. But we doubt if many of our own people, born in Boston, when tolerably comfortable at home, will go, when ill, among strangers to be cured.[15]

When Amory himself was run down by a streetcar in 1886, "a doctor was called and the injured gentleman was removed to his home in a carriage."[16]

The pattern of care obtaining at local railroad accidents is revealing. When a commuter train crashed near Roslindale in 1887, twenty-four passengers were killed and fourteen hospitalized. But most of the nearly one hundred victims were taken to their homes: "The fact that the accident occurred in the midst of a settled suburban district, and that nobody upon the train was more than five miles away from home, made it possible to transport the dead and injured, so far as it was practicable under the circumstances, directly to their homes, and many were so taken."[17] Most of the injured not immediately taken home were brought to the Roslindale station, and the rest to hospitals. Some doctors arriving at the scene were detailed to care for the survivors at the station house, while others accompanied the remaining injured to their homes. The severity of their injuries did not separate those hospitalized from those brought home. Only two of the six admitted to Boston City Hospital were listed as seriously injured, and only one of eight at Massachusetts General. Of the cases brought to their own homes, a doctor making fifty-five home visits the day after the wreck reported nine patients in dangerous condition.[18] This division of cases between home and hospital was not idiosyncratic. The ambulance, a new innovation advocated for Boston in 1871, was intended to take victims of injury or sudden illness "to their homes or to the hospital."[19]

Hospitals offered patients no medical advantages not available in the home; actually, hospital treatment in the 1870s added the risks of sepsis or "hospitalism." When a woman entered Massachusetts General in November 1874 needing an operation for the removal of an ovarian tumor, Dr. Samuel Cabot, the surgeon in charge of the case, deemed it desirable "to remove the patient as much as possible from hospital influences," and "by the liberality of the trustees of the hospital a pleasant, airy room was provided in a private house," where the operation was subsequently performed.[20] The fact that the hospital offered no special medical benefits reinforced a resistance to hospitalization that stemmed both from the role of the home as the traditional setting for those undergoing illness and from a negative image of the hospital. That image derived from the actual danger of hospitalism and the traditional identification of the hospital with the pesthole and almshouse. Thus, even when home care was unavailable, hospital care was sometimes shunned. Though James Haines was away from his Dover, New Hampshire, home, he refused to follow the recommendation of a doctor attending his broken thigh after a streetcar accident, and instead of entering a hospital chose to remain at his hotel.[21]

Facilities did exist for the hospitalization of the relatively well-to-do. As early as 1827 Massachusetts General had some private rooms, and in the '70s private accommodations were moved into a newly built eight-room pavilion that was usually fully occupied.[22] But Massachusetts General had to call attention to the fact that it admitted other than the poor:

> It may not be generally known to the community that there are in the hospital some very elegant and luxurious private apartments for the reception and treatment of a class of patients, whether citizens or strangers, who for peculiar reasons or circumstances would find special advantages here. If a visitor to the city, without relatives or intimate friends, became ill, or met with an accident while transiently staying at one of our hotels, and wished to enjoy all the care and luxuries to which an easy lot may have accustomed him, he would find in one of these apartments, with its attendant resources and accompaniments, a most desirable and privileged refuge.[23]

The people who might be expected to take advantage of private rooms were those well off, yet without homes, or those whose homes were for some reason inadequate. The standard that Massachusetts General used to measure its facilities for paying patients was "their own home." Suffering "a sad and possibly fatal accident" while exercising at the MIT gymnasium, Caleb Cushing was taken to Massachusetts General, though he was the nephew of a judge and the son of the mayor-elect of Newburyport. But since he was a college student from out of town, there was nowhere else for him to be taken. John Kent, Jr., a Harvard graduate and schoolteacher, made his home with his parents. When in a fit of delirium triggered by an attack of typhoid fever Kent jumped through a second story window, he was brought to Massachusetts General. The fall resulted in no serious injury, but his delirium required the constant restraint and attention available only at a hospital. Patients requiring less constant attention, but having no families and living alone, were also suitable candidates. For the fortunate, then, hospitals were a last resort, to be entered only in "peculiar circumstances."[24]

Even the sick poor, for whom hospitals were intended, would avoid hospitalization if possible. One of the stated advantages of a dispensary was that outpatient care sidestepped the "dread" that the prospect of hospitalization evoked among many of the poor. The city's two diet kitchens, founded in the 1870s, supplied home meals for dispensary patients too sick or poor to secure their own food.[25] But force of circumstance often left no alternative. Boston Lying-in received some of its cases from dispensary physicians "who suddenly found themselves called upon to attend some poor woman in quarters utterly unfit for such purposes."[26]

Hospitals replaced comfortless homes "in close courts, narrow alleys, damp cellars, or filthy apartments, which the sunshine never enters, nor fresh air purifies." They made up for the absence of "natural protectors" for those without families. They provided relief for "helpless people, who would suffer tenfold more from neglect and ill-treatment than they now suffer from disease, were it not for the shelter and care of the hospitals."[27] Even "among the poor of a better class," hospitals had a mission. Though their homes were more comfortable, work kept family members away during the day and left them too tired to care for the sick properly at night.[28]

The statistics of hospital use reflected their role in serving the sick and injured victims of a catalog of social ills. Hospital annual reports listed the occupations of patients admitted; when these occupations are classified according to socioeconomic status and then compared with the occupational structure of the city as a whole, we find that patients treated at Massachusetts General and Boston City hospitals in the 1870s were not a cross-section of the population.[29] Such an analysis shows that occupations with high socioeconomic status were underrepresented among hospital patients in 1870 and 1880, while those with low status were overrepresented.

At Massachusetts General in 1870, 16.9 percent of the classifiable male patients were in white collar occupations, while in 1880 that figure was 18.1 percent. In the city population, 32 percent of males were white collar in 1880. Skilled blue collar workers accounted for 41.9 percent of Massachusetts General patients in 1870 and 19.4 percent in 1880, while they provided 36 percent of the general male population in 1880. Among patients, 14.2 percent and 11.1 percent went in semiskilled occupations in 1870 and 1880 respectively, while the city population contained 17 percent in that category in 1880. The unskilled accounted for 26.9 percent and 51.4 percent of the patient population and 15 percent of the city population in 1880.[30]

Much the same pattern prevailed at Boston City Hospital. The largest single occupational category among patients was laborer, consisting of 524 of 1,419 men admitted in 1870/71 and 792 of 2,696 in 1880/81. Patients in white collar occupations totaled 8.2 percent of male admissions in 1870/71 and 10.5 percent in 1880/81. Skilled blue collar workers accounted for 36.3 percent of Boston City patients in 1870/71 and 31.6 percent in 1880/81. Workers in semiskilled and service occupations made up 11.8 percent of city hospital patients in 1870/71 and 21.7 percent in 1880/81. As at Massachusetts General, unskilled (including laborers) and menial workers—43.5 percent and 36.1 percent—were overrepresented.[31]

Unfortunately, the listing of many women patients as simply wives or widows (with no indication of their husbands' occupations), and the absence of a satisfactory analysis of the female occupational structure, make a comparison of female patients with the general female population difficult. But the fact that nearly half the female patients admitted to both hospitals in the 1870s were identified as domestics reinforces the conclusion that hospital patients were drawn disproportionately from among the lower classes.[32]

Though the absolute and relative numbers undergoing hospitalization continued to increase in the '70s as they had since the city's first hospital opened in 1821,[33] the hospital's constituency remained largely the same, with the greater number of patients coming from an expanded lower class. The image of hospitals as refuges for the unfortunate was further heightened by the fact that their patients were not just poor but, after the beginning of the large-scale immigration at mid-century, largely foreign born. The Massachusetts General trustees had at first resisted admitting the Irish, claiming that "the admission of such patients creates in the minds of our citizens a prejudice against the Hospital, making them unwilling to enter it—and thus tends directly to lower the general standing and character of its inmates." Feeling "the excess of foreigners among the patients" to be an evil, they had advised the admitting physician to use "the utmost vigilance," but found that "some such admissions must unavoidably take place." Hospital rules directed that all cases of sudden accident were to be admitted, thus bypassing the screening procedure; a very large proportion of accident cases were Irish. In time, the trustees, "moved by a sense of duty and humanity," opened their wards to the foreign born.[34]

The United States census listed 35.1 percent of Boston's population as foreign born in 1870. In that year, Massachusetts General admitted 718 foregin as against 584 native born patients. The Irish made up the largest segment of its foreign born population, maintaining at least a majority throughout the 1870s, with those born in the Canadian provinces second.[35] From the opening of Boston City Hospital in 1864, a majority of its patients was foreign born. In 1870/71, 1,635 of its patients had been born abroad and 761 in the United States. Throughout the period, Irish patients alone outnumbered the native born.[36]

The image of the lying-in hospital was even worse than that of the general hospital. Maternity care would be among the last reasons the comfortable classes entered hospitals. In the late nineteenth century, women still considered that childbirth could, and should, be performed even in the simplest and poorest home. Hospitals offered no specialized medical paraphernalia or contrivances; puerperal fever was rampant in them and maternal mortality high. The result was that only the most desperate women entered hospitals to have their children. And perhaps the major cause of this desperation was illegitimacy. Small lying-ins, often no more than a few rooms in a tenement or boarding house, kept by midwives or the unscrupulous and untrained, served those seeking "to hide their shame" or having absolutely no alternative. These lying-ins, and the baby farms that sometimes accompanied them, were seen as accessories to vice and degradation, and as adjuncts to brothels. Lying-ins were the first hospitals needing licenses to operate in Massachusetts (1876), but the enforcement problems of the Boston Board of Health suggest that more lying-ins were operated without sanction of law than with it.[37]

Licensed and respectable lying-ins existed, but their patients too were "unfortunate women," often "utterly destitute of money and friends." The New England Hospital for Women and Children, opened in 1862 to train female doctors, provided medical, surgical, and obstetrical services. Cases included in the first volume of its maternity records, covering one and one-half years in the early 1870s, list 61 married and 57 unmarried mothers. Many of those patients not there because of illegitimacy entered because of the most abject poverty; the hospital appealed for old clothing for the women to wear during their stay and after their discharge. Over 51 percent of the more than 1,300 mothers delivered in the 1870s at Boston Lying-in were unmarried. And at St. Mary's Lying-in, only 20 of 550 patients cared for in the decade from 1874 to 1884 were married. The lying-in hospitals of the period reaffirmed the notion that hospitals were for the poor and desperate, and the illegitimacy intimately associated with them added the stigma of immorality to the image of the hospital.[38]

Hospitals were perceived as the kind of place all but the desperate would want to avoid. Yet although they dealt primarily with the poor, their very nature—the omnipresence of death within their walls—imbued their concerns with a powerful attraction. The community at large was curious as to what went on inside them. This desire to know was heightened by the relative newness of the institution; though their history could be traced back to antiquity, hospitals began to emerge in numbers in Boston and the rest of the nation only after the Civil War. Finally, the curiosity as to what went on within hospitals derived from the fact that even the fortunate individual could not be certain that he would not some day be hospitalized.

Horror was a common response to such a prospect. Joseph Chamberlin, for many years the *Transcript*'s "Listener,"[39] reacted strongly after visiting a hospitalized friend.

> If it should fall to the Listener's lot to be called upon to go in sickness to the very best of [hospitals], he would say, "Better a straw cot in an attic at home, with the clumsiest of unprofessional attendance, than the best private room in this place." ... There is something about this all-pervading presence of Sickness, with a large S, this atmosphere of death, either just expected or just escaped, and all of this amiable perfunctoriness of nursing and medical attendance, that is simply horrible. The hospital ...gives one sickness to think about morning, noon and night.[40]

A visitor might be acutely discomfited by the unnatural concentration of disease and death. But for the patient the environment was threatening: "The doctors visit you incessantly, and, in spite of their courtesy, you feel as if you were not exactly an ailing human being, but merely a "case" that was being read as one reads a novel which is interesting enough, no doubt, but which is expected to develop a much more interesting phase, to wit, the catastrophe, at almost any moment. And then the grim disquieting presence of all these people like you in the ward around you!"[41] The hospital reaffirmed the patient's mortality, but denied his humanity.

Chamberlin told the story of a patient hospitalized for an operation. After surgery, she was put to bed. She lived through a night punctuated by the "wailing and crying" of fellow patients, the death "in dreadful agony" of a neighboring patient, and the quiet but quick, and therefore ghostly, movement of attendants. It was terrifying: "Why it was like being dead and conscious of it!" The next day was quiet, but, "spent in anticipating the coming of such another night, was almost as terrible." This particular hospital stay was cut short when a physician inquiring "whether I had not any friend to whom I could go," found she had and "made immediate arrangements to have me taken away." Clearly, this patient and many of her contemporaries shared Chamberlin's conclusion: "What a matter for infinite sorrow it is that there should be homes in the world so dismal, so unhealthy, so ill-attended, that their inmates are better off in the public wards of the hospital, when they are sick, than they are at home."[42]

Because hospitals were strange and frightening places, the public welcomed newspaper articles offering reassurance. This might take the form of a generic history of the hospital, implying that it was not simply a modern aberration but an old institution that had proved its value in the past,[43] or a correspondent's story of a hospital visit, or a patient's description of his stay. These last were often in the style of travelers' accounts.

Chamberlin's story was idiosyncratic; more common in the Boston press were counterphobic presentations that were almost uniformly formulaic, saccharine chronicles which denied the presence in hospitals of death, disease, and pain. Insanity, for example, was not mentioned in an extensive account of an insane asylum, though beautiful flowers and homelike accommodations in cottages were. The smallpox hospital emerged from another narrative as a delightful place, serving wonderful food and providing comfortable beds, while smallpox itself, it was concluded, much improved the system.[44] For those hospitals which depended on the beneficence of the public, reassurances that all was well within served a double function in that they encouraged contributions as well as disarmed anxieties.

Boston's City Hospital was supported as a municipal service, but the hospital tradition in Boston, as in the rest of the United States, had been set by the voluntary hospitals, with groups of private individuals undertaking the care of the sick poor as a public trust. Central to their image and organization in the nineteenth century was the fact that "hospitals are essentially charitable institutions."[45]

Massachusetts General and Children's Hospital formed part of the complex of Boston's Protestant charities that owed their founding and existence, at least in part, to the religious doctrine of stewardship. Social and economic inequalities were legitimized by the notion that God meant them to exist. But the elect, whose heavenly salvation was generally already demonstrated by their earthly riches, held their wealth only as God's trustees. With their wealth came the obligation to aid the less fortunate. The poor provided their economic betters the opportunity, the privilege actually, of spending God's wealth in a way that continually reemphasized their own chosen state.

Doctors James Jackson and John Collins Warren, in their original proposal for Massachusetts General Hospital, assumed that the wealthy of Boston, the "treasurers of God's bounty," would want to do what they could to succor the poor in sickness. Prodding its contributors to continue their beneficence in 1871, Massachusetts General had only to remind them, in religious shorthand, that "the poor are always with us." Supporters of Children's Hospital used the same terms.[46]

Old Boston families supplied the bulk of the names on Massachusetts General's self-perpetuating board of trustees and the list of its financial contributors. Donations came from almost as closed and self-perpetuating a group as the board represented. Donations made in the name of stewardship served to reaffirm an earlier social structure in which the steward's status was unquestioned. But whatever reality there had been in that vision when the doctrine was part of a more viable religious order no longer obtained in post–Civil War Boston. The fortunes that supported the hospital originated before the war, formed largely in Boston's traditional patterns of trade and textiles. In the face of a series of postwar challenges—from new money in new families, from the rising political power of the Irish, and from even greater wealth built on industrialization and urbanization in the nation's new financial centers—Boston's old families turned to defending their standing in the class hierarchy by restricting the access of those with new money to the social elite. The Brahmins thus minimized the value of economic success for their own class as well. Generally eschewing entrepreneurship for financial prudence, they sanctioned few fields for competitive achievement for those born into their class. Some Brahmins still competed successfully, particularly in the professions.[47] But others retreated from the competitive world to practice the virtues that had given their predecessors divine support for their claims to temporal status.

Brahmins continued to display their grace by acting in the name of God and secular humanitarianism as stewards of the poor. The *Boston Transcript,* speaking for the city's established wealth, took the opportunity presented by the readng of the will of Mary Louisa Shaw to point out with pride: "The liberal and judicious bequests of Miss Shaw . . . show what the "blue blood" of Beacon Street not infrequently does for the benefit of the less favored classes of the community. The instances are not rare in which the residents on that street display large and discriminating benevolence. Many of the old families there may proudly point to their munificent gifts as their best title to social position."[48] In a rapidly changing and sometimes threatening world the continuing burden of the stewardship role reassured the Brahmins. The role was central to a life-style which set them apart from those who might equal or exceed their wealth or claims to influence. John Collins Warren (1842–1927), grandson of the founder of Massachusetts General, noted that "the share of their incomes which in other cities would have gone to meet personal wants and provide the luxuries of life was dedicated to the annual needs of the community for public service."[49]

Children's Hospital, founded in 1869, was unable in its early years to enlist the same kind of support among the dominant families as Massachusetts General. Newness was a handicap; Children's lacked the advantage of continuity with the past that made the older hospital so attractive to ancestor-oriented donors. Yet a significant number of benefactors were shared from the beginning; almost one-fourth of the contributors to Children's in its first year were regular subscribers to Massachusetts General. Nathaniel Thayer, Children's Hospital's major contributor ($10,000 of $25,000 collected in 1869) and its first president (1869–83), served Massachusetts General as vice president at the same time. For wealthy non-Brahmins, sponsorship of Children's offered an opportunity to copy the behavior of the more rigidly closed circle around Massachusetts General. In soliciting contributions the managers of Children's stressed that many of "our best citizens" supported it, thus appealing to those who sought identification with the aristocracy. Some prominent patrons of Children's never gained acceptance as members of the Brahmin elite. F. L. Ames, for example, was a major industrialist and railroad magnate who served as a manager of Children's without realizing complete social success. But the very attempts of the newly rich to purchase respectability by supporting the new hospital served to ratify the standing of the old families and the validity of their values.[50] The mix of old and new wealth—present also in the early years of Massachusetts General—led to a heightened sense of social position and hence of social obligation among donors to Children's Hospital.[51]

Fund-raising also took aim at the children of the well-to-do. It often took the form of children's stories, pathos-filled and playing on what was expected to be the natural sympathy of the young for the hospital's juvenile patients. One tale, by Dr. Francis H. Brown, the hospital's founder and chief promoter, told of young children who gave up their luxuries and engaged in other fund-raising efforts in order to secure hospital treatment for an unfortunate waif.[52]

Children might give pennies raised at neighborhood fairs and entertainments, or culled from allowances. These donations were less significant than the sums that the hospital's managers hoped to realize from parents. The managers thought that well-to-do parents might perceive social and personal benefits for themselves in the interest of their children in the hospital, and thus regard the institution as a fit object for their benevolence. The rhetorical question posed by the managers—"What better instruction can be given the children of the city than that which teaches them, in their earliest years, to take their share in the care of the poor?"—broadened the appeal of the institution. While treating the children of the poor, the hospital would help socialize the children of the rich, by teaching appropriate upper class behavior and encouraging appropriate virtues.[53] Brahmins could see their offspring adopting their own life style. Eschewing luxury and waste and carrying on the burden of caring for the unfortunate, their children would prove another generation's claims to hereditary status based on inherited responsibility. They would also be reassured by contributions from children of less privileged status; such gifts testified to the significance of the values of the elite. Non-Brahmin parents liked to see their children reasserting their own claims. Like other voluntary charities, Children's Hospital played a significant role in defining and maintaining upper class status.

The Boston hospitals of 1870 were also instruments of status ascription within the medical profession. Henry J. Bigelow, Boston's leading surgeon, spoke in 1871 of the "two classes of the profession," differentiating those who simply practiced medicine from those who contributed to its development. The latter group was the medical elite; in Boston this group benefited from—and defined itself, in part, in terms of—hospital and dispensary experience. This distinct medical elite was not peculiar to Boston, but existed in other American cities as well.[54]

The medical aristocracy dominated the profession in Boston. The existence of this separate class was most manifest in family names. Oliver Wendell Holmes noted in 1881 that "there has hardly been a year for more than a century in which 'Dr. Warren' or 'Dr. Jeffries' could not be called upon by his Boston fellow-citizens for his service as surgeon or physician." Holmes mentioned the names of other medical families as well, the different lines of which were often bound by marriage: Jackson, Bigelow, Shattuck, Channing, Putnam and Homans.[55] He might also have included Bowditch, Cheever, Minot, and Wyman. This medical elite was part of the city's social elite. The names Cabot, Codman, Holmes, and Lawrence often obscured medical family ties. Oliver Wendell Holmes himself, for example, was married to a niece of James Jackson.

The professional elite was a product of more than family background— Henry Jacob Bigelow probably would not have included all illustruously connected local practitioners in his higher class of the profession—but family background was more than an indicator of medical status. It opened certain options. The upper class medical graduate of the nineteenth century had the means to delay practice and to pursue European study after obtaining his American degree. Further, the properly connected young Boston physician might be motivated to choose the European education that distinguished the best medical work in his community. Both the fortunes of birth, and family and class expectation encouraged him to view his career as more than a nasty struggle for economic success. A succession of these young Bostonians made the medical grand tour. At the turn of the nineteenth century, Great Britain —especially Scotland—was favored; then France became the center of American postgraduate medical education. From midcentury on, the focus shifted to Germany and Austria.[56]

Upper class physicians were also more likely to be members of medical school facilities. Doctors John Collins Warren and James Jackson, for example, had both trained in Europe. Warren had been in London, Edinburgh, and Paris from 1799 to 1802; Jackson had visited London for one year in 1799–1800. Both were professors in the Harvard Medical School.

Dissatisfied with the limited clinical opportunities available for teaching in the Boston Almshouse and aware of the benefits offered European medical schools by hospital facilities, Warren and Jackson sought to have a hospital organized that they could use for their teaching. A hospital would make the medical school more attractive to students and thus increase enrollments. In the largely proprietary Harvard Medical School of the early nineteenth century, instructors received fees from each of their students. Teaching brought other financial benefits, as former students referred difficult cases to former professors for paying consultations. The result of their campaign was Massachusetts General, Boston's first general hospital and the nation's third, chartered in 1811.[57]

A hospital position enabled a medical man to see and treat numbers of special cases, comparatively rare in private practice, and so develop a reputation that would itself be renumerative. Hospital physicians earned their livelihoods in the care of well-to-do private patients who paid for the knowledge gained in hospital work. Private practice remained the norm. And because nineteenth-century hospitals were not the centers of the doctor's work world, the few hours he put in there each day during his term of perhaps three months each year did not represent income lost. Henry J. Bigelow noted in 1889 that hospital connections offered "certain well-understood advantages"; unpaid "hospital offices would command a considerable premium in money from the best class of practitioners were they annually put up at auction."[58] This attractiveness did not derive alone from the prospect of increased earnings, but rather from the style of practice that a hospital or dispensary affiliation might be expected to generate. A report of the Boston Dispensary suggested the interrelatedness of material and psychic rewards: "It is not to be supposed that the motives of the attending physicians have been wholly foreign from considerations of personal advantage. They have doubtless been actuated by the hope of professional improvement and the prospect of building up an honest fame, as well as by the desires of fulfilling the benevolent intentions of this charity."[59] Without this gratuitous service, it was difficult for a young doctor to begin a practice in a city where paying patients had a wide choice among practitioners and would choose experience. With the beginnings of specialization in the mid-nineteenth century, clinics offered even experienced practitioners the best opportunities to see and treat numbers of "special cases," advancing their skills and their reputations.

The roles and experiences sought by practitioners were instrumental in the founding of other hospitals besides Massachusetts General. In 1869, Dr. Francis H. Brown together with three other doctors enlisted the support of lay donors in establishing Children's Hospital. The four practitioners acted as the hospital's first medical staff, while Brown and another of the doctors doubled as managers (trustees). The Free Hospital for Women opened in 1875, a result of the efforts of Dr. William H. Baker, who then served as its first surgeon and later assumed the responsibility of trusteeship. In 1889 the Murdock Liquid Food Company closed the one-hundred-twenty-bed women's hospital it had founded and operated since 1883 as a demonstration of the restorative and healing power of its products. Dr. Ernest W. Cushing of its former medical staff contacted the Woman's Charity Club, encouraged the club to open its own hospital to take up the discontinued work, and volunteered his services. The Woman's Charity Club Hospital opened on New Year's Day, 1890, with Dr. Cushing on its staff.[60]

The organization of a hospital was costly and generally necessitated that physicians secure financial backing from others. But dispensaries, which provided only outpatient care, needed only minimal financial resources. Often no more than a room or two and a collection of drugs, dispensaries could be conducted by practitioners as simple one-man operations offering free advice and treatment to the poor. After Henry J. Bigelow returned from study in Paris in the early 1840s, he opened such a clinic in a church basement. The Dispensary for Skin Diseases and the Dispensary for Diseases of the Nervous System opened in 1872, sharing an address in the city's South End. In 1873, the Dispensary for Diseases of Women and the Dispensary for Children opened in the West End. These latter shared the quarters of the Staniford Street Dispensary, a loosely organized facility located within the offices of Dr. George Cheyne Shattuck, Jr.[61] In these and other dispensaries, doctors took time off from their private practices to set up offices at their own expense in the city's poorer areas, gratuitously treating such patients as came to them. The medical profession traditionally had recognized its responsibility for free treatment to the poor. Dispensaries went well beyond this principle. Shattuck, for example, was dean of Harvard Medical School when he made his office available in 1867 for the informal medical courses that developed into the dispensary. The Staniford Street Dispensary, with its specialty clinics and stated hours, was more than an institutionalization of the care of the poor previously offered on the same site by Shattuck and his father before him.

The recitations and clinics at Staniford Street were staffed by recent Harvard graduates, young men not yet in line for teaching positions in the medical school. The medical school faculty were originally suspicious of this venture, fearing, until they were assured otherwise, that the clinic would serve as the nucleus for a competing school.[62] The establishment of Boston City Hospital had generated the same suspicions. Both the medical faculty and the Massachusetts General staff, which overlapped considerably in membership, had opposed the municipal hospital in the late 1850s and early '60s. They relented only after assurances that no new medical school would be formed at the city hospital.

Harvard and Massachusetts General were again accused of "monopoly" in trying to crush the proposed Children's Hospital in 1869. Dr. Benjamin Shaw, resident physician (superintendent) of Massachusetts General, informed the public through the press that no new hospital was needed in Boston, and that existing facilities, especially in his own institution, were more than adequate to care for the city's sick children. The two hospitals competed with each other once Children's was an accomplished and increasingly threatening fact. Massachusetts General used its annual reports to stress its own fine care for children, advancing its case even to the point of straining credulity. It insisted that mingling children and adults in the same wards was good, because the child patients got attention from the critically ill adults, and the adults were cheered and inspired by the stoicism of the children. Children's countered by describing "the gloomy and forbidding appearance of the ward of a general hospital."[63] When the new Infants' Hospital appealed for funds it was forced by the Massachusetts General trustees not to distribute an already printed circular stating that children under two years of age could not be well cared for in a general hospital and to substitute a more innocuously worded statement of the new hospital's aims.[64] Massachusetts General stood ready to defend aggressively the prerogatives of its medical staff.

As the most prestigious of the city's medical institutions and the one most closely identified with Boston's elite, Massachusetts General was especially attractive to young physicians seeking hospital appointments. New appointments and promotions were made by the board of trustees upon the recommendation of the visiting staff, but family and social ties among the staff and trustees were so intertwined that it becomes difficult to sort through the process to determine who made the decisions. The result, however, was clear; the staff developed largely through inbreeding during the nineteenth century. An elite background not only predisposed the young physician to enter hospital service, but opened the door for him as well.

As hospital positions grew in importance in the late nineteenth century, nepotism did not go unchallenged, but the parceling out of appointments through the network of family and social ties survived at Massachusetts General. In 1873, when President Charles Eliot of Harvard, as part of his program to upgrade the medical school, asked that the hospital appoint house officers on the basis of competitive examinations, his suggestion was rejected. Physicians generally began their careers on the hospital staff as house officers (at that date the description included medical students as well as interns); hence the importance of the position. The next step was advancement to the outpatient staff and then promotion, most often by seniority, to the visiting staff. After consultation with the visiting staff the trustees concluded "that the careful and varied scrutiny to which applicants for the position of House Pupil in the Hospital are now subjected is better than an examination of scholastic and academic character."[65] Eliot's reorganization of the medical school was in part thwarted by his inability to secure the best hospital training for the most able students. Only certain students would be privileged to have "careful and varied scrutiny."

The issue of nepotism surfaced again in 1884 when the trustees requested that the surgical staff reconsider their nominations for extern with a view to having the son of a surgeon long connected with the hospital included among the nominees. Having no objection to the candidate so favored, the visiting surgeons complied, enabling the trustees to make the appointment. At the same time, surgeons C. B. Porter and J. Collins Warren reminded the trustees that five of six house pupils chosen for the coming year were related to hospital trustees or staff members. They warned that the situation was not ideal, and added that "a feeling has grown up among the students and we might say among the profession, that nepotism exerts such an influence in the choice of candidates at the Hospital, that when a relative of any member of the staff applies for a position, he is sure to obtain it, to the exclusion of all others." The trustees, after first reprimanding the surgeons for interfering in hospital policy, determined that allegations of nepotism were baseless. They did, however, institute some changes in the nominating procedure, asking the visiting staff to interview each applicant and also to find out how well each had done at Harvard Medical School.[66]

An anonymous physician familiar with the hospital took issue with the trustees' assertion that nepotism did not exist. In an irony-tinged letter to the *Boston Medical and Surgical Journal,* "XYZ" noted that

The MGH is not yet old enough to appoint all its house pupils from the comparatively few families of its trustees and medical staff, and must fill up its quota from outsiders. Eight appointments in ten years of gentlemen who bear the well known names of members of the staff is by no means a bad showing, but a candid statement with regard to the matter should not be confined to those degrees of relationship which are betrayed by the identity of names. Occasionally a man forces his way in, so to speak, by superior scholarship, provided he takes care to exhibit also those other qualifications mentioned in the statement and it happens to be an 'off year' for favorites.[67]

But XYZ nonetheless went on to defend the system: "Why should not the wishes of a man who helps financially to sustain the institution be regarded? Why should not a physician or surgeon be influenced by the wishes of his dearest friend or most profitable patient? The question is not intended even to suggest improper influence, but simply to say that the gentlemen referred to are subject to like influences as other men, and cannot help trusting the children of their friends, who have grown up around them, rather than the strange young men who may be equally good, but whom they do not know."[68] XYZ's support of nepotism at the hospital was also a defense of Boston's medical aristocracy.

In the late nineteenth century, an appointment to Massachusetts General often seemed implausible to outsiders, predictable to the properly connected. Dr. John Finney remembered that when asked in the late eighties why he had not applied for a house officership he replied: "Well, because to be perfectly frank, it is generally understood among the [Harvard medical] students that only those who are residents of Boston or are known personally to members of the staff have any chance of appointment." Finney, who had come under the patronage of visiting surgeon C. B. Porter, was encouraged to apply and was appointed. More typical was the case of Richard C. Cabot, nephew of visiting surgeon Samuel Cabot, who addressed his gratitude for an appointment to the outpatient staff to "Uncle Edmund" Dwight, then chairman of the trustees.[69] But Cabot's cousin by marriage, Frederick C. Shattuck, was stymied temporarily in his appointment to the position as visiting physician vacated by the retirement of George C. Shattuck, Jr., his father, by clique politics and the "settlement of old scores."[70] His uncle, Samuel Eliot, also chairman of the trustees, helped secure Shattuck's nomination, and the conflict was not typical. But if unusual it suggests that the various factions within the trustees and senior staff were generally able to agree on appointments; candidates favored by the different power blocks were selected each in his turn. The formal division of power, in which staff physicians nominated and trustees appointed, was less important than the informal structure built on family and class.

At other medical institutions as at Massachusetts General, a community of interest united doctors and donors. The wealthy supported hospitals and dispensaries in part to underwrite the work of their medical relatives and friends. Amos Lawrence, the mercantile prince, underwrote the entire cost of a children's hospital under the charge of his son, Dr. William R. Lawrence. The staffing of South Boston's Roman Catholic Carney Hospital by Back Bay physicians brought in financial contributions from their friends and families.[71]

In part, the wealthy supported these institutions because enlightened selfishness led them to share certain of the goals of physicians. The knowledge and experience doctors gained in treating the poor "raised the standard of medical attainments," and thus hospital and dispensary practice "proved a blessing to rich and poor alike." Children's Hospital appealed "to all those who have children of their own," reminding them that they had a "double interest" in the institution, "not only on account of the great benefit it will confer on its little inmates, but also because of the advantages it offers for the study of special diseases by which their own offspring may be afflicted."[72] The *Boston Evening Transcript* warned the fortunate that their own well-being depended on the continued well-being of hospitals: "The aids which society distributes to the hospitals are amply restored by the hospitals to society.... Mainly in these institutions the experience and insight, the methods of observation and treatment, the scientific research, are evolved which become employed for the general health of the country.... If we could imagine the hospitals abolished, the general death rate in all private practice would be increased."[73]

The community of interest extended beyond medical ends to social assumptions. Elite practitioners shared certain of the social values of the lay elite. Simply because physicians had medical motives for hospital service did not mean that they were not serious in also invoking stewardship to explain their voluntary efforts. And while both patron and practitioner understood hospitals to offer medical care, both also expected them to treat their patients in a social context. Children's Hospital provides an instructive case.

In the 1870s, Children's Hospital was characterized by a peculiar amalgam of medical fatalism and social activism. Although the managers listed "medical and surgical treatment of the diseases of children" as their first goal, their early reports expressed much more confidence in the social nature of the hospital's work. Children's had been established to care for the poor; it took as its patients "the little waifs who crowd our poorer streets."[74] The managers noted:

It is known to all medical men that poor food, want of pure air, and uncleanliness are fruitful sources of disease. The condition of ignorance which marks the lower classes of the community is constantly acting to debase the tone of society; it allows the lowest wages for labor, and it leads to the squandering in improvidence for successive generations of that which might afford considerable support. Agencies such as these are constantly at work to lower the vital force of the poorer classes of society, and to render the children an easy prey to the attacks of disease. The aim of all judicious medical treatment is directed not alone to relieve immediate disease, but by a thorough change of life and circumstance, by supplying a rational course of diet and regimen, by substituting for ignorance and thoughtlessness, and the thousand indiscretions which they suggest, judicious and gentle nursing, warmth, nourishment, light and air, to lay the best foundation for relief from disease.[75]

Medicine in the 1870s was broadly defined; environmental manipulation was as much the province of the physician as any narrowly based therapeutics.[76] But Children's Hospital operated outside even the medically limited rubric of health and disease. In cases where physicians and surgeons were helpless to avert a child's death, the managers believed that the hospital had a function in permitting the dying to spend their last days "in a home of purity, comfort, and peace."[77] Besides medical treatment and a conducive physical environment, Children's also offered to care for the spirit.

In its early years, Children's Hospital stressed this spiritual role. Making their first report, the managers stated that the institution would provide its patients "Christian nurture." Sickness provided an opportunity for spiritual healing; the philosophy of Children's reflected that of a local newspaper when it editorially downgraded the function of hospitals in furnishing medical treatment while commending them for giving patients the best gifts of all, "wrought through a ministry of sorrow."[78]

The entire Christian community was invited to participate in the healing process, to visit patients and encourage them "by word or counsel." The first nurses were Anglican nuns, whose strength lay less in medical training than in the "Christian nurture" they provided patients. Sister Letitia was a model of this style of charity untainted by medical pretension: "Though enfeebled by disease of the lungs, which she knew must soon terminate her life, yet entirely forgetful of self," she continued nursing—all the while, of course, exposing her charges to tuberculosis—until she died.[79] Healthy middle and upper class children were encouraged to paint wall decorations of inspirational mottoes that would "cultivate the devotional feelings" of the lower class patients.[80] The theological language in which all this was expressed was largely a carryover from an earlier time; religious terminology provided a familiar and convenient vocabulary. Soon society would no longer justify hospitals in traditional religious terms. One can already sense the beginning of a shift in this period. Within a generation, the mission of hospitals would change drastically, from succoring the sick poor as their role in God's order, to denying that man had to accept God's diseases. But in the 1870s, these religious terms symbolized real moral and social concerns.

Socially, they translated into a program of uplift and social control which it was hoped would help cope with the masses of threatening and increasingly alien poor crowding into the city. The managers had expected that most of their patients would come from the poorest classes of the community. They found that many came "from the very lowest; from abodes of drunkenness, and vice in almost every form, where the most depressing and corrupting influences were acting both on the body and the mind."[81] Hospitalization provided an opportunity to "help the child-soul to lift itself out of the mud in which it had been born, to assert its native purity in spite of unfortunate surroundings."[82]

When a child entered, it was first decontaminated: "On their entrance they are immediately placed in a refreshing bath and clothed in the clean robes of the hospital." Uniform red flannel jackets replaced street clothes. The "visits and attentions of the kind and cultivated" were encouraged at any time of the day, "to bring [patients] under the influence of order, purity and kindness."[83]

At the same time, parents having children in the hospital were severely restricted in the hours they could see their own children. The original parents' visiting hour allowed one relative at a time between eleven and twelve o'clock on weekdays only, raising difficulties for working fathers (or mothers) who wished to visit. Later, parent visiting was further restricted to the hour between eleven and twelve on Monday, Wednesday, and Friday only. The trustees hoped that this regimen would change the children by "quickening their intellects, refining their manners, and encouraging and softening their hearts."[84]

It was hoped that the child leaving the hospital would be different from the child who had entered it,[85] having been "carefully taught cleanliness of habit, purity of thought and word," and with as much attention having been "paid to...moral training as can be found in any cultivated family."[86] But the benefits of the hospital would not stop there:

> Think what a widespreading influence this becomes when the children return to their homes.... Even among the better class of poor people, the children soon notice the discomforts of careless, untidy habits, and are quick to compare such with the "so much better" at the hospital. In the joy of the child's homecoming, the parents are ready to gratify it by trying the new ways, and all unconsciously rise a little in the social scale by so doing.[87]

"In this wise," wrote Dr. Francis H. Brown, the hospital's founder, the institution would "commence the education of the poorer classes."[88]

Even if the child did not go home and improve his family, he himself would be changed by the hospital in a way that would benefit society. The affluent and cultivated were told that they could not tell the difference between their own children and those within the hospital, even though the latter might be immigrant children from the North End. One visitor noted that "the faces of the children quickly lost the expression which we commonly meet in our little street Arabs, and become once more human and civilized."[89] They no longer appeared as threatening as they had on the streets.

The hospital promised other far-reaching improvements. Healthier children would become healthier adults and citizens, better able to support themselves. A promotional article even implied that children might be taught how to read.[90] A hospital stay could help prepare a child for a socially desirable role in adult life.

These perceptions were colored, of course, by expectation. No doubt they express more than actually happened in the hospital in the way of having the children of the poor fulfill the fantasies of the rich. Further, these social expectations were less than the full rationale for the institution. Children's Hospital was founded by physicians, in part for the sorts of professional reasons earlier suggested. At the same time, however, the founding physicians were responsible for much of this socially oriented promotional rhetoric. There is no reason to believe these doctors did not take their own language seriously. They were members of a social class as well as of a professional group, and shared the didactic concerns typical of their culture.

Other hospitals dealt with adults and, getting their patients later in life, could not promise the same complete character building. Carney Hospital claimed that the vision-saving effects of its eye clinic saved many from pauperization and a life in the almshouse.[91] St. Elizabeth's, another Catholic hospital, boarded jobless female domestics, saving them from lives of vice. The Dr. Cullis hospitals, admitting patients with cancer, advanced tuberculosis, and everything else thought incurable, served as "A Work of Faith" promising some miraculous cures as a by-product of their mission of saving souls among the heathen. But Dr. Cullis did not offer the city of Boston the return of better citizens, as patients generally left his grounds bound directly for the City of God.[92]

Supporters of the New England Hospital for Women and Children explained that female patients of good character often could be "restored to their duties, rejoicing in an entire renovation of health and hope." Society profited not just by saving these workers, but also by rekindling in them their faith in the social order. A letter to the *Transcript* on behalf of a fund-raising appeal noted that "in no possible manner can the Commonwealth be more directly benefited than in the restoration of its industrious women to their daily work, as their influence is strong for good over the idle and worthless classes." Even women who had strayed might benefit: "For those who have fallen into the sins of the wayside, in the struggle of life, too weak to resist the temptations which have beset their unguarded footsteps, let us be thankful that when the retributive hour of their pain and peril comes, there is such a retreat where they may be led by the affectionate appeals of noble women; and by the example of their daily lives to see what are the higher aims which hold in abeyance the terrible evils that have so degraded them. Seeing and hearing, they may be led to believe and do."[93]

Massachusetts General, a secularly oriented Protestant hospital like Children's, also began with the mission of uplifting its patients. But overwhelmed by immigrants, it gave up this aspect of its earlier role, and in the 1870s its literature no longer expressed concern for the character of its patients. It kept the support of its donors for a variety of reasons, the chief probably being an inertia in which benefactions served as a quiet reaffirmation of stewardship. As mentioned earlier, an obligation to keep the hospital going because it served the needs of medical practitioners was recognized. And the fact that the McLean Asylum for the Insane was a branch of Massachusetts General and served the upper classes in a very direct way maintained their interest in the corporation. Since the asylum generally met its operating expenses from patient revenues, the contributions it generated helped support the hospital.

Yet the loss of reforming zeal brought no relaxation of discipline within Massachusetts General; if anything, it reinforced it. The "influence of order" which pervaded Children's Hospital, furthering resocialization of its young patients, was a concern in Massachusetts General too, but as a reflection of social reality rather than a vision of social change. Many patients were not bedridden and expected to be able to walk about the grounds and even the city, or enjoy the carriage rides into the countryside furnished by the Young Men's Christian Union. Many were new to urban life (through the 1870s the percentage of its patients born in Boston never approached ten percent) and to the demands of institutional living. To help maintain discipline, the grounds were surrounded by a high wall with guards at the gate. Patients needed signed passes to leave and reenter, and visitors were carefully screened.[94] This discipline was maintained for internal reasons; rather than reform a patient who misbehaved, the hospital expelled him.[95]

Like other hospitals, Massachusetts General was meant to be a guarantor of social stability. As one supporter of Children's Hospital put it, "There is a practical side to this charity, which may commend it to thoughtful men." In the view of the fortunate classes, hospitals provided the working classes with evidence that the wealthy were aware of their responsibilities: "the only sure way to reconcile labor to capital is to show the laborer by actual deeds that the rich man regards himself as the steward of the Master." Until Workmen's Compensation went into effect, accident-plagued corporations, especially railroads and street railways, underwrote free beds at Massachusetts General, thus providing their employees with a paternalistic form of insurance, absolving themselves of responsibility for injury, and attempting to defuse issues that might otherwise build up workers' grievances.[96] One observer noted that "the hospitals act as a kind of insurance system for the laboring classes. They take the risks incidental to their position the more cheerfully, because they know that if injured they are assured of a special provision for their need in our hospitals."[97] Similar reasoning was used to elicit support for Children's Hospital. There would be no telling what even the most respectable worker, distraught over his inability to secure aid for his child, might do. "It is under such circumstances the iron enters a man's soul, and he is ready for a 'strike' or any other desperate remedy that promises better times and money with which to provided good nursing and delicacies for his suffering children." A mother, turned down when applying for admission for her sick child, might go "fiercely on her way, ripe for any evil deed." But assured that the hospital would care for their sick children, the poor would respond with gratitude rather than violence.[98]

In encouraging support for the city's voluntary hospitals, the *Transcript* editorially assured "those who look into the matter [that they would] see that our hospitals are among the very bases of national health and prosperity, and the working of these institutions is, therefore, a matter of general interest and public importance." Hospitals thus served much the same function as the public schools, to which they were sometimes likened by those arguing that they served the entire community and those needing them should use them as a guaranteed right with any cost borne by the community. But this was the view of a minority; Boston's City Registrar complained that too many of those "by mere fortuitous circumstance differently situated" had yet to learn that "the material condition of the whole community is involved in this subject."[99] Though hospital treatment of the poor might protect the established order and add to the wealth of the community, the people for whom it was intended were made to feel recipients of charity and reminded repeatedly that they were enjoying a privilege and that gratitude was expected in return. This attitude was embodied in law. In one case, a man treated gratuitously sued Massachusetts General, claiming his broken leg was set improperly. The court's ruling was in keeping with the common law doctrine of charitable immunity; even if the patient had been treated incompetently and negligently, he was not entitled to recover because the institution was a charity.[100] In another case, a woman charity patient operated on at the Free Hospital for Women sued, claiming her operation was not successful. During the course of protracted litigation, "A Friend to Our Charities" wrote the *Transcript* complaining that such hospital malpractice suits arose because "there are some patients so wholly devoid of ordinary gratitude for favors to which they had not a shadow of a claim, as to make their benefactors suffer by reason of their very kindness." When a verdict for the hospital was finally returned, on the grounds that money given hospitals must not be drained by lawsuits, the *Transcript*'s headline, "A Victory for Charity," translated the jury's decision into a reaffirmation of the status of hospitals.[101]

The social rhetoric generated by hospitals should not obscure their role as medical institutions in the 1870s. They furnished their patients medical care and their physicians the opportunity to keep abreast of medical advance. But hospitals filled both these functions within a social context. For physicians, they were the clinical theater within which elite practitioners shaped their professional roles. Patients were not a cross section of the sick and injured, but were drawn from the unfortunate classes of Boston and its hinterland. A social gulf separated patrons and practitioners from patients. Lay and medical partisans of hospitals defined them and justified them paternalistically. This paternalism was evident in the medical, moral, and social therapeutics that prevailed in them. Hospitals provided their patients with creature comforts and a level of medical attendance they probably could not have secured outside. But hospitals also maintained a rigid discipline and signaled in other ways to their patients that those in control regarded the lower class inmates as perhaps unworthy, their values deficient, and their motives in seeking care—or even becoming ill—sometimes suspect. Hospitals would not cease to be an alien environment for the sick and injured in the next half century, but changes in medicine and society would make them less culturally hostile to their patients. Those changes could affect both their medical and their social role.

## 2. "Bless Almighty God and the City of Boston for This Hospital"

*–a former patient*

Dr. David Cheever, a member of one of Boston's dynastic medical families, testified on January 30, 1880, before a committee of the city council. The committee was considering administrative changes for Boston City Hospital. At issue was a restructuring of the board of trustees: a reduction in their number, a lengthening of their terms of service, selection of them by the mayor rather than the council, and incorporation of the hospital as a state chartered body. These matters were highly technical, but stirred controversy because they raised broader questions about the role of the city hospital, the practice of medicine, and the status and treatment of hospital patients. The committee hearings continued a debate that found the medical staff on one side and representatives of the city's Irish community on the other.

Cheever had been visiting surgeon at Boston City since it opened in 1864; he also taught surgery at Harvard Medical School. The first president of the hospital's medical staff, he held that office until he retired in 1907. More than any other physician, Cheever dominated Boston City Hospital. Cheever informed the committee that the medical staff unanimously favored the administrative changes in question. He personally was dissatisfied with the instability of the lay governing board. The one-year term of office led to frequent turnover, contrasting with the hospital's first decade when, in spite of the same formal terms, many of the trustees had stayed on for longer periods. Cheever pointed specifically to Thomas Amory, Jr., Otis Norcross, Theodore Metcalf, and John T. Bradley; their long service as trustees had given them greater interest in the hospital's well-being. Yet of Cheever's four examples, Amory had served for only one year and Norcross four. Twenty-seven men served as trustees from 1863 through 1870, thirty from 1873 through 1880—a negligible difference considering the enlargement of the board from eight to nine members in 1867.[1] Clearly, Cheever had something other than stability of tenure in mind in describing the board that incorporation was meant to recreate. To replace the board composed of three members of the city council and six citizens chosen at large (though they were often councilmen) by the council, Cheever advocated a seven-man board, only two of whose members would be councilmen serving annual terms, while the other five would be private citizens selected by the mayor for staggered five-year terms. Appointment by the mayor rather than by the council was preferred because the former was responsible to a citywide constituency, and thus more respectable than the ward bosses rising to power in the council. Staggered terms precluded sudden change in board personnel or policy, minimizing the disruption that might be wrought by the electoral process. A board so constituted would be relatively insulated from city politics; in Cheever's judgment, it would "be likely to attract to the position of the trustees, gentlemen who are perhaps not so extremely occupied by their affairs outside that they cannot devote a great deal of time to the institution." Cheever was exact in his use of the term "gentlemen." Changes in administrative structure were intended to produce trustees who exhibited the traits that characterized the moneyed Brahmin elite. Such board members would be more congenial to Cheever and the hospital staff than the politician-trustees especially "noticeable...during the last five or six years."[2]

The expressed fear of those favoring incorporation was that Boston City was becoming enmeshed in city politics. In reality, the hospital staff was troubled by the emergence of a new kind of city politics. Boston's new immigrant based politics—with its professional politicians, ward leaders, and patronage system—had already challenged the political hegemony of the native born merchant elite. But only the first ripples of that challenge had reached the city hospital. Two of the council's 1879 appointments to the hospital board had been opposed—Dr. Michael F. Gavin and Councilman Israel Cohen. Their selection apparently set off the campaign for incorporation that began in 1879. Incorporation was preemptive in nature. It was meant to preclude changes that might occur but had not yet occurred.

Opposing Cheever at the council hearings in 1880 was the newly appointed trustee Dr. Gavin. Gavin testified that the staff had nearly entire control of the hospital and that interference—even from the trustees—was minimal. Only once had the trustees appointed to the staff a physician who had not first been nominated by the staff. Gavin's experience was firsthand. An Irish immigrant and Harvard Medical School graduate, he had won appointment as a house officer at the city hospital in its first year. From the beginning, Boston City—in contrast to Massachusetts General—had selected its house officers from applying medical students by competitive oral examination. When Gavin applied for appointment as a visiting surgeon in 1872, however, he was rejected by the staff. Years later he confided to a colleague that "he had always felt that he had more than sufficient grounds for feeling aggrieved" because of this rejection.[3] In 1879, Gavin capitalized on his political connections in his adopted South Boston to secure appointment as a city hospital trustee. It was in this capacity that he testified in 1880, representing the minority of the board in arguing against incorporation.

Opponents of incorporation claimed that the city's masses found the city hospital attractive precisely because it was vulnerable to the new forces expressing themselves in local politics. Administrative changes would threaten the status of Boston City as the people's hospital. This argument was perhaps as much based on expectations about the future as the argument for incorporation was based on fear. Testifying against incorporation, Thomas C. Brophy noted, "the City Hospital is an institution that all the people take pride in and particularly the poorer portion of the population." Holding opinions similar to those of Brophy about the direction in which city politics was transforming the hospital, opposing witnesses regarded the outcome of unchecked evolution differently. Visiting surgeon Charles Homans advocated the administrative changes because they would put both the hospital and its staff in "a more respectable position in the eyes of medical officers of other hospitals." Visiting physician George Gay echoed the theme of respectability, pointing out that, because the boards of the city library and the city hospital were differently constituted, the public regarded the library more highly. Gay's "public" and Homans's "medical officers of other hospitals" were the city's more substantial citizens.[4]

The controversy over incorporation was a special case of a larger issue fiercely debated in Boston in the late 1870s and early '80s: to which social classes should the city's institutions be responsible? Boston's historic ruling class displayed a siege mentality in developing mechanisms to limit the discretionary power of the alien groups that were achieving political power. Trustees of Massachusetts General, for example, requested the state legislature in December 1883 to amend the hospital's charter, deleting the governor's power to appoint four members of the twelve-man board. In the case of Massachusetts General, the possibility of danger was remote because the social background and outlook of the governor's appointees generally resembled that of the private trustees.[5] The situation at the city hospital seemed more critical. While the governor was responsive to a largely native born state-wide constituency, the city council was responding more and more to the immigrant wards. Massachusetts General failed to secure the revision of its charter, but the state legislature, dominated by rural and small town Protestants, recognized the threat to Boston's Protestant elite and incorporated Boston City Hospital in 1880.

State incorporation duplicated the process and the statute which in 1878 had removed Boston Public Library from the control of the city council and put it under a blue ribbon mayoral board. An Irish witness testifying in 1880 against change in the status of the hospital board complained that the newly incorporated library was serving as a model for the hospital reformers. He noted that the new library board had made proposals "the like of which have never been presented before. In the last annual report of the trustees they say there should be two libraries in two places, one where the literary men could frequent it, and one in another place,—to use the words of the trustees—where the masses could go." The situation in the police department paralleled that in the library and hospital. In 1878, the state legislature removed the police from city council authority and vested control in a mayoral board; in 1885, a newly created state authority removed control of the police from Boston altogether.[6]

The conflict at the city hospital was one of definition; most directly involved were practitioners and representatives of the patient class. Boston City's physicians tried to translate to their institution the assumptions that underlay Massachusetts General. From the outset, voluntary institutions such as Massachusetts General had set the pattern for general hospitals in the United States. But the relationships among patrons, patients, and practitioners that characterized voluntary hospitals did not survive intact in the municipal hospital. Dr. Charles Homans noted in 1880 that the city hospital was "carried on in the same way as all general hospitals, . . . so far as [the staff] have any influence about it."[7] But with the advent of the urban political machine, ward bosses standing in the same relation to the public institution as patrons did to private ones were ready to advocate the interests of the patient classes—their own lower class constituency—against the interests of the elite.

The coming of age of the political machine coincided wth the emergence of modern medicine. The exercise of significant political power by immigrant Americans and their children led to clashes with physicians who were making their own demands of hospitals. As physicians tried to recast the institution to fit their professional agenda, they sometimes found their advocacy of narrowly technical medical care challenged by spokesmen claiming to speak for the patient classes. Each group—physician and patient—had its ideas as to what constituted appropriate hospital organization and proper medical care. It is an oversimplification to place patients and practitioners on opposite sides in all aspects of the debate over the city hospital. The groups were not monolithic. Irish politicians did not always speak for all immigrant groups. Staff physicians had differences of their own. And on some issues, common interests united groups of practitioners and patients. Yet democratization confronted professionalization more fully at the city hospital than at Massachusetts General, where patients had little voice, physicians shared close and inhibiting ties with patrons, and tradition legitimated and maintained earlier patterns.

The advocates of the patient class who emerged out of Boston's ethnic politics in the last third of the nineteenth century had not been the first to challenge the concept of a city hospital modeled on the private Massachusetts General Hospital. The preliminary organization of Boston City Hospital was marked by tension between this model and an opposing one. The propriety of governmental action, in an area that had been reserved previously to the voluntary initiative of private charitable associations, was open to question during the city hospital's early history. Yet by 1857 when sustained activity leading to its founding began, it encountered little resistance, because those normally opposing any expansion in the functions of city government perceived the new institution as a continuation of the city's historic responsibilities rather than as another Massachusetts General.[8]

American cities had historically provided shelter and medical care to two specific elements among the sick and disabled: striken inmates of public institutions and those perceived as threats to the public health. Prisoners and paupers had received medical aid in jail or almshouse and the plague-ridden had been isolated and cared for in pesthouses. Early public discussion of a city hospital had been connected with the city's public health activities. The city government first considered establishing a permanent hospital in the aftermath of the cholera epidemic of 1849 and debated a report proposing that the cholera hospital be utilized as a general hospital. The first bequest to the city for the maintenance of a municipal hospital, contained in the will of Elisha Goodnow, dated from that year. Opponents defeated the proposal by successfully portraying the projected hospital as an expensive duplication of facilities already available at the almshouse for the expected patient population of foreign paupers.[9] In New York and Philadelphia, the first municipal hospitals developed from almshouses; patients treated within them were long subject to the same liabilities as paupers.[10] Boston City Hospital did not share the origins of Bellevue or Philadelphia General, but as a city institution it did not escape all identification with the almshouse. Though suggestions that it be put under the same board as administered the pauper institutions were rejected, perceptions derived from the almshouse experience became expectations of what a city hospital was to be.

But the actual impetus for the hospital's establishment came from the insufficiency of Massachusetts General, with its hundred forty beds. Boston had grown, and that segment of its population potentially in need of hospitalization had been greatly enlarged by Irish immigration. Here was an alternate model for the city's hospital, one under which it was to perform the same service as the private institution. Goodnow, the hospital's first benefactor, had left his money for the city to build "an institution similar to the Massachusetts General Hospital, not such public hospital as may be established or maintained in connection with the City Almshouse or House of Correction."[11]

Probably no one wanted the new city hospital to duplicate the almshouse. Physicians especially were wary of almshouses; in the first half of the nineteenth century they had found these institutions deficient in their medical orientation and unresponsive to the needs of medical men. Generally caring for debilitated and incurable inmates, almshouses held few patients suitable for active medical treatment. But the strongest opposition to the Massachusetts General model for the city hospital had originally come from physicians affiliated with Massachusetts General itself. They favored a new institution which would resemble the almshouse in some respects, but differ in its pronounced medical orientation.

Forces associated with Massachusetts General envisioned a city institution that would not draw its patients from the same class as their hospital. Dr. Samuel Abbot, admitting physician of Massachusetts General, took issue in 1857 with the implication that his institution was unable to handle all the cases it considered its own. He insisted that very few suitable cases were turned away for lack of space. No accident case was ever refused admission. Certainly Boston needed no additional facilities for sick female domestics, the class for which "above all others, . . . the Massachusetts General Hospital was intended." Abbot wanted the new city institution to be a *"free hospital*—a *charity hospital*—such as exists in other cities," meaning a copy of Bellevue or Philadelphia General, hospitals which had developed from poorhouses and were still considered their adjuncts. He wanted the new hospital to treat only the medically and socially offensive; those "suffering from erysipelas, smallpox, fever in any of its forms [and] acute pulmonary disease," receiving "all the sick now sent to Deer Island [the almshouse] and many more."[12]

A plan submitted by city physician Henry G. Clark to the city council in 1860 presented the city hospital as Abbot wanted it. It would care for five categories of patients: (1) cases of contagious disease, like smallpox, or measles; (2) lying-in cases; (3) consumptives and chronic incurables; (4) cases of delirium tremens and delirium convulsions, and other cases from police station houses; and (5) victims of cholera and other epidemics. Confining itself to these categories, the city hospital would not intrude on Massachusetts General's sphere of activity. Further, the new hospital would not represent an expansion of the city government's traditional services. Categories one and five were already recognized as public health responsibilities. Categories three and four were in the almshouse tradition as was, indirectly, category two—it was not uncommon for unwed mothers needing institutional care to receive it in the almshouse.[13]

Clark and Abbot described the projected patient population in medical terms, but except for contagious diseases, the categories actually expressed social distinctions. Diseases recognized as contagious were beyond the scope of Massachusetts General; erysipelas was offensive and a threat to any institution. The station house cases in category four were probably in the very lowest classes. Among accident victims and the sick coming to the attention of the police, only the very poor or vicious (brawling casualties, injured drunkards, debilitated prostitutes, and so forth) were likely to be brought to station houses; those who needed the continued care of the city were especially forlorn. Alcoholics and unwed mothers needing public relief fell into the same class. And the chronically ill, consumptive or otherwise, without the resources to have themselves cared for privately, were the staple almshouse population. Advocates of a city institution oriented toward these groups noted that it would benefit Massachusetts General "by aiding in restoring it to the uses originally intended by its founders"[14]—perhaps implying that a city institution, dealing with the socially marginal, would relieve pressure on Massachusetts General to admit the foreign born.

Those on the other hand who envisioned a city hospital that would duplicate the functions of Massachusetts General used both explicit social terms and socially laden medical terms in defining the prospective patient population. In asking the city council to consider establishing a hospital in 1857, Mayor Rice suggested that it would serve "those plunged into poverty by sickness or sudden reverses, who ought not to be sent to the almshouse."[15] Only those whose poverty was respectable would be entitled to hospital rather than almshouse care. The city council committee considering the mayor's address defined hospital patients more carefully:

Hence we would not have this a hospital for the reception of the degraded victims of vice and intemperance, or a home for the hopeless pauper; but we would have it regarded as an asylum for the industrious and honest mechanic and laborer, who by sudden injury or disease is temporarily prevented from laboring for the support of himself and his family; and who by proper care and medical treatment, may have his sufferings alleviated, and sooner be restored to his health and his family, and enabled to resume his labor.

We would have it a home, to which the respectable domestic may be sent, when struck down by sickness, whose attic chambers cannot be made comfortable, and who cannot receive the requisite attendance, however well disposed may be the family in which she resides. We would open its doors to the stranger overtaken by disease, when absent from friends and home, and to all others among the various classes of society who in sickness require that comfort and medical advice which their means and homes cannot afford.[16]

It was this 1857 report with which Clark and Abbot took issue. When the Clark plan was rejected in 1862, those who did not wish Boston City to intrude upon Massachusetts General were dealt a setback.[17]

By the time the city hospital was dedicated in 1864, it was presented as a departure from municipal tradition. Rather than caring for patients for whom the city had been responsible historically, it was to assist instead "the honest, temperate and industrious poor." Soon after the first patient had been admitted, the trustees voted that no applicant, except for accident or emergency cases, "be admitted to the Hospital who cannot give a satisfactory reference as to character when requested to do so."[18] Delivering the keys to the board, Mayor Lincoln reminded them of their responsibility to distinguish "between the virtuous poor who have a claim on your sympathy, and the vicious who are suffering the penalties of their vices." Though the hospital's president, Otis Norcross, admitted in his remarks the difficulty of drawing "the line which separates temporary necessity from pauperism," he pledged the vigilance of the trustees in keeping the institution from becoming a pauper hospital.[19]

In his address, Thomas C. Amory, Jr., the outgoing president, referred to Massachusetts General as the "parent institution" and set out a program duplicating that available at the older hospital, which was no longer adequate to care for an expanded and dispersed population. The new hospital would treat the "respectable poor, virtuous, neat and well-conducted" and exclude "the profligate," whose "unseemly habits, profane and rude conversation" might drive all others away. Rather than function as a repository for categories of cases refused admission by Massachusetts General, the city hospital would also deny entry to the chronically ill, incurable, or contagious, and provide no lying-in facilities.[20]

Though the city hospital's opening marked a new departure in governmental activity, it did not represent a complete break from government's traditional responsibilities in public health and the maintenance of paupers. The institution originally contained no facilities for contagious diseases, but the ordinance creating it vested in its board of trustees control over any small-pox or other epidemic hospital which the city council might establish. Presidents Amory and Norcross foresaw the possibility of separate buildings on the hospital grounds to care for "infectious and contagious diseases," and those judged incurable during their hospital stays might be transferred to the almshouse. Further, the original hospital rules copied those of the almshouse in compelling free patients able to work to do so.[21] Not fully severed from the almshouse tradition when it opened, Boston City Hospital—like municipal hospitals elsewhere—would revert at times to that tradition.

In actual practice, the patients at Boston City Hospital came from a lower class overall than that which used Massachusetts General.[22] In part this was because the voluntary hospital reserved its right to refuse all but emergency patients who could not pay something toward the cost of their maintenance or were unable to secure nomination to a free bed. As a public institution, Boston City could not exercise such discrimination. Furthermore, popular opinion perceived the city hospital as obligated to admit all seeking entry. Trying to hold to their goal of duplicating Massachusetts General, the trustees bemoaned the "misapprehension on the part of many citizens regarding the class of persons for whom the hospital was intended." The trustees denied statements "by those who are interested in [the applicants'] behalf, that there is no reason for debarring them from this privilege, as the institution is a 'Free Hospital,' and the expenses thereof are borne by the taxpayers of the city." From the beginning, the trustees rejected "the erroneous title of *Free* City Hospital." (The title was used in the mayor's 1857 message, and in common parlance). Norcross stated, "That it will be free to a certain extent is very true, but not to the extent such a title would imply."[23] The early trustees did not consider free care at the city hospital a right, but a gift, as it was at Massachusetts General.

Though the city hospital was supported by local taxpayers, its use was not to be restricted to Boston citizens. The Massachusetts poor laws obligated the city to care only for residents who had met the requirements of legal settlement (residential longevity, tax payment, and so on). But it was clear that few settled Bostonians would care to use the hospital. Thomas Amory acknowledged that "should the benefits of the Institution be confined to such alone as have acquired or inherited a legal settlement, it would remain much of the time untenanted. Whoever are familiar with Boston and its people, know well that there are but few of this class who do not prefer the privacy of their own dwellings, and the attendance of their own kindred, to any advantage to be gained from the best scientific care in a hospital. This feeling is deeply seated."[24] Those who had acquired settlements were people of some means and had spent at least ten years in Boston.[25] Those who inherited legal settlements might not have means but certainly had roots and family in the city. Neither were likely candidates for hospitalization in the first decade of the city hospital.

It was among those without legal settlements that the city hospital was expected to concentrate its work. Boston was a "great emporium of commercial and social activity," and while many of its own sons and daughters sought their fortunes abroad or in the west, the city had attracted great numbers of workers who constituted "the great mass of [its] industry, enterprise and thrift":

> It was often the expressed opinion of the early advocates for the establishment of this Institution, that young men and women from other towns or States, engaged here in earning their livelihood, would derive from it the principal advantages. Their meagre recompense furnishes no supplies for illness. They reside in crowded dwellings, whose proprietors, by rigid economy, just meeting their own obligations, cannot afford to be generous. In cold rooms, with unsuitable nourishment, they are often driven to distant homes to perish. Their toil contributes to our prosperity; they form an important part of our population; many among them, in the future, will be the most useful members of our society. They would seem, of all others, entitled, by a liberal interpretation of the statute, to enjoy its benefits.[26]

While the city hospital was in its planning stage and in its early years, it was influenced "by a liberal interpretation of the statute."

This liberality culminated in the administration of Dr. Edward Cowles, superintendent of Boston City Hospital from 1872 to 1879 (and later superintendent of the McLean Asylum, 1879–1904). Recognizing the responsibility inherent in his duty of admitting patients, Cowles explained how he applied the guidelines developed by the trustees. Confronted by an applicant not meeting the rigorous standards, Cowles asked: "Is it *humane* to reject this applicant?" He felt the question necessary in view of the difficulty of strictly applying the formal rules. Though only the deserving were to be admitted, Cowles would not exclude any accident case "although not a few of them may be vicious and intemperate." Though paupers were to be excluded and referred to the almshouse, they included in their number many of the "honest and virtuous, who, pursued by misfortune and disease, are forced at last to overcome their pride, and ask for aid." Some of them might benefit from temporary aid, and perhaps even recuperate enough to return to their homes "saved from being pauperized and becoming charges of the public during the remainder of their lives." Though those suffering the consequences of their own vices were to be turned away, Cowles admitted the vicious if they were ill, and refused them only if it did not "endanger their lives, or prolong suffering that may be alleviated here."[27]

Cowles saw the city hospital as saving patients from a worse fate. For the undeserving it might stave off death or disability from otherwise untreated illness or accident. For those on the verge of pauperism because of disease or injury, it presented an opportunity to regain their strength. For all in distress, the city hospital functioned as an alternative to the almshouse. For many, it provided humane treatment available nowhere else in the city. All that it lacked were expanded facilities that would allow the admission of "all persons who are very sick, and *needing aid* from the Hospital, whatever be their moral condition." Expansion would enable further classification among the patients so that the worthy would not be forced to share quarters with the vicious or intemperate.[28]

Cowles saw that the city hospital was dealing with a class of patients different from that admitted to Massachusetts General. He responded by abandoning the Massachusetts General model and loosening institutional restrictions. Witnessing the same phenomenon as Cowles, the trustees determined even more that their institution would replicate the private hospital and not be forced by its patients to the level of the almshouse. Whereas the Massachusetts General model had earlier been invoked to plan a hospital more liberally managed than the almshouses, by the 1870s the trustees used the same model to justify an authoritarian policy.

The trustees found their original expectations, that the city hospital would cater to worthy young New Englanders drawn into the city to make their fortunes, dashed by 1870 in the face of overwhelming majorities of foreign born patients. The trustees' first inclination was restrictive; to admit only the "legitimate, acutely sick, and deserving citizen." But because theirs was not a private institution, they resigned themselves to admitting some patients "more fitly placed in some 'other appropriate public institution.'"[29] Forced to admit patients they considered unworthy, they took care to define the city hospital's services as not a right but a privilege. While its planners had originally believed that patients would pay voluntarily for board—there being "no class in the community in which this sentiment or desire of independence is so strong as among that class for whose special benefit this Hospital is intended"—by the 1870s the trustees increasingly stressed the obligation of patients to pay for their care. Boston City started formally charging all who could pay in 1877.[30]

The trustees also determined to examine the settlement of nonpaying patients to see if the cost of their care might be recovered. An 1865 state law provided that localities could be reimbursed by the state for the care of nonsettled sick persons too ill to be moved to the state almshouse. The law had been designed to cover sick paupers without local settlements confined to local almshouses. Claims made against the state under the law would not only raise money for the city hospital but might also discourage nonpaying patients the trustees deemed undesirable, since they would now be subject to the same legal liabilities as almshouse inmates, including pauperization, one consequence of which was disenfranchisement. The same liabilities held for nonpaying patients settled in other Massachusetts cities and towns. It is unclear whether this penalty was invoked in practice. The Associated Charities *Directory* (1891) warned that anyone receiving free aid at Boston

City Hospital would be legally pauperized and thus disenfranchized. Legal scholar Charles T. Russell, Jr., noted, however, that only persons receiving aid under the poor laws on the day of voter registration would be disenfranchised. That the threat was nonetheless clear is evident in the objections raised after the practice of seeking reimbursement for nonsettled and nonpaying patients was instituted: "It is said that the effect of the payment of these would be to pauperize the patients."[31]

At the request of the trustees, superintendent Cowles conducted a month-long investigation of patient settlements in 1873. He found that of 249 admissions, 49 were not settled and could come under the provisions of the 1865 law. The other 200 were not all Boston settled and included nonpaying patients for whom the state could not be charged because they were "able to bear transportation to the almshouse." The nonsettled who entered the hospital were, as President Amory had foreseen, not strangers to Boston. In Cowles's study, 10 of the 49 nonsettled cases had lived in Boston more than ten years, failing to gain settlement only by reason of insufficient property, while no less than 28 of the 49 had lived in the city for more than two years at the time of hospital admission. When Cowles was directed to repeat the study in 1877/78, he found 154 non–Boston settled, nonpaying patients out of a total of 347 admitted in one month. (Ten of the 347 were nonsettled who paid, while 183 were legal residents of Boston.) Of the 154, 42 had lived in Boston at least ten years, 79 at least five years, and 111 at least two years. Twenty-seven of the 66 nonminor males in the group had paid at least one city tax and 12 of the nonsettled patients had been born in Boston. But 122 of the 154 were foreign born. Except for the fact of their foreign birth, these were the patients for whom the city hospital had been intended. The policy of the trustees was to legally pauperize these patients if they entered as free patients. In 1882, about forty percent of the city hospital's patients were not legally settled in Boston and, if not paying, were subject to pauperization.[32] The care of nonpaying Boston settled patients continued to be paid for out of the city hospital appropriation, and consequently these patients could not suffer the legal penalty of pauperization.

The trustees used settlement as a tool to force patients to pay something for their care: "Many poor and respectable persons, legally resident and non-resident, parents of families, serving women, domestics, laborers, young men in the various trades, would without doubt willingly pay for their board in a hospital such small sums as they are able, if the rule and custom were established for the sake of the feeling it may give them that they are not *dependent* on charity, and *to save themselves the liability of being made the subjects of claims against the state for their care.*"[33] The nonsettled patient refusing to pay would come under the poor law; the nonpaying settled patient could at least be made to feel "dependent" and stigmatized.

The trustees' stress on settlement—like the desire to have patients pay—no doubt in part reflected the fear of being imposed upon that pervaded much of the charitable sentiment of the period. In the broader society, this attitude toward the poor was implicit in warnings about indiscriminate almsgiving and led to the founding, in 1879, of Boston's Associated Charities.[34] The city hospital trustees tried to avoid unwarranted benevolence toward patients. When, for example, physicians complained that the food given patients was both meagre and "not such that they can take it with relish or even without disgust," the trustees responded that it was all that people of average means should expect.[35] Among the administrators and theoreticians of Boston's charities, many feared that lavishly or unwisely bestowed gifts would destroy the character of the recipient and make him unfit to support himself. Free hospital care was a first step to a dissolute life. But the crucial influence on the trustees' attitude was their expectation of what the city hospital was to be. Forcing patients to pay was, in the main, an attempt to bring an unpleasant reality in line with the trustees' earlier, Massachusetts General influenced model. The trustees concluded that encouraging patients to pay had a positive effect: "The presence of paying patients in the wards has had an effect of elevating the character of the Hospital, and evidently of attracting increased public interest to it."[36]

While Edward Cowles remained superintendent, his humane attitude minimized the effect of the trustees on the actual operation of the hospital. His valedictory reports in 1878 and 1879 were catalogs of rules he had broken and strictures he had neglected in promiscuously opening the institution to all. Patients who could not pay had not been pauperized. He had not rejected—if they could benefit from admission—the "professional invalids, shiftless and improvident persons, frequent applicants for relief [and] victims of their own vices with alcoholism or injuries from drunken quarrels or accidents." The same held for the chronic and incurably ill. The police had been encouraged to bring in "doubtful cases" that might otherwise have spent time in station houses or jails. Even those suffering attacks of insanity had been welcomed, and the hospital had responded to their needs by organizing a department for diseases of the nervous system. In parting, Cowles noted with pleasure that the public was pleased: "As in other kinds of business, an institution like the City Hospital gains the goodwill of the public by being always ready to promptly render the aid needed and asked for, with as little circumlocution and as few obstructive rules as possible, and thereby making itself valuable to the public." Cowles's parting advice was that the hospital foster "its growth in the direction of the obvious needs of the public."[37]

With Cowles's replacement as superintendent in 1879 by Dr. George H. M. Rowe, hospital policy shifted. Rowe, a martinet, was sympathetic to the work of the Associated Charities and was well suited to be the instrument of the incorporated, "nonpolitical" board of trustees that began to manage Boston City in 1880. While Cowles had been superintendent, the trustees had occasionally requested the city council to take steps that would allow the hospital to enter claims against the state and other towns for nonsettled patients. But starting in 1880, the trustees repeatedly brought the settlement issue to the attention of the city council, and these requests no longer contained the qualifications they had had under Cowles. The trustees warned of the venality of those who had no claim on the city but insinuated themselves into its hospital: "large numbers of patients are treated in this Hospital who, by reason of misrepresentation or by accidents or urgent illness, procured admission to the City Hospital of the City of Boston."[38]

One of the first items of business of the incorporated board of trustees was to discuss with the city government "collecting from the State and from other cities and towns the cost of supporting patients chargeable to them." After making arrangements with the Overseers of the Poor, the trustees voted to hire an agent to examine settlements and begin the work of charging the state and the various cities and towns for care.[39] Since the state was not obligated to consider claims for the care of state settled poor who could bear removal to a state almshouse, the work of refusing admission to state settled (that is, having no settlement in any Massachusetts town) applicants who were not in immediate jeopardy began in earnest. In 1882, Rowe estimated he was referring twenty prospective patients a week to the state, "whose duty it is to look out for them," for removal to the state almshouse.[40] While Cowles had been superintendent, state settled cases had been admitted even if they could bear removal.[41]

Malingerers, the shiftless, and victims of their own vices were also put on notice that they would not be admitted. Patients considered incurable—and thus of limited clinical interest—were discharged to the city almshouse. Superintendent Rowe rejoiced that the increase in other facilities, represented by the city prison, and a less cumbersome asylum commitment law made it possible to reject cases of insanity more frequently. He also suggested that the city provide accommodations for tuberculosis cases elsewhere.[42]

Because it was a public hospital, however, these restrictions did not go unchallenged. Envying other local hospitals "free to admit or reject such applicants as they deem best," Rowe reported that the public's expectations complicated the enforcement of hospital policy. It was "not uncommon for persons to make journeys of considerable length, coming to the hospital with their baggage expecting to be received because it is supported by the tax levy of the city." Applicants used "every possible lever to open our doors." Rowe's solution was an enlightened public that would accept restrictions imposed by the hospital: "complaints always have been made by the public because these applicants are not received and always will be made until there is a more general apprehension of the true purpose of the hospital, and what constitutes a proper case, and the legal right for admission."[43]

By the 1880s, then, those controlling the hospital—the incorporated board of trustees, the medical staff for whom they often spoke, and the superintendent—had developed a unified view of it as an instrument for grudging and inexpensive relief to the sick poor, an agency of social control, and an arena for the professional aspirations of elite physicians. Had the lay board and the medical staff been free to implement the program implicit in this understanding, the city hospital would have been much like Massachusetts General. But Boston City—even as an incorporated institution—remained a municipal hospital. Local ethnic politicians, styling themselves representatives of the patient class, stood ready to challenge the hospital's governors.

Because the hospital budget remained subject to city council appropriations, the influence of democratic politics could not be wholly abated. Formal city council resolutions make visible—to the historian, at least—the intermediacy of politicians representing their constituents before the hospital authorities. Fearing rejection when applying for admission, for example, potential patients carried letters from ward leaders or other persons they considered powerful or well connected. In some cases, elected officials personally contacted trustees—a difficult task, according to Alderman Martin Lomasney, both because Boston's upper classes had deserted other sections of the city for the Back Bay and because they deserted the city entirely for summer vacations. In the face of mounting demands that patients pay something for their care, politicians broadened their patronage with requests to excuse individual patients from whatever charges the hospital might assess.[44] In securing admission or the remission of fees, ward leaders, in effect, duplicated the function of wealthy donors to voluntary hospitals. At the same time, politicians were more accessible and were perceived as more benign than elite subscribers to free bed funds.

Those dissatisfied with admitting policies set by the hospital trustees also sought to use the political process and the weight of public opinion to change those policies. Opposition to the hospital's restrictive admissions policy sometimes crystallized around the difficulty encountered in gaining hospital admission for the inebriated or apparently drunk. The poor were suspicious of the use of alcoholism as an excuse for withholding medical services, fearing that legitimate medical complaints mght be mistaken for alcoholic stupor and denied admission. It was not uncommon for poor drunkards, picked up by the police, to die unattended in station house lockups. The police either could not secure their admission to the city hospital, or else did not attempt to do so because, on the basis of prior experience, they judged the task impossible. Such incidents might be followed by public investigations or inquests finding that obvious drunkenness had masked pneumonia or serious injury, and that inebriates had died in police custody when medical care might have saved their lives.[45] As the incorporated governing board adopted increasingly restrictive admissions policies for Boston City Hospital in the 1880s, the city council sponsored investigations of individual cases and asked the trustees to consider changing their procedures to effect a more generous policy toward intoxicated persons who were injured or sick.[46]

The debate was not only over whom the institution should serve but also over how it should serve them. In accident cases, for example, was the hospital to facilitate the victim's right to sue for damages, or was it to side with the employers and property owners who might be sued? The first inclination of the trustees was to benefit employers, or those who might be held responsible for accidents. When it was learned that lawyers and law students were "visiting patients with the purpose of instigating suits," the trustees ordered the superintendent to "take particular care to prevent others than friends visiting patients on visiting days."[47] These attorneys may have appeared unscrupulous in soliciting cases, but their ambulance-chasing activities could also promote settlements for injured patients who might otherwise not have pursued their claims.

While patients were constrained from suing, physicians retained to provide expert testimony by insurance companies and employers were free to consult the hospital's medical records to prepare cases. When the surgical staff voted to request the trustees to restrict access to medical records to hospital staff members only, the action was undertaken not to secure the privacy of patients, but to further the monopoly of Boston City Hospital staff members on lucrative insurance company positions. The trustees complied. When Dr. Edwin Wells Dwight asked permission to consult the files to obtain information in behalf of the Employers Liability Insurance Company, he was refused; but within the year, he was appointed to the hospital staff, giving him and the company he represented unlimited access to all the hospital's records.[48] Finally popular pressure caused a change in policy. The trustees informed the staff in 1905 that "recent criticism have been made relative to the alleged use of the Medical Records of the Hospital, by some members of the Medical and Surgical Staff, in matters of settlement and in suits in Court, and it has been said that this use had been more especially made against the interests of patients whose records are given." Patient records were ordered to be held confidential and released only by authority of the patient concerned, the trustees, or a subpoena. Doctors serving corporations in obtaining such informations were told that such action was "inconsistent" with their holding hospital positions.[49]

Popular dissatisfaction did not end there. In 1909, Alderman James Michael Curley complained of the abuse that resulted from the employment of hospital doctors by insurance companies and corporations in the defense of accident claims. The problem lay not with the doctors' making records available, but rather with what they entered in those records. As Curley explained: "Quite often, where a man, either in the employ of some public service corporation or while at work on a building, meets with an accident and is rendered unconscious it is customary to give him a little drink of brandy, and if it happens that the physician who attends him when he arrives at the hospital is in close touch with the corporations in whose employ the man has met with the accident it is customary to give him a little brandy in order to bring him around to consciousness and then to mark his card at the hospital 'Alcoholism.'" Physicians and surgeons did well under the system, receiving, Curley charged, large retainers and witness fees of fifty dollars a case from corporations (railroads and street railways in particular). Patients suffered, however, as their cases were prejudiced by a medical record that indicated they were injured while intoxicated.[50] The trustees responded by changing the hospital rules to require that notation be made in the medical record if alcohol were administered to an accident case.[51]

The original, loosely defined regulations that were sometimes exploited to the detriment of hospital patients in the case of their records were on the other hand often rigidly enforced against them in other areas. Thomas Amory expected that the city hospital would be operating with the same rigidity as Massachusetts General when, in his dedicatory speech, he stated that "its decrees may often involve considerations not to be explained or communicated, and should be final without question or appeal."[52]

The hospital's electric clock system exemplified this rigidity. The clocks were constructed to minimize any irregularity in timekeeping. The main clock was located in the superintendent's office and connected with "electric companion clocks" in the wards and main hall, assuring "uniformity of time in the different parts of the Institution." The superintendent would not only be able to tell, at a glance, the exact time throughout the hospital, but as the whole system was attached to an "electro-magnetic watch clock" he could also be certain of "the precise time of [the watchman's] passing through the different parts of the buildings."[53]

Duplicating the clockwork as a mechanism for controlling the institution were the laws adopted for internal governance. The activities of patients were to be thoroughly regulated, their contacts with the outside world carefully controlled. Patients were not to leave their wards without permission of their nurses, a precaution necessary because many patients were not bedridden. Nor were patients to leave and reenter the hospital grounds without a pass from the superintendent. In one of its first actions, the visiting staff asked that this regulation be strictly enforced. The comings and goings of all patients, staff, and visitors were regulated by a gatekeeper, and the hospital gate locked every evening. Patients were prohibited from receiving any article from the outside without the consent of the superintendent.[54] Interaction between patients and outsiders was also to be minimized by a great wall enclosing the hospital, a pet project of Superintendent Rowe. Rowe sought the eight-foot-high brick wall to replace a wooden fence constructed when the hospital was built. He complained of "the great detriment to discipline" caused by the "too free communication...now held between patients and unscrupulous passers by." The wall would also prevent "the smuggling of liquor and other pernicious things to patients." When completed, Rowe was pleased with its effect in improving hospital discipline.[55] Although necessary to enforce appropriate behavior, rules, practices and even institutional design could result in petty tyrannies and oppressive discipline. While the sources for documenting patient response to the moralistic and authoritarian hospital regimen are limited, there can be little doubt that the interaction of lower class patients with upper class perceptions and proscriptions added to the discomfort of a city hospital stay.

In response to demands expressed through the political system, however, the emphasis on control decreased.[56] This was most evident in the policy of visiting hours, which had at first served the same functions as the wall and restrictive passes in minimizing patient contact with the outside. During the debate over incorporation in 1879-80, advocates of a hospital responsive to the popular will contrasted the ease of access to patients at the city hospital to the situation at Massachusetts General. Councilman P. F. McGargle noted his constituents' feelings that "the latter was so private that one might as well attempt to get into the vaults of the savings banks as into it, even to see a friend." Before incorporation, the hospital trustees had already refused Sunday visiting, necessary if workingmen were to visit family and friends. But the fear was that an incorporated hospital board, like the incorporated library board, which refused to open the public library on Sunday, would be even more adamant in refusing to accede to Sunday visiting.[57]

Original policy allowed one visitor per patient per day, with visits to occur during one afternoon hour on each of four weekdays. Intensive city council pressures in the 1880s and '90s led to a more generous policy. Two visitors were allowed each day instead of one; the visiting hour expanded from four to six days each week; and city councilmen won the right to issue passes to admit visitors outside of regular hours. In 1902 the hospital instituted Sunday visiting and also added an early evening visiting period on weekdays.[58]

The hospital was further humanized by its increasing responsiveness to the wishes its users expressed through the political system. The trustees went along with a common council request that they no longer charge messenger fees for notifying relatives of the death of a patient. They heeded the wishes of the board of aldermen in making it easier for relatives to collect corpses by reducing the waiting period after death and lengthening the hours during which bodies could be removed from the hospital. The rule against card-playing was dropped. When a Father Mahoney complained of the unspecified behavior of a hospital physician, the trustees, increasingly sensitive to the Catholic community, ordered the physician immediately discharged. And when the Boston Central Labor Union complained that one of its members had received inadequate care at the outpatient department, the trustees arranged a meeting between representatives of the union and the staff. Though the trustees decided that most of the charges aired at the meeting were unsubstantiated, they agreed that the original complaint had merit and took steps to monitor the work of the outpatient department more closely and cut down the time patients had to wait for medical attention.[59] To further safeguard the interests of the working classes, the Central Labor Union asked the mayor, in 1903, to appoint one of the city hospital trustees from the ranks of labor, for "inasmuch as working men are the chief patrons of the institution, they should have a voice in its management." In practice, the board consisted of one physician, one lawyer, and three businessmen. Protecting the already attenuated position of the elite in the direction of the hospital, organized medicine opposed the labor union request: "The fallacy and possible danger of such a principle of representation is apparent."[60]

By the turn of the century, the very composition of the hospital elite—the professional staff—was no longer beyond the influence of the political system. According to city hospital rules, new staff members were nominated by the senior staff and then appointed by the trustees. In the same way that ward heelers had brought many of the hospital's wage workers under the patronage system—turning election day, St. Patrick's Day, and Jewish high holidays into paid days off in the process—trustees and politicians responsive to groups not usually represented in hospital staffs used their positions to encourage the nomination of physicians from these outside groups. By the 1890s, Jewish politicians were urging the claims of their medical coreligionists.[61] The process had begun earlier with Irish Catholic politicians and Irish Catholic medical men. Dr. Michael F. Gavin, disappointed in his first attempts to be appointed to the visiting staff, successfully capitalized on his later position as trustee—the fruit of his political involvement—to gain admission to the surgical staff in 1884. Dr. Francis J. Keany followed the same tack in 1897. Selected as a trustee by the mayor, Keany nevertheless failed in his goal of securing a position on the medical staff in the dermatological department, but even his failure suggests the power of politicians over the city hospital by the end of the century. Rather than offend the mayor by simply refusing Keany the nomination, the cautious visiting staff abolished the position.[62] The advocacy of nonelite physicians by politicians made the hospital less threatening to Irish Catholic and Jewish patients and reinforced their feeling that Boston City, unlike Massachusetts General, was the people's hospital. Benefits to the nonelite physicians—who were otherwise largely denied the increasingly necessary opportunity of hospital practice—were even more tangible.

By the mid-1880s, in a parallel development, requests from women medical students, a homeopathic school, and other regular but less favored medical schools that the hospital be opened for clinical instruction to all students on an equal basis seem to have been granted, at least formally, to a limited degree.[63] Meager though this victory was—instruction remained under the control of the Harvard dominated staff until the twentieth century—it contrasted starkly with the situation at Massachusetts General, where in an unsuccessful plea for a limited teaching affiliation, Tufts Medical School felt compelled to promise that none of its female or black students would enter the hospital.[64]

Implicit in the questions about hospital staffing and admissions was the definition of a hospital. What services was it to provide? Who was to decide how it could be of greatest benefit to the community? Physicians might think one type of service appropriate; patients might prefer another. "Good medicine" as doctors understood it was sometimes not the supportive and personal care that the public seemed to want. Opposing incorporation at the hearings in 1880, city councilman William Whitmore acknowledged the contradictory—and equally valid—conceptions of the hospital: the practitioners wanted "to make it a great institution,...to create a great scientific school and do other things in their own way"; Whitmore's constituents wanted " a simple charity [for] the poor needing it."[65] The tension between the wishes of representatives of the patient class and those of practitioners determined the nature of the hospital. Because Boston City Hospital was a municipal institution, these conflicts were expressed in the political arena.

The dichotomous standards noted by Whitmore permeated discussions of the location of hospital services and the hours of their availability. Spokesmen for patients stressed accessibility. Hospital staffs favored the centralization of services that the logic of modern medicine seemed to imply. Doctors also wished to shape the institution to their professional roles. The case of Dr. George Galvin illustrates these dichotomous standards.

An entrepreneur as well as a physician, Galvin competed for a time in the 1890s with the city hospital. Galvin was a transitional figure, dividing the period when hospital appointments characterized an elite style of medical practice from the time when such positions became necessities of medical practice.

Galvin presented his paper "The Necessity of an Emergency Hospital in the Business District of Boston" to a meeting of the Suffolk District Medical Society in November 1890. He explained that he had been led to a consideration of the topic by his practice in the thickly settled, industrial and commercial South Cove district. As a young surgeon without an established practice, he found his patients among the many accident cases in which the district abounded. He had come to see the need for an emergency hospital in the area for the great number of casualties that required immediate medical or surgical aid. The seriously injured had to wait up to twenty minutes for the police ambulance and then endure a "long ride over rough and uneven pavements" that might take another half hour before arriving at Massachusetts General or Boston City Hospital. Most of the accident cases Galvin had seen were mild, involving "mangled fingers and toes, fractures and dislocations of the shoulder, forearm and ankle, scalp wounds and moderate concussion of the brain." These patients faced long waits in outpatient clinics, and in traveling and waiting lost time that could otherwise be spent on the job drawing pay.[66] Cases of both types would benefit immeasurably from immediate medical care, available twenty-four hours a day, directly in the area where accidents frequently occurred.

Galvin based his observations and proposal on experience. Five years before, he had gone to the general managers of the three railroads having stations in the South Cove area and had secured their cooperation in setting up an accident room in the United States Hotel. Railway accidents provided much of Galvin's practice, but industrial accidents involving machinery, elevators, and chemicals had also come to his attention in great numbers. He also saw many streetcar accidents and cases of sudden sickness from the crowds who filled the district's large stores, depots, warehouses, and streets.[67]

Galvin's assertion of an extremely high accident rate in the central business district was not challenged at the medical society meeting. As Boston's population had grown, its central business district served increasingly larger numbers of people brought into the area by the very streetcars that enabled the city to expand. Those streetcars themselves were, in part, directly responsible for the increasing number of accidents—as was the construction of the ever taller buildings that street railways made necessary. But the meeting rejected the call for an emergency hospital. For one thing, no acute sense of the medical "emergency" had developed by 1890. The "ordinary period of delay" was not perceived as harmful. It would require further advances in medical therapeutics before the difference between immediate and less immediate treatment translated into a better prognosis for the patient.

Arthur Tracy Cabot, surgeon at Massachusetts General, cited Boston's limited geography to disprove the need for a downtown relief station. Every populated section of Boston was within one and one-half miles of one of the city's three major hospitals. Dr. George H. M. Rowe, superintendent of the city hospital, also opposed Galvin's plan. Rowe thought that any difficulties in handling accident cases could be resolved easily by better coordinating the city's ambulances. He agreed with Cabot that Boston's limited size made any concern for additional or decentralized facilities unnecessary.[68]

Criticism did not dissuade Galvin. With support from the railroads and industrial and commercial concerns, he opened his Boston Emergency Hospital in July 1891. In its first year, the hospital served primarily as a first aid station treating over four thousand generally minor accident cases. Though it provided for stays of only up to twelve hours, very few of its patients needed more extended care in other hospitals after treatment. The Emergency Hospital drew its patients from the high risk occupations of the district. Laborers, with nearly a thousand admissions, provided the largest group of cases, followed by teamsters (432), brakemen (391), machine workmen (380), machinists, (210), clerks (192), and factory employees (187).[69] Galvin stated that his purpose in operating the hospital was to demonstrate its usefulness. He hoped to conduct it for perhaps three years and then have the city take it over.[70] By having his emergency facility merged into the city hospital, Galvin probably hoped to work his way into a desirable staff position at an established hospital, with increased prestige and income for himself.

Unlike clinical positions at the city's established hospitals, positions at the Emergency Hospital were directly remunerative. Galvin and his fellow surgeons drew salaries and charged professional fees of patients considered capable of paying. This practice, and Galvin's style, changed the attitude of Boston's medical establishment from mild skepticism to open disapproval and hostility.[71] This hostility closed off the possibility of an immediate merger into the city hospital and led Galvin to recast his institution as a long-term proposition, aggressively competing with the city hospital. He diverted his appeal from the medical profession to the public at large and the political process.[72] Forsaking the medical arguments of his 1890 lecture and his 1892 report, in the Emergency Hospital's next published report, issued in 1895, Galvin was demagogic. He blamed medical politics for hampering the work of the Emergency Hospital and attacked the city's other hospitals for the inadequate care they offered the working classes. Hospital outpatient departments were open only during limited morning hours; they should be open afternoons, evenings, and Sundays and holidays as well. Other institutions should follow the lead of the Emergency Hospital in having staff physicians and surgeons in attendance at all times. Galvin apparently hoped that popular pressure would force the city hospital to accept both him and his institution; he wrote that these expanded services at the established hospitals "would furnish appointments to worthy and capable physicians and surgeons."[73]

While leaving himself open to accepting a hospital appointment should it materialize, Galvin also announced his intention to continue pursuing an independent course should that be necessary. Galvin implied that the city hospital had failed in its mission; he expanded his populist advocacy by suggesting that there be in Boston "a hospital maintained by the working people." He presented a plan for a hospital association that could be operated by prepaid annual contributions of one dollar per person from its membership. This payment would entitle members, recruited from among the working classes, to free medical and surgical inpatient and outpatient care, obviating any need to continue the city hospital.[74]

At this point, the response of the Boston City Hospital staff changed. Galvin's original plan had been rejected in 1890, and in 1892 the staff had specifically rejected any need for an emergency hospital, repeating that only improved ambulance service was required. This attitude was maintained well into 1895.[75] But after Galvin's report appeared in November 1895, Dr. David Cheever, senior surgeon at Boston City, quickly presented a "plan in regard to the need, location and details of an Emergency Station for the reception and treatment of accidents." The staff agreed unanimously to the need for such a station, operated in the central business district as a branch of Boston City Hospital, and located at least one but not more than two miles away from it. This vote followed earlier agreement that there was no significant difference between an ambulance ride of one as opposed to two miles.[76] The trustees overcame earlier fiscal objections to an emergency branch and immediately voted their approval of the plan, forwarding it with a request for an appropriation to Mayor Josiah Quincy.[77] Apparently pressure on the city hospital abated at this time, for although the trustees continued to mention the need for an emergency hospital, nothing further was done. The city did meet one of Galvin's criticisms in 1897 when the city hospital opened a new surgical outpatient building, housing house officers available for emergencies on a twenty-four-hour basis.[78]

The issue flared again in 1899, sparked by Galvin's financial problems. Overwhelmed by debt and with its support in the commercial community alienated, the Emergency Hospital was forced to close in August 1899. The local medical establishment seized upon this occasion to press for a new emergency hospital under city hospital management. But Galvin's discomfiture was temporary. In September, he announced the opening of his "Wage Earners' Emergency and General Cooperative Hospital Association," and again the city hospital was on the defensive. The new hospital was to be operated in accordance with the plans Galvin had set out in his November 1895 report. With the support of the city's Central Labor Union, the association raised just under $30,000 through the sale of one-dollar membership certificates. No funds were solicited from businessmen; the balance of the first year budget of over $50,000 came largely from the board of patients, not members of the association, and from insurance companies and businesses assuming responsibility for the care of injured employees. The staff included Galvin and seven other surgeons practicing in the South Cove and old South End areas, who were paid nearly $20,000 in salaries. There was also a visiting committee which included some of the city's active social reformers, among them Professor Frank Parsons, Rabbi Charles Fleisher, and Benjamin Orange Flower. During its first year, the new hospital answered 943 ambulance calls, recorded 94,000 outpatient visits, and claimed to have treated nearly 2,500 bed patients.[79]

The new hospital's program suggested some of what those using other hospitals considered to be their failings. It advertised itself as directly supported by and therefore highly responsive to working men and women. Its doctors and nurses were experienced professionals rather than students, so that there was no feeling among the poor that they were being practiced upon. There was a minimum of red tape. Patients enjoyed privacy of a sort generally available only in a physician's private office; surgical records were kept only because of the frequent court cases arising from accidents, but there were no medical records. The Wage Earners' Emergency Hospital promised to treat its patients with little delay, and kept its outpatient department open around the clock every day of the week.[80]

In maintaining practices different from Galvin's, established hospitals were acting both out of self-interest and in keeping with their own notion of good medicine. Hospital outpatient facilities, for example, were designed primarily to offer experience to young physicians and to serve as clinics for medical schools. Traditionally, hospitals had not considered seriously the convenience of patients in setting the hours for outpatient care. At Massachusetts General, in 1885, patients could apply at medical and surgical clinics only from 9:00 to 10:00 A.M. on weekdays. In 1890 Boston City provided outpatient care from 9:00 to 11:00 A.M. weekdays for surgical cases and from 9:00 to 11:00 A.M. on Tuesday, Thursday, and Saturday for medical cases, with specialty clinics on various weekday mornings. For those most likely to resort to outpatient care, attendance at a free clinic involved the loss of work and pay and jeopardized job security. Recognizing this, Trinity Church in 1886 had opened an evening dispensary for working women who could not spare time for outpatient departments open only during working hours. The following year, the Women's Industrial and Educational Union started an evening clinic for working women. Both were staffed by female physicians.[81]

With other facilities offering evening care, pressure developed in 1899 for the city hospital to do the same. The trustees announced they were favorably inclined and asked the opinion of the visiting staff. By majority vote, the senior physicians and surgeons opposed the suggestion, citing the danger that extended service would be more liable to abuse. If men could not come to the morning clinics because they had jobs, then they also had incomes from which they could certainly spare the one-dollar-or-so fee charged by younger doctors for private visits. Even if the public were complaining, the staff also had to take into account the resentment of physicians in private practice whose incomes would be threatened by any expansion of free medical services. Even limited outpatient care encouraged pauperism and socialism. All that excused such clinics was their value in instruction. An evening clinic, coming after the fatigue of a long day, would be useless for teaching and learning.[82]

The staff minority, favoring an evening clinic, pointed to the hospital's public rationale: it was maintained by the people for the people. The public perceived that an evening clinic was in its own interest. A decision based primarily on the interests of the medical profession was improper. Considering the high fixed cost incurred in operating the institution, the hours the department was open were clearly inadequate. In restricting outpatient care to hours that required its patients to miss work, the hospital failed "to help people to help themselves." An evening clinic would "encourage and help men and women to continue at work," increase the total number of days labored in the city, and even keep patients from becoming hospital ward cases.[83]

Aside from principle, the minority report stressed practical politics. Criticism was mounting against the limited hours patients could attend the outpatient clinics. That criticism was coming even from "Boston's respected and worthy citizens." An evening clinic was necessary if the hospital hoped "to continue to receive the favor of the popular element of the City Government." Without that support, it would be difficult to obtain money for new buildings and perhaps even annual appropriations. The lack of a city hospital evening clinic was being exploited to solicit private contributions and governmental appropriations for private institutions, alienating those sources from the city hospital. The staff voted that the medical outpatient department be expanded from three to six mornings weekly and that the hospital pursue more vigorously its goal of establishing a relief station in the central business district under city hospital auspices, but it voted down the evening clinic.[84]

The public also expected that the city hospital would respond to Boston's growth by growing along with it. From the beginning, all elements connected with Boston City were committed to its expansion. Its doctors wanted more beds to increase their opportunities for research and teaching. Modern medicine—and the specialization it implied—was dependent on institutional size and the classification of patients. Superintendent Rowe complained in 1892 that no new wards had been built in three years.[85]

In his valedictory, Superintendent Cowles had suggested that the hospital commit itself to expansion for reasons of democratic ideology rather than of professional self-interest. The hospital had to meet the increasing demands that a growing population would make.[86] As a larger proportion of the public and a greater population looked to the hospital for care and treatment, those expectations became more pronounced. Attracted to the hospital no doubt in part because of the sense that it was their own, middle class patients swelled the constituency of use in the 1890s and added their often more articulate and influential voices to the discussion of the city hospital's needs. Complaining about overcrowding and at the same time noting the changing public using the hospital, Superintendent Rowe remarked that this placed the institution "in a position to be more carefully scrutinized and more intelligently criticized." Rowe repeated the hospital's need for continued expansion if it hoped to keep pace "with the large amount of sickness and surgical injuries inevitable with the growth of the city."[87] Constant expansion was supported by consensus.

There was no agreement, however, about which direction the hospital's growth should take. Was it to be a centralized institution expanding only at its South End site, or was it to spread branches throughout Boston? Until late in 1891, aldermen and councilmen from Boston's outlying neighborhoods—Roxbury, Dorchester, South Boston, East Boston, Charlestown, and Brighton—had lobbied for improved ambulance service for their areas rather than branches.[88] Hospitals were not perceived as advantageous to neighborhoods. Prior to the 1890s, Boston had witnessed several cases in which residents and property owners had frustrated the attempts of hospitals to locate in their areas. Quite often, the same democratic process that from the 1890s on forced hospitals to build in certain areas had been used earlier to keep hospitals out. Boston City Hospital itself had been a victim, stopped in its first attempt to locate by an aroused neighborhood. Searching for a site in 1857, the city council committee on the hospital had come upon a building constructed for and originally used as a hospital by the Boston Lying-in Association. On Springfield Street in the South End, it had been closed for want of funds, and the city was able to purchase it. But when the city government asked the legislature for authority to establish a city hospital, the city received a charter into which had been written a prohibition against locating the hospital within three hundred feet of any existing church or schoolhouse. This clause had been inserted through the efforts of neighbors of the proposed hospital building. Because the Springfield Street site was within three hundred feet of a school, the clause effectively stopped the city's plans.[89] This same kind of law was used to regulate objectionable establishments like public health nuisances or saloons. Perhaps because of lessons learned from the fears aroused by the city hospital's first proposed location, one of the plans submitted to the trustees in a design competition for the hospital stipulated an indoor courtyard, thereby allowing patients to exercise while at the same time sparing outsiders the misfortune of seeing them.[90] The city hospital was finally constructed beyond the line of settlement (several hundred yards south of the Boston Lying-in building) on mud flats south of Boston Neck in an area that was gradually being filled in to form the South End.[91] The neighbors which soon surrounded it included wharves, coal sheds, and the Roxbury drainage canal.

Residents might have opposed the location of a hospital in their area because of its association with foul or contagious disease. South End residents and businessmen later saw the smallpox hospital, on the water side of Albany Street across from the city hospital, as "jeopardizing the health and lives of the inhabitants and destroying their business." They forced the city government to close it just as the epidemic of 1872–73 began. For a new site, the city council could agree only on one of the unpopulated islands in Boston Harbor. Because the boat ride to this pesthouse was life-threatening for the sick—and also evoked the image of a seemingly irreversible journey—patients refused to be transported there and so were reluctant to have their cases reported. Consequently, the hospital failed to slow the epidemic.[92]

The council attempted to choose yet another site, but except for the uninhabited harbor islands, every area of the city was represented in the council, and thus every proposal met opposition. At one point, the council voted to buy an unspecified but already chosen piece of property.[93] The land, purchased in mid-October, was on Pine Island in the South Bay, between the South End and South Boston. A temporary building was quickly put up in the tidal swamp and, just as quickly, mysteriously burned down. It was rebuilt but, surrounded by the effluent from Boston's sewers and threatened by every tide, was not successful in drawing patients. Finally, with the death toll rising, the democratic process was abandoned. Out of the sense of crisis there developed popular sentiment for an appointed board of health with almost unlimited power. The council had been able to agree only on uninhabitable sites. At the very meeting at which the board of aldermen approved the mayor's appointments to the new board of health, the aldermen once again rejected the old Town of Roxbury almshouse as a site for the smallpox hospital. That property had been advocated by many thoughtful observers since the epidemic began; the first act of the new board of health was to seize it, designate it Boston's smallpox hospital over local objections, and open it for patients the same day.[94]

The hostile neighborhood reaction that greeted the original plans for the city hospital and almost all plans to isolate smallpox was repeated with private hospitals. In 1876, Dr. Charles Cullis encountered local opposition when he attempted to expand his religiously oriented Cullis Consumptives Hospital. He wished to build an additional structure on his site in the Grove Hall section of Dorchester. The new facility would be devoted to cancer victims, adding another class of patients to the incurables for whom Cullis provided a home.

Though his good intentions were almost universally lauded, more pragmatic considerations prevailed. At hearings held by the board of health, the president of the Home Savings Bank explained that the cancer hospital would injure real estate values and thus diminish city revenue: "He gave as an example the city hospital. . . ." Stressing the loathsome nature of the disease, other remonstrants pointed out that the project would be detrimental to the health of the neighborhood and destroy its attractive residential character. The tuberculosis home itself would be hurt and the entire area would be subject to unpleasant odors. One objector, referring by implication to the grotesque disfiguration often wrought by cancer, noted that "the patients would have to go out on the horse cars and the line running there was one of the best in the city." The board of health sided with the protesters. The area was too important to the city's continued growth to permit such a hospital.[95]

St. Elizabeth's Hospital encountered the same response in 1880 when it began to use a house in Roxbury as a hospital for the chronically ill. The building, bordering Highland Park, was in a desirable residential area. Petitions forced city council hearings. An officer of the Home Savings Bank, one of the petitioners, explained that his bank was concerned because it held extensive mortgages in the area. To protect these, property values had to be maintained, and experience showed that they would depreciate if the hospital stayed. Property values in the neighborhood suffered when the smallpox hospital (since removed) had been established a quarter mile away in 1873. Neighbors and others with real estate interests testified to the drop in property values that had accompanied the smallpox hospital. In one case, a parcel of land dropped from one dollar per foot to twelve and one-half cents. St. Elizabeth's was expected to reduce values by from twenty-five to fifty percent.

Several witnesses commented on the damage the hospital would do to the park. Supporting this argument, one alderman noted that "the patients will be on the park and their different diseases will be constantly before the eyes of the citizens." This would clearly lead to the end of the park as a source of pleasurable relaxation and recreation. The solution recommended by petitioners and adopted by the council was to ask the park commissioners to use their power of eminent domain to take the hospital site and add it to the park.[96]

A park was also involved when the issue of the Cullis Consumptives

Hospital surfaced again. In 1895 the institution requested a building permit to allow it to replace its old structures with new facilities at the same location. This turned into a public discussion of whether to permit the continuation of the home. Twenty years before, there had been no attempt to dislodge it, but since that time the Grove Hall section of Dorchester had changed greatly. Franklin Park, the city's largest, had been completed, and the Cullis Home bordered the park and sat opposite its main entrance.

Supporters of the home argued that mortally ill consumptives should not be denied the pleasure of strolls in the park, but opponents swept aside such sentimental appeals. The park commissioners opposed a concentration of tubercular patients on the park's edge. One physician noted with horror that the hospital's location was "evidently intended to afford the inmates the advantages of roaming over the five or six hundred acres which the city had set apart as 'lungs' for its inhabitants." Consumption was no longer perceived as a romantic disease; one physician after another testified that since 1882 it had come to be understood as contagious. More than the perception of tuberculosis had changed. What had been a sparsely settled area in the 1870s was, by the mid-1890s, a pleasant suburban community. Residents complained that inmates were walking about the area, visiting homes and shops, and even using public drinking fountains. Perhaps the most frequently heard protest was that the consumptives home was hurting property values. Responding to popular pressures, the city council voted to prohibit the use of the Cullis site as a consumption hospital after 1900.[97]

In responding to citizen complaints about the location of hospitals, the city government had available a variety of powers to control hospitals. It could use its police power to abate nuisances, its authority to issue or refuse building permits, and even its power of eminent domain to take hospital property for city purposes. But except for the three-hundred-foot-law extended by the state to cover hospitals, no specific statutes existed covering the location of any but lying-in hospitals. There was no coherent public policy toward hospital location.[98] Government played no role unless neighborhood outcry brought an individual case to its attention.

The city clearly had authority to regulate the location of lying-in-hospitals. Because of their notoriety, the Massachusetts legislature had, in 1876, enacted a law giving local boards of health the responsibility for licensing them. Beginning in 1876, Boston's board of health used that authority to pass on the suitability of applicants for licenses and the suitability of the premises they proposed to occupy. In making this latter judgment, the board took into account the well-being of prospective patients and the interests of the neighborhood. Between 1876 and 1909, citizen complaints which reached the floor of the city council were always effective in stopping licenses.[99]

It is possible to generalize, at least in the case of Boston, about why hospitals located where they did until the end of the nineteenth century. Though the hospital literature is replete with references to the need for sunshine, fresh air, and dry soil,[100] hospitals located where they encountered the least opposition, and most people did not want them nearby. Massachusetts General and Boston City hospitals were able to locate near concentrations of population because they built in tidal land beyond the edge of settlement. Boston filled in around them.

But Galvin, by locating both his Emergency Hospital and his Wage Earners' Hospital in a specific area of the city believed inconvenient to existing hospitals, struck a responsive chord and, after his Emergency Hospital opened, the city's neighborhoods began to request local branches of Boston City Hospital. Responsive to the pulls of localism, the city government asked the city hospital trustees to develop a comprehensive plan for Boston City's continued growth. Otherwise, further requests to fund hospital additions piecemeal would not be considered. Specifically, the council asked the trustees to examine the possibility of locating hospital branches in the city's outlying districts.[101]

Acting with the advice of the professional staff, the trustees reported that the establishment of branch hospitals was unnecessary. They repeated the argument of distance raised against Galvin's proposal, asserting that none of Boston's districts was really remote from the center. They restated the issue as being one not so much of miles as of transportation. And they found "every day the matter of miles . . . more and more overcome by improvements in transportation." Because the city's major arteries ran outward from its center rather than circularly around it, they found that with the exception of East Boston, "major portions of every outlying district [were] by means of the existing means of public communication . . . more accessible to the center of the city than they [were] to any one point within the limits of the district." By using either an ambulance system that they hoped would soon be improved, or the very streetcars that had allowed population to build up in the outlying districts, residents of those districts could get to the city hospital for treatment.[102]

The trustees also cited the logic of modern organization. The report noted "the tendency of the times amongst those asking for outpatient advice and treatment . . . to seek it in dispensaries having special departments for special diseases. This has been especially true, and in an increased degree, since the improved communication by horse-cars has made the larger dispensaries easier to access." A growing city had led to larger hospitals, able to support a more extensive division of labor with its promise of more sophisticated medical knowledge. Here was an argument for building Boston City larger rather than fragmenting it. The trustees claimed: "So long as it is possible to afford reasonably convenient access to a great metropolitan hospital, its superior facilities for treatment and cure should be extended alike to the citizens of every section of the city needing its care and through the building of small or local hospitals, absolutely or substantially to exclude the citizens of certain districts from its benefits, might well be charged as an injustice and wrong to them."[103] This was the professional argument of good medicine.

Far from putting to rest the agitation for branch hospitals, the report stimulated it. An almost constant stream of requests began to flow from local aldermen and councilmen through the city council. These either asked the city hospital board to study the feasibility of a branch in a particular area, suggested the appointment of a council committee to select sites, or sought appropriations to build. Even the West End, site of six hospitals including Massachusetts General, asked for a city hospital branch because Massachusetts General was a private corporation, taking cases "just as they please." Representatives of the North End joined those of Brighton, East Boston, Charlestown, South Boston, Roxbury, West Roxbury, and Dorchester in asking for branches.[104] Finally, the city hospital trustees and staff took over sponsorship of proposals to build an emergency hospital in Haymarket Square to serve the business district. It opened in 1902. And over especially strenuous objections from the hospital, the city council voted to establish a branch in East Boston, opened in 1908.[105]

Before people thought of themselves as potential hospital patients, all hospitals were perceived as somehow contagious—morally if not medically. By the 1890s, neighborhoods might differentiate between hospitals that served local needs and others which remained objectionable. In 1891, the West End remonstrated against a new private, and therefore potentially disreputable, lying-in which opened among six existing hospitals—including Massachusetts General and Boston Lying-in.[106] In the same year, residents of suburban Brookline, which had no need for a charity hospital, protested the proposed move of the Free Hospital for Women into their town.[107] Yet private hospitals serving the middle classes opened in this period in Brookline and fashionable Boston neighborhoods.[108] Hospital location in the second half of the nineteenth century was subject to local pulls expressed through the political system. Hospital policy—in the case of the public Boston City Hospital—became enmeshed in that system as local politics itself grew more responsive to the patient class.

Dr. David Cheever retired from Boston City Hospital in 1907, having exercised his considerable influence for over forty years. Publishing a memoir in 1911, Cheever reaffirmed the conservatism that had guided his professional life. Though he had seen great changes in medical practice—the rise of specialties and the conquest of sepsis—he continued to believe that traditional values should shape medical institutions. Social and medical authority exercised by gentlemen was proper. Acknowledging, for example, that the use of patients in clinical teaching created a socially awkward situation, he noted that "the doctor in command, if a gentleman, can much alleviate the inconveniences." Cheever was direct in expressing his continued oposition to certain forces of change. He found the possible admission of women to Harvard Medical School "hideous" and "the most repulsive form of co-education." He complained that "in the City Hospital municipal influences induced the trustees to admit both women and homeopaths to the [operating] amphitheater." Yet, even with the intrusion of the political process, Cheever's conservatism had not suffered a complete defeat. Cheever noted that women medical students were still not admitted to the hospital wards, and that "one distinguished surgeon [presumably Cheever] never operated before mixed classes." In another area, the trustees had rarely disregarded the nominations of the staff in making medical appointments.[109]

Cheever died in 1915 at the age of eighty-four. He had lived to see his vision of the city hospital battered by political realities. The autocratic institution, governed by elite lay trustees sympathetic to the elite practitioners of the medical staff, had been compromised. Boston City's patients were no longer simply the powerless, accepting the charitable care grudgingly dispensed by their betters. Politicians representing the immigrant and working class constituencies had exercised the role of intermediaries. In departing from the charitable orientation of institutions like Massachusetts General and becoming more responsive to patients, municipal hospitals—though in the minority in the United States—influenced the public perception and role of all general hospitals. One factor in the legitimation of the hospital as a community institution was the success of municipal hospitals in countering the image of hospital patients as a socially marginal, dependent class. City hospitals also gave patients a voice in the discussion of good medicine, a discussion from which they had heretofore been excluded.

# 3. The Impact of Modern Medicine

The annual address to the Massachusetts Medical Society was an occasion for the profession to reflect on its history, accomplishments, and prospects. In honoring one of its members with responsibility for the oration, the society identified its luminaries, paid them homage, and received their wisdom. The orator in 1888 was Dr. Benjamin Joy Jeffries, descendent of a prominent Boston medical family, Harvard graduate, and pioneer ophthalmologist. Jeffries chose as his topic, "Re-establishment of the Medical Profession."

Jeffries spoke first of the problems confronting the profession, making assumptions that were not uncommon among thoughtful practitioners in the middle and late nineteenth century. The status of the physician, he noted, had once been exalted; the "position was one of trust and confidence."[1] But this situation no longer obtained. The leaven of democracy had opened the profession to large numbers deficient in education and breeding, whose lack of distinction reflected on every physician. At the same time, Jeffries keenly felt the domination that new fortunes were exercising over every aspect of a society that had been unloosed from its traditions since the Civil War. Millionaires were eclipsing medical men in their communities. One force was pulling the profession down from below, another was pushing it down from above.

Jeffries's anxieties about the diminished status accorded medicine were exaggerated. But his fears cannot be disregarded. Jeffries was nostalgic for a past when the elevated position of the profession had depended, to some extent, on the social origins of practitioners. To say—as Jeffries and others have done—that medicine fell in public esteem during the nineteenth century is misleading, but Jeffries was right in his assessment that the post-Civil War profession could no longer derive its status from the backgrounds of its practitioners. The oration, however, was infused with optimism, not despair. Jeffries understood that he was witness to a period of profound change. New values, institutions, and practices were displacing "the village life of former days." These changes bred an insecurity that made Jeffries especially sensitive to the drop he perceived in professional status. Yet change also signaled opportunity. Speaking of "our duty to right ourselves before the community, if our efforts have again placed us in a position to be trusted and confided in," Jeffries noted that the profession could control its own destiny—receiving "social recognition for itself, through itself." In the past, the world view and values of practitioners had reflected those of their society; even medical therapeutics, in some cases, had been influenced by values that physicians shared with the laity. Now, physicians—mostly those younger and better educated than the profession at large—were turning to an expanding science. Medicine had to take full advantage of science and the enhanced skills it promised. The achievements of highly educated practitioners would determine the status of the profession.[2]

An expanding scientific base furnished only part of the substructure of the emerging professional culture. Enhanced diagnostic and therapeutic skills did not alone lead to the rationalization of medicine in the late nineteenth and early twentieth centuries. But medical science played the most significant role in this process; it was central to parallel developments in the process of professionalization—developments in specialization, education, professional societies, and hospitals.

The agenda set for the medical profession by B. Joy Jeffries was first realized by doctors practicing in hospitals. The impact of modern medicine on hospitals is the focus here.

The tempo of medical advance had begun to quicken by the early 1870s, but medicine remained comparatively primitive. Physicians elaborated theoretical etiologies for some disease processes, but still diagnosed many disorders by their superficial symptoms. At Boston City Hospital's medical outpatient department in 1867, "pain" was diagnosed as the patient's ailment in 158 cases. The only diseases listed more frequently were cough, constipation, bronchitis, and debility—categories barely more precise.[3] The public and profession were often fatalistic in their attitudes toward accident and disease. Newspapers anticipated results in describing still living accident victims as fatally injured. Conscious of the limitations of their art, physicians excluded large categories of patients from the sick and injured they might be expected to help. Boston City explained away its mortality rate by pointing to the large proportion of patients dying within forty-eight hours of admission, a time span considered too short for medicine to have much impact.[4] Yet medicine stood on the threshold of the modern era.

The development of antisepsis in the 1860s provided a major breakthrough. Joseph Lister's carbolic spray and chemical cleansing of the field of operation, instruments, and the surgeon's hands made possible the consistent healing of wounds without suppuration and dramatically reduced mortality in surgical cases. Rounding out his education in Europe, John Collins Warren had been impressed with Lister's results in Glasgow; upon his return Warren introduced the process at Massachusetts General when he began work there as an outpatient physician in 1869. Listerism did not take hold immediately in Boston or elsewhere.[5] It was tried sporadically at Massachusetts General during the 1870s, but not until the end of the decade was it systematically applied. Boston City Hospital's first completely antiseptic operation was performed in 1879. By the late 1880s, asepsis—which differed from antisepsis in requiring a scrupulously clean surgical environment rather than relying on a disinfectant spray during operations—was replacing antisepsis. In 1888 Massachusetts General began to construct an aseptic operating theater, and in 1891 Children's Hospital refitted its operating room with aseptic furnishing and an up-to-date sterilization system.[6]

Surgeons whose careers spanned both eras testified to changes wrought in hospitals by antisepsis and asepsis. Before antisepsis, surgery was generally followed by infection. Dressings had to be changed daily, a painful process and one carried out in wards permeated by the odor of pus. Compound fractures often resulted in infection, and the subsequent necessary amputations carried a high mortality rate. With antisepsis, the healing process was much less painful, dressings needed to be changed less frequently, and patients recuperated in wards free of infection. When asepsis replaced antisepsis the healing process became even less unpleasant, as black urine and other symptoms of carbolic acid poisioning disappeared. Results also spoke eloquently. From 1864 to 1869, sixty-six percent of 120 compound fractures treated at Boston City Hospital required amputation, and amputations were followed by a mortality of forty-nine percent. Between 1889 and 1894 a greatly enlarged hospital recorded only 82 amputations, and those had a mortality of seventeen percent. In 1903, Massachusetts General proudly announced that although it recorded 83 cases of sepsis in the year, only ten had acquired their infections after entering the hospital.[7]

Neither antisepsis nor asepsis made hospitalization necessary for surgery. In many cases these precautions could be observed just as easily in the home.[8] But these procedures did combat hospital germ concentrations and made hospital surgery relatively safe. They also made more adventuresome surgery possible. Surgeons expanded their field of activity and began to operate successfully even on the abdominal cavity. A string of seven fatalities gave way to better results as John Homans introduced complete antisepsis in his ovariotomies at Carney Hospital.[9]

The expansion of surgery fashioned a new image of the doctor. Appendicitis provides a case in point. Its symptoms—severe abdominal pain, sometimes accompanied by nausea, vomiting, and/or fever—had been treated medically and passively. In the 1860s and '70s, "no operative interference was thought of." The disease "was left to progress undiagnosed, or was mistaken for gastritis, enteritis, idiopathic peritonitis or colitis" and allowed to go its often fatal course.[10]

Reginald Heber Fitz presented his paper "Perforating Inflammation of the Veriform Appendix" to the Association of American Physicians in 1886. The Massachusetts General and Harvard Medical School physician cleared the confusion which had associated the disease symptoms with a variety of different organs and demonstrated conclusively that the appendix was the problem and surgery the solution. Aware of the inadequacy of their treatment, practitioners were prepared to accept a convincing demonstration of the nature and treatment of the disease. Fitz's work provided eagerly accepted answers. A diminished reluctance to expand surgery also contributed to the widespread adoption of Fitz's treatment. After 1890, operation on the appendix "multiplied with great rapidity" and "became comparatively common." Results were excellent. Fitz coined the term *appendicitis* to focus professional attention on the organ and the disease process.[11] The term also focused public attention on a "new" disease, discovered and conquered at the same time.

Surgical treatment for appendicitis produced startling results. Modern medicine demonstrated its ability to diagnose and treat successfully a widespread, hitherto baffling and frequently fatal malady. Where families had once observed physicians helplessly watching patients die, they saw them instead intervening actively. Dramatic treatment and likely cure reflected well on the medical profession, as did the treatment's quick adoption. No protracted debated revealed splits in the profession. Knowledge of appendicitis was advanced not through medieval disputation, but through scientific inquiry. Medicine faced the public vested with the authority of modern science.

Diphtheria provided another example of the increased efficacy of medicine. The disease was often epidemic in Boston and a prime cause of childhood mortality. Boston City, the only hospital admitting contagious diseases, confessed in its annual reports its inability to treat diphtheria. Beginning with the opening of a diphtheria ward in 1888, the hospital amended its gross mortality statistics by deducting deaths due to diphtheria (as well as deaths within forty-eight hours of admission), implying that diphtheria was so far beyond the reach of medical science that the hospital took no responsibility in these cases.[12] In fact only the most serious cases were brought to the hospital, those often marked by the inability to expel the membranous obstruction in the larynx, leaving no alternative but tracheotomy or intubation to forestall suffocation. These surgical procedures were acts of desperation, performed on already weakened children, and required hospitalization because they demanded round-the-clock attention available at home only to wealthier families.[13] Mortality rates were staggering. At Boston City Hospital in 1888, 54 of 61 tracheotomies for diphtheria resulted in death, as did 78 of 107 intubations and all 17 combination intubation-tracheotomies. A Boston City surgeon weighing the comparative benefits of intubation and tracheotomy could not assess the procedures on the basis of their almost equally disastrous mortalities, but had to discuss instead whether surgery brought some relief in breathing to dying patients. Of the hospital's 371 diphtheria patients in 1888, 176 died (47.4 percent), as did 239 of 511 in 1889 (46.8 percent). From February 1876 through February 1894 the hospital's diphtheria mortality rate was 46 percent.[14]

In 1894 and 1895 diphtheria antitoxin was introduced in both private and hospital practice in Boston. Remarkably effective, antitoxin reduced mortality and permitted health officers to limit the spread of the disease. As parental objections to the board of health's removing children from home diminished in the face of dramatically successful treatment at the city hospital, hospitalization became an effective weapon against contagion.[15]

The hospital's new contagious disease department, coincidentally opened in 1895, provided more and better facilities for the care of patients. Diphtheria mortality at Boston City dropped to 14 percent in 1896/97, 13 percent in 1897, 12.8 percent in 1898, and 9.9 percent in 1899/1900. City-wide mortality fell from 18.03 deaths per 10,000 inhabitants in 1894 to 11.73 in 1895, 9.8 in 1896, 7.77 in 1897, and 3.15 per 10,000 in 1898. The rate of incidence of the disease fell from an average of 30.7 cases per 10,000 inhabitants in the sixteen years preceding 1895 to 12.27 per 10,000 in 1895–98, and to 4.9 per 10,000 in 1899. Boasting that it treated 51 percent of Boston's reported diphtheria patients in 1898, the city hospital assigned credit for the conquest of the disease to its new contagious disease department,[16] but the discovery and introduction of diphtheria antitoxin was the most significant factor. It unquestionably enhanced the esteem in which the public held both the hospital and physicians, and increased the self-confidence of the medical profession.

When Children's Hospital was founded in 1869, its physicians listed medical treatment and the advance of medical knowledge among its purposes. But, as noted earlier, Children's focused the attention of its supporters not on its medical functions, but on the "moral benefit" it provided its charges. Not until their tenth annual report did the managers more than casually mention medical orientation. Rewriting their history after ten years of operation the managers admitted for the first time the primacy of physicians in the founding.[17] This historical revisionism marked the beginnings of a shift in emphasis. At the suggestion of its medical staff, Children's had opened an outpatient department in 1875.[18] Though it followed tradition in drawing its patients exclusively from among the poor, the new department was overwhelmingly medical in its orientation, departing from the earlier moral and social rationale. Treated as outpatients, children were not removed from their unfortunate home environments, nor did their short visits provide the beneficent moral influences available with extended inpatient care.

The 1880s provided further evidence of the shift at Children's. In 1883 the number of surgical patients exceeded that of medical patients by a wide margin for the first time, setting at trend that was to continue into the twentieth century.[19] The dominance of surgery reflected unequal rates of progress in medical science. Internal medicine lagged. At the same time, Children's pioneered the study of orthopedics. Encouraged in part by the safety provided by antisepsis and asepsis and the relative painlessness of surgical anaesthesia, doctors operated on children's deformities with new surgical techniques. Wracked limbs, previously untreatable, were reshaped under the surgeon's scalpel. In the last two decades of the nineteenth century the hospital's orthopedists successfully treated "hip disease, caries of the spine, deformities of infantile paralysis, the contractions of spastic paralysis, bow legs, knock knee and other deformities of rickets, osteomyelitis and deformities following diseases of the bone, club foot and other deformities of the feet, wry neck and congenital dislocation of the hip," reducing the list of "irremedial afflictions of childhood."[20]

Orthopedic surgery brought Children's into the era of active medical treatment and established it as a hospital in the modern sense of the term. Children's redefined both its mission and its accomplishments. Moral uplift disappeared completely by the time its history was revised for its twentieth anniversary, replaced by the treatment of disease, injury, and deformity. Whereas once the hospital had taken pride in removing threatening urchins from the streets and transforming them into cultured and disciplined children, the 1895 report took credit for a different change visible in the streets: "We can point to the fact that the presence of cases of club foot and cracked backs and lame legs is noticeably less on our streets than it was twenty years ago."[21]

Advancements in orthopedics established a national reputation for Children's Hospital. Its fund-raising stressed the quality of medical care provided and its role in the advance of medicine. Where once it had boasted of the religious and moral background of its nurses, by 1887 it was complimenting them on their skill. Secular, trained nurses joined the staff, and the original nurses—sisters of St. Margaret's—undertook studies at the training school of Boston City Hospital. Having at first hidden the role of physicians in its founding, by 1887 it was advertising that several of its staff held appointments in Harvard Medical School.[22]

In the 1890s Children's continued its metamorphosis, by redefining who its patients were and should be. Pointing to the scientific treatment offered, the managers encouraged parents of "*all* medical cases" to have their sick children admitted for care. For although the hospital had been established to serve the poor, orthopedic surgery had brought "the children of the wealthy, as well as those of the middle and poorer classes [to] meet within our walls." The hospital's rationale had changed. So too had the reasons for some of its policies. Parental visiting, for example, remained highly restricted. But parents were kept out of the wards because of an expressed fear of medical contagion, and no longer because of an implied fear of moral contagion. The hospital had moved from a philosophy of medical fatalism and social activism directed at the poor, to a medical activism designed to serve directly the children of the whole community.[23]

The demands of science increasingly confronted the charity mentality in the operation of hospitals. When charity had been the primary function, a careful stewardship on the part of lay trustees demanded that they oversee the smallest expenditure with care and maintain a healthy skepticism toward any expense that seemed unnecessary in providing refuge for the poor. When demands of space forced the managers of Children's Hospital to consider a new building, they hastened to reassure the contributors "that they have no intention at any time of erecting any elaborate or unnecessarily costly building."[24] As hospitals developed into more than homes, however, a new level of expenditure became necessary to maintain them.

Those not fully conscious of the new role resisted rising costs. When the seventh annual conference of the Association of Hospital Superintendents turned its attention to steadily mounting expenses, Dr. S. S. Goldwater of New York's Mt. Sinai Hospital defended the costs as necessary "because improvements in medical science demand improved and enlarged facilities." Dr. Thomas Howell of Worcester took a more traditional view. Physicians trained at hospitals equipped with modern paraphernalia would be handicapped when they had to adjust to private practice: "Not having been taught to improvise, they do not realize how much can be accomplished with the crude implements to be found in the ordinary household. The graduates of cheaply equipped institutions, on the other hand, have been required to exercise ingenuity throughout their apprenticeship, and, as a result, they are not only more resourceful in emergencies, but their adaptability enhances their professional reputation." Asepsis provided excuses for the most lavish expenditures of all. These costs were obviously unnecessary. Did not mortality rates from home surgery compare favorably with those of the most lavishly equipped operating rooms?[25]

To some accustomed to medicine as it had been and the tradition of hospitals as a charity, the new requirements fell into the category of lavishness and extravagance. George Ludlam, lay superintendent of New York Hospital and president of the American Hospital Association in 1906, commented on the difficulty of working with doctors trained in scientific medicine: "Familiarity with these methods engenders a spirit of extravagance which permeates the whole establishment and which it is exceedingly difficult to check or control." Wedded to the concept of hospitals as a charity, Ludlam made a fetish of controlling extravagance. He was proud of New York Hospital's answer to the spiraling cost of maintaining a medical library. Stating, "I am absolutely at a loss for an understanding of the value of a medical library in a hospital," he announced that his hospital had shut its library, given away the books, and put the space to better use as a nurses' reception room. Ludlam saved his most righteous indignation for the rubber gloves then becoming a necessary condition for maintaining asepsis.

There has grown up in the hospital with which I am connected, a custom which I do not think I characterize by an exaggerated expression when I call it a craze for the use of rubber gloves. Beginning in a small way, our consumption of that item has increased from year to year until, absolutely and positively, I should be ashamed to tell you what we spent for rubber gloves last year. I go to our attending staff and call their attention to it. They say it is deplorable, but rubber gloves have come to be a very important item in the treatment of surgical cases.... I went to one doctor recently, and said, "Doctor, I notice that all your assistants now in the operating theatre, even down to the orderlies, are wearing rubber gloves at the operation. I notice that the house staff in their ordinary attention to the patients in the ward making ordinary ward dressings and the nurses who attend them are all wearing rubber gloves. Now is this last necessary?" . . . "Oh, no [they respond], it is far more important to use rubber gloves in the ward dressing than in the operating department."[26]

In a milder way, the Massachusetts General trustees shared this bewilderment at the mounting financial demands made by modern medicine. Upset in 1893 with rising expenditures for oxygen, they asked the visiting staff to restrict its use.[27] Steadily rising expenses prompted the trustees to order expenditures for 1896 kept within 1891 levels. Trying to reduce costs at the city hospital, the trustees in 1900 asked the medical staff to use fewer dressings.[28]

At Massachusetts General resistance to the level of expenditure necessary for scientific work did not last long. But Children's Hospital, as Boston's medically most progressive, was the city's first to develop a new view in which the requirements of science justified hitherto extravagant costs. In 1899 the managers followed an explanation of some major capital expenses designed to "ensure the attainment of favorable results in the one direction aimed at—the successful treatment of the diseases and injuries of children," by reminding donors of the "reputation for excellent work" the hospital had earned. In the mid-1890s the hospital turned to raising the larger sums needed to see that everything medically possible could be done for patients. In 1895 the managers followed a description of the hospital's power to save lives and combat invalidism by remarking, "It is thought best to make this statement at this time in order that the patrons of the Hospital may recognize the importance of, and may be tolerant of, the demands made upon them to carry out the good work."[29]

Once medicine began to produce results and medical research promised further results, a new level of expenditure was considered appropriate. Massachusetts General Superintendent Herbert B. Howard had answered denunciations of extravagance at a conference of hospital superintendents by declaring justifiable any expenditure that provided better patient care. According to hospital authority Dr. John A. Hornsby, hospital efficiency depended not on cutting costs, but "on the fidelity with which we carry out the doctor's orders, and that hospital will succeed best which is equipped with the most modern appliances and the skilled people to handle them."[30] The Massachusetts General trustees pointed with pride, in 1898, to the effectiveness of their antiseptic procedures: "The staff has introduced many improvements in antisepsis; for example, the use of gloves by the operators and assistants has materially lessened the danger of spreading sepsis." By 1900 the trustees had forsaken attempts to keep expenditures within earlier levels and were calling attention to "the steadily increasing gravity of the average case." The hospital was dealing with the sick rather than the poor. In 1902 the trustees announced that, considering "the newer scientific improvements," a steadily increasing cost per patient could be anticipated if Massachusetts General expected to preserve its high standards. A scientific hospital could not be funded under the restraints traditionally imposed on a charity for the poor. The final break with the presumption that a hospital could be managed primarily as a charity came in 1907 when the trustees decreed that mounting deficits be met by increasing patient rates.[31]

As the twentieth century began, hospitals existed for purposes different from those for which they had been founded. As charities, money had been their most important resource. With the expansion of medical knowledge, the skill of their physicians and surgeons became paramount. Annual lists of staff publications joined donor beneficence in the Children's Hospital annual report for 1895, in Massachusetts General's in 1898, and in Boston City's in 1903.[32] Scientific accomplishment led to a mounting sense of professionalism; as the relative value of the contribution made by physicians and surgeons increased, they become more assertive in managing the hospital and setting its goals.[33] This shifting pattern of control would eventually crystallize in the movement for hospital standards which put the ultimate power of accreditation in the hands of medical professionals.[34]

When hospital care meant mostly food, comfort, and shelter for the needy, trustees and financial contributors made many of the basic decisions as to who was to be admitted as a patient. The Boston Dispensary, in its early years, accepted for treatment only those patients bearing "a ticket of admission from a subscriber or manager."[35] Massachusetts General admissions were from the first controlled by the medical staff, but trustees interviewed each new patient and fixed his rate of board. In 1825 the trustees set up a system of "free beds" through which each contributor of one hundred dollars received the right to control the use of one bed for a year.[36] At first limited to 40 beds, this system expanded until a financial crisis in 1876 forced the board to limit the total number of free beds in use at any one time to 140. Of these, only 72 were controlled through subscriptions to the free bed fund in 1876 but, in response to a special appeal, the increased total of 118 beds was so controlled in 1877.[37] Until the trustees restricted the total number of free beds, they also reserved for themselves an almost unlimited right to admit free bed patients. Such free beds were filled either during the weekly visit of a committee of trustees, or by the superintendent. These decisions were subject to the approval of the board.[38]

The decision to monitor more carefully the number of free patients did not spell the end of the free bed system. Restrictions on the total number of free patients allowed at any one time did not apply to "parties who have brought letters from parties maintaining free beds." The New England Hospital for Women and Children made the same exception in its policy of limitation: "When application is made by a donor or yearly subscriber for a free bed, or by a society who pays for a free bed, the patient shall be admitted even though all the free beds are filled at the time."[39] In 1875, Massachusetts

General had allowed a $1,000 subscription to buy a lifetime free bed. In 1884 this right was codified more carefully: $5,000 bought control of a free bed for two designated lifetimes. In 1888, the American Bell Telephone Company traded "the use of 14 telephone sets in consideration of the right to the use of a free bed at the hospital by the Company."[40]

Control of free beds, whether by doctors or trustees, meant control over most hospital admissions. Patients not admitted on free beds at Massachusetts General had to pay several weeks' board in advance. To be admitted, the poor patients who were the hospital's natural constituency needed to be sponsored by a subscriber or at least approved by the trustees. In 1877, the same year in which the number of free beds was reduced from 160 to 140, the hospital had an average patient census of 164, with an average of 143 patients in free beds.[41]

For the sick entering the hospital for food, comfort, and shelter, the length of stay allowed was an important consideration. In this as in admission, donor and trustee control prevailed at midcentury. Seeking to discourage the applications of long-term invalids, the directors of the New England Hospital for Women and Children instructed their resident physician in 1877 to admit on free beds only patients who could be benefited by a maximum stay of two months. Within a year, subscribers to the free bed fund had forced the directors to back away from this position. Hospital policy would henceforth allow a six-month stay for patients admitted by donors of free beds; longer stays were at the discretion of the directors. Reporting to the Massachusetts General trustees on the average length of stay, the resident physician cited the wishes of the patient's "patrons" as a factor. At Boston City Hospital, the original rules gave the trustees ultimate authority in admissions, and they retained the right to "dismiss any patient whom they thought improperly admitted." This right extended even to accident victims, who could be admitted either by a trustee or an attending practitioner. At most institutions, physicians and surgeons generally suggested to the trustees names of patients ready for discharge. This practice obtained at Massachusetts General until the trustees ruled in 1873 that ordinary discharges need not be held up pending the approval of the trustees' committee visiting the hospital.[42]

By the end of the nineteenth century, professional staffs had increased their control over admissions and thus over the character of the institutions they worked in. This change from lay to medical control over the patient population was evident first at the Boston Dispensary, where the system of admission by subscriber's or manger's ticket was abolished in 1856.[43] This early date is explained by the fact that as an outpatient institution offering neither board nor shelter, the dispensary was less dependent than hospitals were on the financial contributions of donors and trustees. The Boston Dispensary provided only the medical advice and treatment gratuitously given by practitioners.

More significant in the shift from lay to medical control was Boston City

Hospital, where the broadened scope of medical work, together with the increased competence of the professional staff, led to rule changes. In the annual report for 1897/98 the provision that trustees might admit patients was dropped, along with the power of trustees visiting the hospital to deny any admission they thought improper or dismiss any patient they thought wrongly admitted.[44]

The Massachusetts General trustees in 1895 restricted the lattitude allowed free bed subscribers in selecting patients by adding a provision that the use of the beds was subject to "the rules of the Hospital." How this worked in practice is suggested by letters nominating patients for admission. In 1897, trustee William Endicott, Jr., wrote to resident physician Herbert B. Howard: "If Mr. B. C. Raymond of Beverly is found to be a suitable patient for the Hospital, I will thank you to admit him upon my bed, and oblige." Someone other than the free bed subscriber, who in this case was also a trustee, decided whether the prospective patient was "suitable" for the hospital. This same lanaguage appeared in free bed nominations by Endicott in 1898 and 1901.[45]

By the twentieth century, members of the visiting staff were regularly playing a role in admitting individual patients on free beds. Dr. Francis B. Harrington wrote the admitting physician in 1905: "Will you please admit the bearer Mrs. Miriaity to the MGH as a free patient for operation. . . . She is a poor widow who must support herself by hard work." Hospital physicians even shared in the authority to set rates for patients, a power previously reserved to the trustees and the resident physician acting for them. Dr. Harrington asked that a patient he proposed be charged no more than one dollar and a half a day. Dr. H. H. A. Beach asked: "Will you kindly admit to my service Mrs. A. Shannon. . . . Her husband is a policeman and she can pay $5 a week board."[46] The decline in the power of donors to select patients was emphasized in 1920 when the trustees endorsed a memorandum noting that "subscriptions for beds are useful to the Hospital where they are substantially gifts to the Hospital."[47]

The shift in hospital goals and pattern of control also affected the treatment accorded syphilitics. Concerned in large measure with the morality of their patients, many nineteenth-century hospitals refused them admission. Trustees set hospital policy; they shared the prevalent popular assumption that patients with venereal diseases, as the degraded victims of their own vices, were not worthy of the philanthropic effort hospitals represented. Boston's medical journal reported that "there is an old-fashioned feeling in Boston that venereal disease is not a respectable thing to have to do with under any circumstances; that the victims are suffering for their sins or those of their fathers, and that it is almost flying in the face of Providence to assist them."[48]

This policy was not yet well defined when Massachusetts General first opened in 1821, and its very first patient was treated for syphilis. In 1822, however, the trustees determined to exclude venereal patients. Between 1856 and 1881 the hospital's rules provided for the admission of syphilitics only by vote of the board of trustees and required that the patient pay double the rate of board. From 1881 to 1900 such patients were theoretically inadmissible. In the 1870s syphilis often ranked second to tuberculosis, the fairly consistent leader, as the reason given for rejecting applicants.[49]

Practice at the city hospital largely followed that at Massachusetts General. The first set of rules forbade the admission of patients with acute syphilis as charity patients, and set a minimum rate of twenty-five dollars a week for those admitted. Patients suffering "mania-a-potu" (alcoholism) were also penalized, but their minimum rate was fifteen dollars.[50] Few syphilis patients were admitted, and throughout the century the disease remained a major reason for rejecting applicants. Some syphilitics entered under a waiver of the rule when their cases were "so complicated by other physical conditions as to make the urgencies paramount to the rule."[51] Because of its origins as in part a contagious disease institution, the city hospital accepted some responsibility for the care of syphilis and treated the disease on an outpatient basis, thus keeping it out of the wards. In 1868 the hospital organized an outpatient department for skin diseases, a classification which included "syphilodermata."[52] The Boston Dispensary, an entirely outpatient institution, also maintained a clinic for syphilis. But when financially pressed in 1877, its lay managers chose the venereal disease department as the one to be closed to cut expenses.[53]

Physicians, enjoying the social status of trustees, largely shared their perceptions. As the scientific basis of medicine expanded, the experience and training of doctors would increasingly differentiate them from their fellow citizens. Yet even in 1822, when the Massachusetts General trustees questioned the wisdom of admitting syphilitics, the hospital staff opposed exclusion. Though conceding that the viciousness of the patients concerned might justify their exclusion, Drs. Jackson and Warren cited "the more intimate acquaintance with this subject to which our professional duties have led us" as having "induced in us a different opinion." But at the same time Jackson and Warren articulated medical views consonant with popular assumptions in concluding that women with syphilis be more subject to exclusion than men; though men could get the disease through an occasional indiscretion, for all but very few women it came as the result of a life of infamy.[54]

During the century physicians began to depart from the static view of the trustees. The Boston Medical Association dropped discriminatory charges for syphilis patients from its fee table in 1876. In 1877 members of the Harvard Medical School faculty sought to have the Boston Dispensary revoke its decision to close its syphilis department.[55] The *Boston Medical and Surgical Journal* criticized the closing, blaming it on "cruel superstitions." The *Journal* reminded the managers that many who contracted the disease were blameless: "Virtuous wives almost without number are suffering for the

sins of dissolute husbands, and bringing children into the world doomed to
lives of suffering and disease." Without explaining the reversal in medical
attitudes toward the sexes—men had been innocent and women vicious in
Jackson and Warren's statement in 1822—the *Journal* argued that even the
vicious deserved medical care: "We imagine that this movement [to shut the
department] may have been suggested by the number of cases of gonorrhoea,
which of late appears to have been unusually prevalent among the rough
element. We own we do not see why one of these scamps should not be
treated as readily as his brother who has had his nose bitten off in a drunken
brawl."[56] Nothing came of a suggestion offered in 1885 by Dr. Edward
Wigglesworth that the city hospital set aside beds for skin disease and
syphilis. The same response greeted a suggestion by Dr. C. Irving Fisher,
chairman of the committee on the Massachusetts State Almshouse (Infirmary) at Tewksbury, that municipal and other general hospitals establish
wards for treatment of venereal diseases.[57]

A major cause of inaction was lack of commitment on the part of physicians. In 1890 the Suffolk district of the Massachusetts Medical Society
notified the Massachusetts General trustees of the urgency of their providing
in-hospital care for syphilitic patients. The matter was referred to the visiting
staff for their opinion. The staff recommended no change in existing policies; active cases of syphilis were to be barred, and only those who could be
benefited by surgery were to be admitted.[58] The staff decision mixed
morality and medicine, citizenship and professionalism. Where medicine
was effective, in the cure of chancres for example, even a disease perceived
as degrading did not prevent admission. In cases where medicine was less
effective, moralistic prejudices and proscriptions remained undisturbed.[59]

As late as 1899, Boston's only in-hospital facilities for venereal diseases
were at the Long Island Hospital, one of the city's pauper institutions.
Popular attitudes assigned the diseases to a netherworld, and physicians,
though they maintained a professional interest in syphilis and gonorrhoea,
were reluctant to reject too openly the popular wisdom. When, around the
turn of the century, Dr. David Cheever agreed to Charles Eliot's request that
he give two lectures on venereal diseases at Harvard Medical School, Cheever
stipulated "that there shall be no chance of their being advertised, or
noticed by the press."[60]

The impetus that led doctors to break more completely with the traditional
treatment accorded syphilitics came in the early years of the twentieth
century. In 1910, the first samples of 606 or salvarsan, an experimental drug
developed by Paul Ehrlich in Germany, reached Boston.[61] Compared with
earlier drugs salvarsan was dramatically successful and revolutionized
treatment for syphilis. Able to treat syphilis, physicians declared their independence of popular taboos and saw to it that syphilitics were admitted to
hospitals.[62] From 1905 through 1910 the number of cases admitted to
Massachusetts General increased slowly from 5 to 45, but jumped to 133 in
1911 and 194 in 1912. In 1913 the disease was raised to departmental status

and an entire ward assigned to it.[63] The hospital began actively to recruit syphilitic patients. Pregnant women at Boston Lying-in diagnosed as syphilitic were brought to Massachusetts General for treatment.[64] The public responded positively to salvarsan, in effect acknowledging the increased therapeutic power of physicians. When the outbreak of World War I interrupted supply and the unpleasant mercury treatments previously used were resumed, Carney Hospital reported "a rather considerable falling off" in the number of patients coming for treatment.[65]

The significance of salvarsan was amplified by the Wassermann reaction for the diagnosis of syphilis. Though physicians as early as the 1880s had understood the role of syphilis in causing some neurological disorders, the test developed in 1906 showed the infection responsible for a variety of poorly diagnosed cases already subject to hospitalization. The test was not perfectly reliable, and it was viewed initially with skepticism. If used with more confidence than it should have been following its acceptance in the years after 1909, the Wassermann was nonetheless a diagnostic triumph. Testing for syphilis at Massachusetts General increased dramatically; from experimental tests on "a large number of patients" in 1909, it "greatly increased in 1912" to 2,262 blood specimens tested, and 5,502 in 1913.[66] Beginning in 1915, all patients admitted to the medical wards of the new Peter Bent Brigham Hospital were tested routinely. More than twelve percent of the first 1700 tests were positive. Physician-in-chief Henry A. Christian reported that "very often this knowledge of syphilis infection greated aided us in diagnosis and treatment."[67] With the Wassermann reaction and salvarsan, syphilis took a step out of the medical netherworld.

To be sure, even when doctors acted as scientists they found it difficult to free themselves completely of moralistic assumptions. Involved in serious research into the nature of syphilis, the head of the department at Massachusetts General noted: "The clinic is watching the relations of syphilitic disease to various employments, and especially to idleness."[68] It was not until 1929, when the syphilis department was reintegrated into the department of dermatology, that the hospital ended the demeaning practice of having a separate entrance and separate benches reserved for syphilitics.[69] Yet once physicians developed the ability to discover and handle syphilis, it started to become a disease like any other. The decision to admit or exclude it became a narrowly medical rather than a moralistic decision, one made by physicians and scientifically attuned trustees rather than by trustees and morally oriented physicians.

Changes in the way patients used hospitals duplicated changes in the way hospital medicine was practiced. In the mid-nineteenth century, Massachusetts General tried to avoid having a permanent population of the chronically ill by narrowing its use to those "requiring a physician's daily care." But even with this restriction it functioned in the 1870s largely as a shelter providing no medical services not available in the average home. In one exceptional case the hospital maintained an old man with nowhere else to go from October 1887 to March 1888 and from July 1888 until his death in June 1899. The managers of Children's Hospital admitted, in retrospect, that "in its early days [it] was in fact merely a nursery for sick children."[70]

Hospital stays tended to be long; patients entered for the duration of an illness and a convalescence rather than for a brief episode of special medical or surgical intervention. In 1855, the average stay at Massachusetts General was 81 days.[71] Free patients stayed an average of 4.82 weeks in 1870, 3.92 in 1871, 4.35 in 1872, 6.09 in 1873, 5.64 in 1874, 5.18 in 1875, 5.73 in 1876, 5.54 in 1877, 5.27 in 1878, and 5.16 in 1879. Administering a shelter, the trustees reviewed quarterly lists of those patients in the hospital for more than three months, to grant permission for extended stays and perhaps to ensure that the charity was not debilitating. Paid patients (23 percent of the patients in 1870-79 were listed as paying) remained for significantly shorter stays—3.37 weeks in 1870, 3.12 in 1871, 3.15 in 1872, 3.28 in 1873, 2.73 in 1874, 2.82 in 1875, 3.22 in 1876, 2.84 in 1877, 2.80 in 1878, and 2.84 in 1879—suggesting that the poor needed more of the social care and support component of hospital medicine than patients with means. A hospital stay for the poor was therapeutic—in terms of the nineteenth century's holistic understanding of medicine—simply because it enabled the disadvantaged to escape their often unwholesome home environments.[72]

Patients were not uniformly bedridden. They used the hospital grounds. Guarded gates at both Boston City and Massachusetts General kept patients from entering and leaving freely without the signed passes that permitted excursions into the city. The Young Men's Christian Union provided carriage rides into the countryside for convalescents at both hospitals. Considering the condition of ninteenth-century roads, this suggests that at least some patients availing themselves of this charity were not seriously ill.

The experience of the Roman Catholic Carney Hospital illustrates the changed pattern of hospital use that evolved in the last decades of the century. When opened in 1869, the institution devoted one of its five floors to "old people who may not be sick, but come here for a home." Embodying Christian charity, the hospital was an undifferentiated welfare institution. The nuns who managed it and begged door to door to support it measured its usefulness by the neediness of the inmates it cared for.[73]

Though Carney was called a hospital from the beginning, medicine seemed at times to be an afterthought. Staff surgeons described their work as involving largely "cases of a more or less chronic nature." Few recent accident cases arrived at Carney; doctors had to find surgical work among the debilitated. For a time at the end of the 1870s and beginning of the '80s Carney was the site of the most active surgical work in the city as John Homans pioneered his techniques in ovariotomy there. But when Homans returned to Massachusetts General in 1882, Carney gave up its position in this field.[74] Active medicine had a precarious hold on the hospital's attention. The hospital had few surgical instruments in the early 1880s. Surgeons complained that not only did they personally have to supply the instruments for major operations, but they also had to underwrite the cost of such surgery themselves by paying for special diets and nursing for their patients.[75]

Perhaps encouraged by Homans's successes, the Carney staff began to express a different conception of what a hospital should do. While praising the sisters' goals, the physicians and surgeons suggested those goals limited medical activity and repeatedly pressed for the admission of more acutely ill patients. In the report of 1883, the medical department openly labeled the large numbers of chronic cases filling its beds as a burden and insisted that "the usefulness of the Hospital would be increased by admitting a greater number of curable cases." The Sisters of Mercy gradually capitulated to their increasingly aggressive professional staff. By the late 1880s the medical report stated that "the hospital does not wish to receive permanently chronic invalids who may live for years, and are not in need of specialized medical attendance."[76] An 1892 *Boston Medical and Surgical Journal* article lamenting Boston's inadequate provisions for the chronically ill found Carney receiving few such cases.[77]

Increasing their medical orientation, hospitals restricted their work to the more acutely ill. Hospitalization was prescribed not for entire illnesses but only for the more critical segments requiring active medical intervention.[78] As the century drew to a close, patient stays at Boston's general hospitals grew progressively shorter. At Massachusetts General the average stay for free patients dropped below four weeks in 1886 and remained there. In 1896 the hospital started reporting the average patient stay in days rather than weeks. Meanwhile, the difference between the average stays of paid and free patients narrowed considerably, and in 1897 the annual report stopped listing average stays for paid and free patients separately. The obliteration of this difference stemmed from changes in professional perception and institutional practice. Modern medicine, as it emerged from the nineteenth century, shed many of its nontechnical, social concerns. Poor patients were treated solely as medical cases and discharged once they became candidates for what was being redefined as sheltered care. Between 1897 and 1910 the average patient stay hovered between 17 and 20 days, very nearly in the same range that had existed for paid patients in the 1870s and '80s. In October 1901, the Massachusetts General trustees received their first quarterly report in at least thirty years that listed no patient in the hospital for more than three months.[79]

The same pattern prevailed at Boston City Hospital. There the average stay decreased steadily from 27 days in 1870/71 to 24.2 in 1875/76, 22.6 in 1880/81, 21.76 in 1885, 20.46 in 1890, 19.4 in 1895/96, and 17.8 in 1900/ 1901.[80] The hospital attributed shorter stays to increased pressures for admission. Physicians even canvassed the wards for dischargeable patients, bringing the institution's practices into line with their perceptions of its role. As early as 1871 the visiting staff had asked for a convalescent home where patients who had no suitable place to go could be sent, so that the wards could be cleared of convalescent patients no longer receiving active medical treatment.[81]

The first convalescent homes connected with Boston hospitals were meant to serve as country branches, to allow an extra period of recuperation before the transition to a home environment where poor patients would again be subject to the same conditions that had originally led to hospitalization. Children's Hospital set up a country sanitarium in Weston in 1874, where "pleasant sights and sounds of the country" were made available to children from the "narrow and gloomy courts and alleys of the city." Operating during the summer only, the home continued the hospital's benign influence for an average of three weeks after children were discharged from the wards.[82] In 1880, Massachusetts General began a similar institution in Belmont. Designed for patients no longer needing hospital care "either for their own advantage or that of the institution," the cottage served a small number who were "unfit to return to their homes and renew at once their cares and work."[83]

These early homes changed as the hospitals changed, their goal shifting to speeding the hospital discharge date rather than putting additional time between the end of hospitalization and the return home. The Children's Hospital convalescent home became an integral part of the hospital during the 1890s. A new expanded building opened in 1892 in Wellesley. Gradually lengthening its season, it began to stay open year round in 1894 so that physicians and surgeons could use it as a recovery ward. Removal of ward cases to the home, at first only once a week, became more frequent; the managers reported that "many cases which a few years ago would have remained in the hospital from four to six weeks, are now sent to the Convalescent Hospital on the third or fourth day after operation." By 1912, surgeons ceased compiling for the annual report the condition of patients upon discharge, because cases were sent to Wellesley "before the results can be stated." The extremely delicate condition of some children sent to the home necessitated, in 1913, and arrangement with nearby Newton Hospital to provide emergency services.[84] In 1910, Massachusetts General began to press for a country branch where surgical cases could be sent soon after operation, freeing hospital beds for more operative cases. By this time the hospital had few traditional convalescents. In 1906, Superintendent H. B. Howard, in thanking the Young Men's Christian Union for its convalescent rides, mentioned that the hospital retained very few convalescents who were well enough to take the rides.[85]

One consequence of the advent of modern medicine was that hospitals excluded convalescence; another consequence was a new institutional attitude toward death. Hospitals as charities had been wary of being associated with death. Fear of offending popular prejudices had been evident in the decision of the city hospital to tunnel under a bordering street so that stretchers might be carried unseen from hospital to morgue.[86] But scientific hospitals, reflecting the confidence that medical attainments had bred in physicians and surgeons, began to regard the percentage of deaths followed by autopsy as a reflection of their scientific orientation. At Boston City, the new pathology building constructed in the 1890s contained a mortuary chapel, ostensibly to allow "friends and relatives of the deceased patients opportunities for holding burial services without the expense of church or the inconvenience and cost of a funeral at home."[87] City hospital pathologist William T. Councilman explained the real purpose of the chapel when he encouraged John Collins Warren to press for the same feature at Massachusetts General. With a mortuary chapel, "encouragement could be given to the people to have the funerals of their friends take place from the hospital. Bodies could be embalmed and prepared for burial here, they could remain in a suitable place to be inspected by their friends, and the funeral services could be held in the chapel. In this way a great many more autopsies could be obtained than under the present conditions."[88] An institution trying to divert attention from deaths on its grounds would not offer to host funeral services. The first annual report of Peter Bent Brigham Hospital proudly announced the highest autopsy rate in the city. The surgeon in chief, Harvey Cushing, declared that the results were so favorable that Brigham would not participate in the common practice of arranging "a timely transfer to other surroundings" for dying patients so as to reduce the death rate. Brigham's annual report discussed each surgical death in detail. Even the lay trustees were pleased with the system that exposed possible error in order to advance scientific understanding.[89]

Cushing went further and claimed that a high hospital mortality rate reflected excellence. Difficult cases—and here Cushing implicitly offered his own pioneering work in neurosurgery as an example—would of course result less favorably than simpler traditional medical work. The fact that an institution was in the forefront of medical advance and treated the hitherto untreatable and presumably fatally ill would show in its high mortality. When Cushing temporarily left for war service, his replacement was almost apologetic in explaining the hospital's lessened surgical mortality; it was "due to the partial cessation of the hazardous neurological surgery after the departure of Dr. Cushing."[90]

Boston Lying-in moved to much the same position. Though continuing to note, in 1923 as it had before, that a considerable number of patient deaths occurred within a few hours of admission, the hospital report handled the matter boldly.

There has been a considerable increase in the number of seriously sick patients referred to us by the general medical profession for the treatment of obstetric emergencies which is extremely gratifying...we welcome all such cases. We feel that our responsibility to the community involves the attempt to give such aid as we can to the patients who are sure to die at home, and feel that the saving of one such patient means more to the hospital, even though it entails a high mortality in our work, than an attempt to bolster up the hospital statistics by refusing sick patients.[91]

Deriving their legitimacy from a self-confident scientific medicine, hospitals were less vulnerable than before to the interpretation of a patient's death as an institutional failure.

For much of the nineteenth century, hospitals had been—to a greater or lesser extent—asylums for invalids, marginal institutions treating the socially marginal. In the span of a few decades they evolved into embodiments of modern medical science. Contributing to this development were the invention and introduction of a steady stream of complex medical equipment, beginning with the x-ray apparatus near the end of the century and following with elaborate machinery for physiotherapy.[92] At first difficult and later impossible to duplicate outside of central locations, this technology provided physical artifacts to which a society growing attuned to scientific progress and endowed with an appreciation for its material expression responded favorably. Dr. Frederick C. Shattuck defined a hospital, in 1906, as "a collection of the sick, [which] concentrates means and appliances for their care and cure which in private practice must be scattered, and thus difficult or impossible of full use, even by the rich."[93]

Scientific medicine, while only one of a number of factors shaping the modern hospital, had a decided impact on practitioners. As they augmented their diagnostic and therapeutic skills, they expressed greater professional self-confidence. Theirs became the dominant voice in hospital management and control. They recast the institution to fit their professional agenda. As the definition of medicine became more technical and narrow in the twentieth century, the rationale of the hospital changed. Patients came to be treated less for their social and personal failings than for physiological manifestations of accident and disease. While perhaps no less authoritarian, hospitals became less judgmental. Freeing their patients of stigma, they escaped much of their own stigma.

# 4. A Modern Arena for Training and Practice

Medical science opened new possibilities for medical practice and institutions, but the realization of these possibilities was not automatic. Science was not simply imposed on the existing substructure of medicine; rather, new possibilities and old realities were mutually adapted to each other. Decisions to improve medical education, introduce specialization, or augment the laboratory component of clinical medicine were made in a social context and often implied the necessity to alter the relationships among physicians that underlay earlier styles of practice. Decisions to expand the scientific base of medical practice exacerbated strains within the medical profession, both among practitioners within hospitals and between hospital and nonhospital doctors.

A complaint and a celebration, separated from each other by a few years in the 1890s, suggest the difficulties encountered in adapting medical institutions and practices to the evolutionary dynamic of modern medicine. The two phenomena were peculiarly local, but their significance for the hospital as an institution transcends the provincial concerns of Boston's hospital practitioners.

Maurice Howe Richardson, visiting surgeon at Massachusetts General, complained to trustee William Sturgis Bigelow in December 1893:

> We hear of nothing but the John [sic] Hopkins Hospital and what they do there. Some of our hospital graduates are now working at John Hopkins, and we are sending on to them to find out what they are doing. The medical side have sent to learn from Dr. Thayer, of John Hopkins Hospital, an interne within two years, what he is doing in the examination of the blood. Now I for one want John Hopkins to sent [sic] to the Massachusetts Hospital to find out what we are doing in the examination of the blood. Not that it is not well to learn what other institutions are doing, but it is better to have other cities send here once in a while to find out what we are doing.

Richardson was sensitive to the fact that the best scientific work of the day was being done elsewhere; that Boston had become a medical backwater. Richardson's lament pointed to the damage wrought by institutional conservatism: "It grates upon me very much," he noted, "that we should be forced to fall in the wake of other institutions. We have got to do this, however, unless we recognize at once the necessities of modern hospitals."[1]

Baltimore's Johns Hopkins was the American hospital in which scientific medicine had been integrated most thoroughly. Opened in 1889, Hopkins was the first hospital in America to seize the opportunities newly made available by the revolution in European medicine. The hospital and its medical school—the latter opened in 1893—capitalized on the absence of institutional precedent in pioneering the professional relations that a generation of physicians came to associate with scientific medicine. The hospital was integrated completely with the medical school. Heads of hospital services were department chairmen in the medical school and were appointed after a national search. Since they came to the hospital without local practices in Baltimore, they were able to concentrate their work in the hospital. Johns Hopkins closely linked the basic sciences and clinical (bedside) medicine, and stressed laboratory medicine and research. From the first it committed itself to advanced medical training; in its program of residencies, it provided the most thorough articulation of specialty training in the country.[2] In Boston, such change would come only with a struggle.

Medicine in Boston was not the anomalous case; Johns Hopkins, rather, was the exception. With national and international medical attention focused on Baltimore, Maurice Howe Richardson was not alone in his discomfort in Boston. One refuge from the relative decline of Boston medicine was a return to the past and a glorification of earlier accomplishments. In 1846 Massachusetts General had been the scene of one of the earliest applications of ether as an anaesthetic, an event which revolutionized surgery. Boston had always taken credit for this conquest of pain and the expansion of surgery which it made possible. The city's physicians and its medical journal staunchly defended ether and attacked its competitor, chloroform, as a killer. One local practitioner noted, with uncharacteristic dispassion, that "there is little doubt that proportionately more ether is used in Boston than in any other city in the world. A keen interest in ether administration always exists in this vicinity."[3]

Ether had first been used in the operating room under the Bulfinch dome at Massachusetts General. Yet when the operating room was moved out in 1868, the dome was forgotten. J. Collins Warren later noted: "In abandoning the old amphitheatre in the Dome, it had not occurred to the Hospital authorities that a great opportunity existed to preserve the memory of the greatest of all the contributions of the MGH. Here was the home of as momentous and dramatic an event as any that had occurred in the history of surgery up to that time. . . . No better use was found for it in 1868 than to turn it into a storeroom." Continuing his narrative of the hospital in the early days of his practice there, Warren unwittingly explained why the Massachusetts General of 1868 had made no effort to preserve its history. "The hospital of the early 1870's was as fine a representative of the surgery of the day as could be found in the country. It was also quite on a par with the best that was to be found in Europe."[4]

The discovery of ether took on new significance as other medical centers surpassed Boston. The Massachusetts General staff took the initiative in pressing for a commemoration of the discovery that would advertise the hospital's attainments. Seizing upon the upcoming fiftieth anniversary of the hospital's first ether operation, the staff proposed a celebration. After years without special notice of the anniversary, ether day began in 1896 as an annual event bringing the great names in medicine to Boston. Ironically, William H. Welch of Johns Hopkins was chosen to give the major address, as if the event could be legitimized only if recognized by the medical institution then foremost in the nation. Ether day took place under the old dome, in an operating theater rescued from obscurity and restored as a shrine.[5]

Ether day was at first an exercise in self-reassurance; later it would bear witness to the continuity of medical traditions. Medical tradition itself was challenged, however, in the debates over teaching and specialization at the end of the nineteenth and the beginning of the twentieth centuries. The accommodation of the new medical style with the old would be fought out within the profession itself. But the ramifications of those struggles would affect hospitals and their role in the community.

Harvard Medical School took the lead in trying to revitalize Boston medicine. The school itself had been hurt by the appointments policies pursued by Massachusetts General and Boston City hospitals.[6] Without a hospital of its own the medical school was dependent on the clinical facilities provided by the hospitals and had to appoint to its faculty men with hospital positions. Harvard's clinical faculty was therefore preselected for it by the hospitals.[7] Revitalization meant bringing in faculty from outside, ensuring that Harvard's appointments would go not to men qualified chiefly by their position in Boston but to the best men in the nation.

With the example provided by the University of Pennsylvania in luring William Osler from McGill, the Harvard medical faculty considered replacing the resigning clinical professor of medicine in 1886 with a physician from outside Boston. But once selected, the new teacher would have to be furnished with a local clinic, and unable to secure clinical facilities for someone not already a hospital staff member, the faculty dropped the idea. The disappointment came soon after the medical school moved in 1883 from its location next to Massachusetts General to a new site in the Back Bay. One motivation for the relocation was the hope that Harvard might take fuller advantage of clinical opportunities available at Boston hospitals other than Massachusetts General. But these expectations were unmet, and the faculty became even more aware of how dependent they were on Massachusetts General. Frustrated in their search for other affiliations, they sought closer ties with Massachusetts General, hoping that this would give them some say in hospital appointments.[8]

Encouraged by President Charles Eliot, the medical faculty began to negotiate with the Massachusetts General trustees in 1889. The school offered to donate its old building to the hospital, asking in return that it be equipped and maintained as a medical ward, for which Harvard would appoint the staff. When the hospital rejected this proposal, a faculty committee began to draw up plans for a new, university controlled hospital. But with President Eliot casting the deciding vote, the medical faculty voted against the university hospital for financial reasons. At the same time, the faculty voted unanimously to set up a hospital under the exclusive control of the school "as soon as necessary funds become available." Yet when the former Murdock Liquid Food Hospital was offered to the faculty in 1891, little enthusiasm was exhibited. And when Frederick C. Shattuck anonymously offered the university $5,000 to begin such a project, the Harvard Corporation refused to accept the responsibility entailed in the grant.[9] The inability to muster support for a university hospital did not mean that the medical school had lost interest in controlling its own faculty appointments. Rather, as one participant later recalled, the inconclusive outcome of the events of 1890 through 1892 meant that the school had become aware that it might be able to take advantage of the will of Peter Bent Brigham. Brigham, who died in 1877, had left a large fortune to be used twenty-five years after his death to establish and endow a hospital in Boston.[10]

Another opportunity for the medical school to select its clinical faculty came before the Brigham hospital approached realization. When the chair of clinical medicine fell vacant in 1899, the possibility developed that the school might be able to appoint William Sydney Thayer, a promising scholar then serving under William Osler at Johns Hopkins. Thayer was doubly attractive because he was not a complete outsider. He was born and grew up in Boston and had the proper family background. His father, James, was professor of law at Harvard and his brother Ezra was to become dean of the law school. He himself had received his undergraduate and medical education at Harvard and had interned at Massachusetts General.[11] Thayer was interested in Harvard; all that stood in the way of his appointment was the provision of a satisfactory clinic.

Charles Eliot took personal charge of the matter. Since Massachusetts General had already provided a clinic for Frederick Shattuck, Harvard's Jackson Professor of Clinical Medicine, Boston City Hospital was the logical choice for the new professor. The visiting physicians at Boston City resisted, however, the intrusion of someone not in the hospital's seniority system. They tried to force Harvard to appoint one of their own number. Visiting physician George B. Shattuck suggested his colleague George Sears for the professorship. He recommended Sears as "a good practitioner and a good teacher" and added that "there is probably no man at the City Hospital at present more available as a teacher." Sears had not impressed Eliot, but he had the traditional qualifications.[12]

More than city hospital traditions operated against the appointment of Thayer. Chosen specifically for his brilliance he might outshine the other professor of clinical medicine, Frederick Shattuck, and emerge as his rival. This fear was probably made more real to Shattuck because of the terms under which Thayer proposed to come to Harvard. Thayer wanted a clinic on the Hopkins model, with a continuous full-year service for himself rather than the three- and four-month annual terms prevailing at Boston hospitals.

Thayer also asked for complete independence in his teaching and a salary which would be out of line with what Harvard paid clinical professors in its medical school. Eliot's response to Thayer's terms also made Shattuck uneasy. Eliot saw nothing unusual about the conditions and wrote Shattuck what he had been told by another Hopkins professor whom Harvard was trying to lure: "He frankly said he would not exchange Johns Hopkins for Harvard on any terms which he thought it would be suitable for Harvard to offer him." Eliot was willing to admit that Harvard was having "difficulties" and saw an admission of the superiority of Hopkins as the first step in elevating the Harvard faculty.[13]

Frederick Shattuck chose to fight Thayer's appointment. In this he was aided by his brother George, visiting physician at Boston City Hospital. George Shattuck dominated the visiting physicians at Boston City and engineered their rejection of the Thayer appointment in the face of pressure from the medical faculty. Frederick Shattuck was alone among the senior faculty in opposing Thayer, as Eliot, who had learned of George Shattuck's obstructionism, took obvious pleasure in writing him after the committee of full professors refused to appoint the Shattucks' candidate, Sears. Besides pushing the less able Sears, Frederick Shattuck guarded against any untoward outcome by advocating the reorganization of the department of clinical medicine, with himself as sole chief and any new appointee as his subordinate.[14]

To salvage an appointment he believed "of the utmost importance to the future welfare of the school," Reginald Heber Fitz proposed a compromise in which Thayer would begin his service as an assistant professor. This, he hoped, would diminish the threat perceived by Shattuck and lessen his objections. Thayer refused to consider Harvard on those terms.[15] Finally, after more than a year of wrangling, Eliot and the medical faculty capitulated to Shattuck, and Sears was appointed assistant professor of clinical medicine. Summing up the affair, Henry Pickering Walcott of the Harvard Corporation wrote that because of Sears's connections at the city hospital he might be able to do some good teaching there. But Walcott, a leading Boston physician and chairman of the State Board of Health, went on to conclude that Harvard would have to woo the Brigham fund, and "give them the land, if necessary, for the right of nominating the medical staffs." The Thayer affair had made inescapable, in the judgment of the research oriented former dean of the medical school, Henry P. Bowditch, as well, "how absolutely essential it is for us to have a hospital under our own control."[16]

Harvard's opportunity to control a hospital and nominate its staff grew out of the will of Peter Bent Brigham. Brigham, like Johns Hopkins, was a self-made millionaire merchant with railroad interests who had made his fortune in urban real estate. At his death in 1877, he left the bulk of his estate to be managed as a trust for twenty-five years and then applied to the building and endowment of a hospital for the sick poor of his adopted

Boston.[17] Brigham's $1.3 million had grown to $4.3 million by 1902 when the trust was transformed into a hospital corporation.

From the standpoint of the medical school the Brigham will contained a grave defect. Unlike the provisions made by Johns Hopkins, it made no mention of connecting the proposed hospital with a medical school. In a period when public opinion did not automatically equate medical training and research with proper care of the sick poor, attempts to remedy Brigham's omission had to be pursued delicately.[18]

Active wooing of the Brigham fund began in 1899, when it became clear that the medical school had outgrown the Boylson Street building into which it had moved in 1883. Gifts to the medical school had raised the possibility that the "scientific" and preclinical departments, such as embryology, morphology, physiology, and histology, might be moved out of the medical school building to the university's Bussey Institute in Forest Hills. There they might have the laboratory space impossible at the existing site. The clinical departments would remain at Boylston Street, convenient to the city's hospitals. The preclinical faculty were unhappy with this prospect because it seemed to deny the interrelationship of the medical sciences and medical practice. Charles S. Minot, professor of embryology, sought the help of President Eliot in consolidating clinical instruction and the laboratories at a single site. Minot proposed that a new school be built on the Francis estate, a large lot within the Roxbury section of Boston. The clinical faculty were at first opposed to Minot's scheme. But Henry Bowditch raised the prospect that a new consolidated medical school might be able to attract a new Brigham hospital as its neighbor. This could give the clinical faculty control of a hospital. In a vote of February 1900, the medical faculty unanimously approved Bowditch's plan.[19]

The faculty began to plan its new school with the expectation that the Brigham fund would build its hospital next door. Since the Brigham will specified that the hospital was to serve Suffolk County, a medical school site close to the university's other departments in Cambridge (Middlesex County) was impossible.[20] Early in 1900, the medical faculty selected and approved the Francis estate, which had room for both a medical school and a hospital.

With the cost of the land underwritten by a group of twenty Bostonians headed by Henry Lee Higginson, Drs. J. Collins Warren and Henry Bowditch turned their attention to raising funds for the school buildings. The possibility of a heavily endowed hospital apparently contributed to their vision of an extraordinary school. A school controlling appointments in a great new hospital would no longer be operating on only the local scene. It would be a national institution reaching beyond Boston for a distinguished staff. In seeking national status for the school, Warren knowingly weakened the position of his family in the Boston medical scene. Since the vision required funds beyond the resources of Boston's traditional elite, the school would have to be national in its financing as well. Though discouraged by men of more

local vision,[21] Warren and Bowditch succeeded in raising $2.385 million of
$4.950 million for the school from Morgan, Rockefeller, and Huntington,
New York millionaires whose money derived from a new national economy.[22]
The physicians used the prospect of the school's connection with the Brigham hospital to justify their large hopes and needs to potential donors and to
explain the haste in which they were working.[23]

The Peter Bent Brigham Hospital corporation was to be organized in May
1902, and the university wanted to use its projected and already financed
medical school to convince the hospital board to establish close ties. These
ties did not exist while money was being raised for the school. Robert
Codman, one of the two original executors of the Brigham estate, had
apparently rebuffed Harvard representatives in their earliest approaches.
Reporting to Eliot on a conversation held with Edmund Codman, son of the
deceased Robert and his successor as a Brigham executor, John Collins
Warren wrote in September 1901 that "he spoke encouragingly about the
Brigham Hospital—perhaps [illegible] to say that he was not opposed like his
father."[24] To tie the two institutions together, the university offered the
hospital a portion of the Francis lot.

Harvard's argument for a close affiliation was largely effective. By May
1902, when the Brigham corporation first met formally, some understanding
had probably been reached between Edmund Codman and Harvard.
Codman and his fellow executor, Laurence H. H. Johnson, selected six men
to serve with them as the hospital's first board. Three of the six, Alexander
Cochrane, Eben S. Draper, and Augustus Hemenway, had been members of
the twenty-man group underwriting the medical school's purchase of the
Francis lot.[25] The Brigham committee, appointed in May 1902 to find a
location for the hospital, reported back in October with not only a site but
also the beginnings of a gentlemen's agreement with the Harvard Corporation. The committee found the Francis lot's location in the Roxbury-Long-
wood-Jamaica Plain area "the most desirable section of the City" for a new
hospital: "Part of this district is close to the centre of the City's population
and at the same time land values are comparatively low. It is convenient of
access for both patients and doctors, and is in the general direction of the
City's growth. In addition neither the City Hospital nor the Massachusetts
General Hospital are near enough to this section to give it adequate service."
The committee recommended the purchase of ten acres of the site from
Harvard.[26]

What ties the two institutions should have was less clear. It was agreed to be
to the advantage of all that the medical school use the hospital for teaching
and research. But after conferring with Dr. George H. M. Rowe of the city
hospital, the Brigham trustees expressed reservations about the desire of the
medical school to appoint the hospital staff. Rowe encouraged the trustees to
press for complete independence from the school.[27] Bowditch, Warren, and
Dean William L. Richardson, acting as a committee of the school, asked the
Harvard Corporation to make no agreement with the Brigham trustees that

did not establish the new institution as a university hospital. They thought the trustees should be honored to accept the title "The Brigham Hospital of Harvard University" and feared that the school might someday regret having on its grounds a hospital in which it did not have explicit written authority to nominate staff. Warren was especially afraid of repeating the experience of his grandfather, John Collins Warren. The earlier Warren had helped found Massachusetts General as a teaching hospital for Harvard—and the hospital had later exerted its independence, to the detriment of the medical school. When he began his memoirs in 1900, Warren wrote of those earlier hospital founders: "They made the mistake of placing this hospital in the hands of an independent board of trustees, instead of uniting it intimately with the medical school." In their letter to the Harvard Corporation, the medical school committee suggested that if Harvard could not secure an ironclad agreement as to the right of the university to nominate Brigham staff, they write in instead a clause giving Harvard the right to purchase the hospital at a fair price should the school's nominations ever be thwarted.[28] Rather than try to settle on a contract with detailed language acceptable to both university and hospital, both institutions agreed to enter into their records correspondence setting forth their positions as they understood them. Harvard stated its expectation that the trustees would allow the university to nominate the hospital's medical staff, and the trustees agreed to give careful consideration to Harvard's nominations.[29]

Lawsuits filed by the Brigham heirs delayed hospital construction until 1911, but the university began to consider its staff appointments before then. After the disappointment of the Thayer affair, it had become clear to President Eliot that the medical faculty was as marked by ambitions and jealousies as the hospital staffs, and could not be trusted to nominate men for Brigham. When Eliot understood Henry Walcott to say that the Thayer case meant that the medical faculty should control hospital appointments, Walcott was quick to clarify: "I did not mean to be understood that the Medical Faculty should have to nominate for the hospital service—if such were established on the Francis lot—but the Corporation. I quite agree that the work can be better done in the taller body."[30] There was apprehension that if Harvard chose unwisely in its first critical nominations—chief of medicine and chief of surgery—the new hospital might go the way of Boston's existing institutions and become a medically inbred family operation. William T. Councilman confided to Eliot his "fear that when it comes to the critical point the Back Bayer's will not relax their grip but will demand that the new hospital shall be a Back Bay institution."[31]

Councilman was in a unique position to influence the first nominations. He had worked with Welch at Johns Hopkins and had been called to Harvard in 1892 as a professor of pathological anatomy. His appointment was the first in the medical school in line with Eliot's ambition of applying the same standard of national excellence there as in other university departments. The university had been able to invite him because as a pathologist he was not dependent on a hospital position to the same degree as a clinical teacher. As an outsider he was greeted with suspicion by the established medical hierarchy. Though appointed pathologist to Boston City Hospital, he was at first not accepted by fellow doctors unwilling to share power with him as a voting member of the visiting staff. Councilman's desire not to be limited to local physicians in the choice of his assistants led to difficulties with city hospital trustees as well. The board requested the pathological department "to encourage, as far as possible, the application and acceptance by said department of local men in carrying on the work of the department, rather than to introduce assistants from other states."[32]

Councilman shared President Eliot's commitment to upgrading the medical school. Himself evidence of Harvard's potential when untrammeled by traditional forces, he became a close advisor to the university president on medical school matters. Councilman advanced the interests of two young outsiders for Harvard's Brigham nominations. For surgeon in chief he suggested Harvey Cushing, a Harvard Medical School graduate then serving at Hopkins. Councilman coupled repeated pleas for Cushing's appointment with dire predictions for the future of both the hospital and the school should traditional forces hold sway instead.[33] He supported Henry A. Christian, a Johns Hopkins medical graduate, as physician in chief. Christian had served under Councilman as a pathologist until 1907, when Christian began teaching clinical medicine at Harvard and the school secured a favorable appointment for him as physician in chief at South Boston's Roman Catholic Carney Hospital.[34] Councilman argued that Harvard should now give Christian a substantial salary increase so that he could be kept at Carney until the opening of Brigham. After Councilman fought the appointment of a man not committed to scientific medicine as dean of Harvard Medical School, Christian was offered the position in 1908.[35] Before accepting, however, Christian asked for and received assurances that Harvard would nominate him physician in chief of Brigham. The Brigham trustees officially appointed Christian and Cushing in 1910, and the appointment of Councilman as pathologist in chief followed in 1912.[36]

Between the reading of the will in 1877 and the opening of the hospital in 1913, the entire project had undergone drastic change. Brigham had been underwritten as a hospital in the traditional, nineteenth-century sense of the term, a charity and refuge for the sick poor of Suffolk County. It opened committed to the best in medical science, perceiving its role as that of a laboratory for the advancement of medicine. The narrow geographic limitations determining eligibility for admission were swept aside just before the hospital opened when its surgeon in chief argued that a scientifically oriented clinic needed to be able to admit all seeking its specialized treatment.[37] Further, its relations with the medical community were different from those of nineteenth-century institutions. Brigham did not make its appointments from a local, inbred medical family which perceived its service in part in terms of a narrow stewardship. Rather, it turned over its appointments to a medical school seeking a national reputation and willing to hire men for what they could contribute to medical science.[38] As Brigham flourished, Harvey Cushing called attention to "the cultivation of an ingrowing staff" as "one of the dangers of institutional age." Inbreeding would foster conservatism and slacken the quest for scientific knowledge. Cushing was pleased that the Brigham staff included "a succession of capable men who have received a portion of their training elsewhere." The changed nature of the student population of Harvard Medical School also delighted Cushing. In the academic year 1901/2, ninety-three percent of the student body was from New England; by 1924/25, that percentage had been reduced to thirty-five. Cushing pointed out that the emergence of Harvard as a national medical school followed its tie with Brigham.[39]

Peter Bent Brigham was not the only scientific hospital in Boston. Before Brigham opened, Children's Hospital and Infants' Hospital had placed their chief staff positions under the control of the medical school and announced their plans to move to Harvard's Francis Avenue lot.[40] Prodded by the growing bonds between Harvard and other hospitals, Massachusetts General began to reorganize after the turn of the century, countering the effects of seniority by instituting and then lowering retirement age, rearranging its services to benefit teaching and stress research, and seeking better relations with the medical school. Massachusetts General even began to appoint outsiders, nominated by the medical school, to major clinical positions. The first such appointment was that of David Linn Edsall of the University of Pennsylvania as visiting physician and chief of the east medical service (1912).[41] One of the small symbols that sometimes mark large changes was noted in the 1905 annual report. With the retirement of J. Collins Warren from the visiting staff, the hospital observed that "for the first time in our history the Annual Report appears without the well known name of Warren upon its pages.[42]

More than the needs of medical schooling encouraged hospital reorganization. The fact that an increasing proportion of hospital patients were in critical condition provided additional pressure. Surgeons at Boston City Hospital noted in 1890 that "the severe character of the cases demanded more time and care." As a result, a third surgical service was established and the heavier work load was split among more surgeons.[43] This was an early but very limited reorganization, carried out on the supposition that the hospital was the site of only a limited part of a practitioner's professional activity. If each case required more time, the solution was to give each practitioner fewer cases. But implicit in this early reorganization was the future recognition by staff members that hospital service was no longer peripheral to their occupations. The titles of visiting surgeon and visiting physician would be retained but would grow anachronistic as hospital service moved away from a part-time charity and developed into a full-time professional role.

Among the leaders in this shift were specialists. Their own activities the product of scientific medicine, specialists often took the initiative in advocating scientific medicine and the new relationships to which it pointed. The logic of specialization led to changes in hospital organization and rationale.

Medical specialization came into its own in the latter half of the nineteenth century; one contemporary Boston physician called the period "the age of specialism."[44] Initially, the regular profession reacted to the emergence of specialties with some hostility. James Clarke White, speaking in 1905 about the situation in Boston which greeted his return in 1857 from a year of medical study in Vienna, noted that "young men of the present day cannot in the least appreciate the animosity on the part of the general profession felt and expressed regarding the specialist, however accomplished he might be, and however great the ignorance of the general practitioner in such departments of medicine."[45] In Boston, institutional facilities for the treatment of specific diseases—as opposed to simply the quarantine of infectious diseases—dated from the founding of the Massachusetts Charitable Eye and Ear Infirmary (1827) and from the variety of institutions devoted to the treatment of women and children in the mid-nineteenth century. Within the general hospitals, the development of formal specialties was somewhat delayed, though the functional separation of women's diseases through separate wards for men and women existed from the start.

The original development of specialities in the general hospital was as outpatient departments. These were established at Boston City Hospital, for example, in dermatology (1868), otology (1869), gynecology (1873), neurology (1877), and laryngology, (1877). At Massachusetts General, laryngology and neurology were established as outpatient departments in 1872, ophthalmology in 1873, and otology in 1884. At Boston City, an ophthalmological service had beds in the hospital from the start, but other specialities had to struggle to be reorganized as inpatient services. Jealous of their prerogatives, the senior members of the inpatient staff—that is, the visiting staff—refused to allow the more junior outpatient staff to separate interesting cases out of the patient population. Such separation was the essence of specialization; it was necessary for the scientific study, understanding, and mastery of a specific organ or organ group. As long as specialities did not have beds, outpatient specialists might find patients worth study but would have to transfer such cases into the wards if they were acutely ill; there patients would come under the control of a visiting staff not divided into specialties. With the establishment in 1868 of an outpatient department for skin diseases at the city hospital, the visiting staff cautioned the physician directing the new department that acute and rare cases were to be sent into the wards for treatment and observation. The visiting staff further monopolized interesting work by warning in 1870 that "no operating whatever should be performed, no incisions be made, nor any important dislocations be reduced" in the outpatient department unless specifically authorized.[46] At the urging of the newly appointed staff neurologist or "electrician," a ward service was set aside in 1878 for diseases of the nervous system. With a later change in personnel, however, whatever reasons had compelled compliance with this request disappeared, and the ward was abolished in 1886. In the 1870s, '80s, and early '90s, the visiting staff rejected requests for ward beds from outpatient specialists for skin, throat, and nervous diseases, and diseases of women.[47]

Specialists faced much the same situation at Massachusettts General. James Clarke White, first appointed physician to outpatients in 1865, recalled his partially successful struggle: "In 1870, after long-continued agitation on my part, a ward for the care of skin diseases was established by the trustees in the face of great opposition on the part of the surgical staff, and placed under my charge." This was the first such ward in the United States. White's victory was short-lived. The superintendent, sympathizing with the visiting staff, used his authority over patient assignments to deny White the cases he wished. The trustees gave in to pressure from the visiting surgeons in 1872 and closed the ward. White remained at the hospital as physician to outpatients with skin diseases.[48]

Limited to the outpatient staff until the very end of the century, specialists at Massachusetts General often functioned as an out-group. They were more ready than their senior brethren to define themselves professionally in terms of their growing expertise and their teaching interests. James Clarke White had begun his campaign for a special ward to further his teaching activities in dermatology at Harvard; he attributed part of the hostility of the established medical community to his forthrightness in criticizing traditional medical education.[49] Older clinicians, whose loyalties tended to be to a more holistic style of medical practice, were less likely to take stands advocating the new scientific medicine.

The less traditional attitudes of specialists were evidenced on a variety of issues. In the 1880s, Edward Wigglesworth, a specialist in skin diseases with an appointment in the outpatient department at the city hospital, took the lead in urging the hospital admission of syphilitics. Wigglesworth exemplified the role of specialists as leading advocates of the replacement of moralistic by scientific standards in medicine. He himself was conscious of the link. In pleading for ward facilities for specialization at Massachusetts General, he wrote trustee F. H. Peabody: "Specialization is the essence of civilization, and syphilisation is the spectre of selfish surgery." "Selfish surgery" referred to the refusal of general surgeons to give up any of their cases to better qualified specialists; "syphilisation," or infection, was sometimes the result of this selfishness. Wiggleworth's request to Massachusetts General, like his later request to the city hospital for the admission of syphilitics, brought no action.[50]

Specialists also took an early and vigorous stand against complaints that hospitals were being used by other than the poor for whom they were intended. The trustees of Massachusetts General, fearing in 1874 that the increasing use of their outpatient department indicated such abuse, suggested that financially able outpatients be encouraged to pay something in return for treatment. The outpatient staff was hesitant about such action, and expressed its fear that the policy might diminish the number of outpatients. After first ordering the installation of locked boxes into which outpatients might contribute anonymously, the trustees decided that the hardships of the depression of the mid-1870s rendered any more aggressive policy inexpedient.[51]

The controversy over abuse, and the contrast in the attitudes of specialists on the one hand and charitably inclined laymen and general practitioners on the other, was made more explicit a few years later. With the successful organization of Boston's Associated Charities in 1879, the issue of charity abuse received widespread public attention. How well hospitals functioned as charities was also discussed.[52] The *Boston Medical and Surgical Journal* editorially castigated the city's hospitals and dispensaries for their lax management; by caring for outpatients who could pay for the services of physicians, they deprived struggling private practitioners of their livelihoods. Reform was imperative. The *Journal* suggested cooperation with the Associated Charities.[53]

Resident physician James H. Whittemore attacked the problem at Massachusetts General. In a lengthy communication to the trustees, he criticized the policy of virtually open admission to the outpatient department. Whittemore presented a more extensive analysis to the Boston Society for Medical Improvement and published his remarks in the *Journal*. The gravity of the situation, Whittemore pointed out, was clear in the figures for outpatient attendance. In 1860, the city's two outpatient facilities, the Boston Dispensary and Massachusetts General, had logged just over twenty thousand visits. With Boston's population at 178,000, the ratio of free outpatient visits to population was 1:8.8. By 1870, three facilities, now including the city hospital, had counted 43,594 visits. With a city population of 250,256, the ratio was 1:5.7. Reports for 1880 were staggering. Six dispensaries with published figures accounted for 83,664 visits. In a population of about 360,000, this amounted to one outpatient for every 4.3 Bostonians. And these figures did not include the activities of fourteen other free outpatient facilities in Boston. Assuming the increased use to be a product of increased abuse, Whittemore then recounted the English success in reducing abuse by establishing provident dispensaries which cared for the working classes in return for paid memberships. The best answer for Boston, however, was trained inspectors to investigate thoroughly all applicants and exclude all but the deserving poor.[54]

All but one of the recorded comments of Whittemore's audience were favorable. In pointing out the harm that reducing outpatient clinics would do to medical education, James Clarke White argued that "the question of the supply of the necessary clinical material for the proper education of future members of the profession far outweighed . . . any possible injury to physi-

cians by depriving them of fees or any remote danger of encouraging pauperism, as had been so generally urged against the present system in this
discussion."[55] After ritualistically seeking the advice of the senior staff as to
whether to restrict outpatient admissions, the Massachusetts General
trustees disregarded their negative recommendation and in 1881 set about to
end abuse. They hired an investigative agent, sent notice to the press, and
posted a sign in the outpatient department warning away all but the deserving poor.[56] The senior staff apparently acquiesced, but the outpatient
specialists protested. To the visiting staff's mild assertion that the danger of
abuse was probably exaggerated, dermatologist James C. White, neurologist
James Jackson Putnam, laryngologist F. L. Knight, and ophthalmologist
O. F. Wadsworth added the complaint that the new system would curtail
the study of disease and deprive medical education of needed clinical
material. Nonetheless, the plan went into effect.[57]

A year later, the outpatient specialists renewed their plea, asking that their
protest be reconsidered and the investigation of applicants suspended.
Having operated under the restrictive rules for one year, the specialists
reported that the "educational resources of these departments are being
seriously crippled." The new procedures had been especially harmful in
limiting the patients from Boston's vast rural hinterland. Many of these
residents of New England and the Canadian maritime provinces had been
referred previously for consultation to the Massachusetts General outpatient
department. These "rare and obscure" cases had baffled local doctors and
had been used to great benefit in clinical instruction. But if these patients
could afford to travel to Boston they could not be considered poor enough to
enter the clinics. Further, the very fact of investigation kept away patients
with interesting diseases of venereal origin, "who naturally shun investigation."[58]

Examining the situation, a committee of the trustees agreed. The hospital
from its beginning had undertaken responsibilities as an educational institution; it was clear that those duties should not be forsaken. Yet the danger to
the community from pauperization was real, the trustees concluded, and the
system of investigation might bring good results, "not so much to a rigid
exclusion of actual applicants, as to the general dissemination of the knowledge that such an examination is made, in place of the opposite conception
of the Hospital as a place where gratuitous treatment can always be had
whatever the means of the applicant." By keeping its investigator, the
hospital could continue to educate the community. But the imperatives of
medical education could not be dismissed: "The standard of admission
should be a liberal one, that the sieve should have a wide mesh, and exclude
only the manifestly unfit." Even that standard could be forgotten on a
physician's testimony to "the obscurity and educational value of the disease." The committee thus advised no public action, and the petitioners,
their request largely granted, were simply given leave to withdraw.[59]

Faced with another crisis in outpatient abuse in 1893—this time the problem was not complaints based on a philosophic consideration of charity, but rather the strain put on the hospital's resources by the increased out-patient load of the depression—the trustees again studied the issue and asked the advice of the staff. This time, however, unlike in 1881, the trustees decided to take only minimal action. A ten-cent charge was instituted for surgical outpatients, partly to help balance the budget and partly to limit the patient load.[60] But the trustees conceded that the paid investigator had been unsatisfactory and reverted to trusting the outpatient staff to handle applicants on a case-by-case basis:

> The Trustees will be able to protect the hospital from an inconvenient number of patients, partly by money charges, partly by the pressure of inconvenience and the loss of time involved in the nature of the service. Extreme cases of imposition will be detected and rejected by the staff, unless they are afflicted by an interesting disease, in which case they will be received with enthusiasm. Any attempt at further restriction of gratuitous service to the deserving poor is now frankly abandoned. Much good will be done, because the sick and wounded will be healed, but a considerable amount of imposition will be submitted to in the cause of science.[61]

Even the restriction in patient load was in the cause of science and not of charity; if outpatient doctors were kept from being overwhelmed, their work would be maintained at a high level. This would not be the last crisis over outpatient abuse, but by the early 1890s the trustees had accepted the vocabulary of the outpatient specialists, and the possible danger of abuse would henceforth be measured against the certain benefits of medical research and education.

The growing influence of specialists, and thus also of scientific medicine, in hospital affairs was institutionalized at Massachusetts General in 1898 when the trustees installed the senior practitioner in each of the outpatient departments as a regular voting member of the visiting staff. Nathaniel Faxon, later administrator of the hospital, remembered the growing influence of the specialties while he was an intern in 1905-6. They brought "new men with new ideas" into positions of power and played a significant role in reshaping the hospital in the early years of the twentieth century.[62] When the Boston City Hospital trustees decided to include the senior dermatologist and neurologist in the visiting staff in 1899, the visiting staff protested, but to no avail.[63] Medical specialization dictated new organizational patterns in hospitals.

The changing nature of hospitals exacerbated strains in the medical profession. Nonhospital practitioners had long complained that hospitals did them an injustice in treating patients who pleaded poverty. When hospital wards and outpatient departments began to offer treatment superior to that available in private practice, the problem for nonhospital doctors grew more serious. In one of the periodic crises over outpatient abuse in 1893, Dr.

Maurice Howe Richardson defended patients who came to the Massachusetts General outpatient department even though able to pay small fees. He noted that many came because of the hospital's reputation. Patients often thought neighborhood practitioners less competent than the physicians who inhabited the temples of modern science. Local doctors sometimes reinforced this public attitude by sending difficult cases to the hospital for diagnosis and/or treatment. A special manifestation of this problem existed in immigrant communities. The self-deprecation common among the foreign born in America colored their perception of doctors who shared their immigrant origins. Jewish practitioners, for example, complained their Jewish patients thought them too backward to handle difficult cases. In such cases, immigrants might abandon their own physicians for the imposing—and thoroughly American—hospital clinics.[64]

The rise of the scientific hospital began a reorganization of medical practice. Outside general practitioners, fearing they would lose their place in the new order and that their income and status would decline, resisted. One letter to the *Boston Medical and Surgical Journal* interpreted Children's Hospital's program of providing aftercare as a conspiracy to keep people from paying their private doctors. A physician wrote that after he had taken charge of a case of hip disease discharged from the hospital, a hospital nurse had called at the child's home, inspected his work, remarked that "the child's leg would become shortened without the hospital traction treatment," and requested the child be readmitted. The physician did not deny the hospital's prognosis or the validity of its plan of treatment. Rather than answer the hospital's implication that its treatment was superior, he simply asserted that "persons who can afford to pay for treatment outside of clinics should be encouraged to do so, instead of attempts being made to prevent them from doing so as in the above instance." In December 1909, the Boston Medical Society sent a circular letter to the hospitals of the city complaining against the "rising feeling" that surgery could be performed only in institutions, "thus depriving all ordinary private physicians and surgeons of a class of cases." The society condemned the city's hospitals and dispensaries for "inculcating in the minds of the laity a lack of confidence in the abilities of the ordinary private practitioner."[65]

The clearest expression of this conflict came in a case involving Dr. Richard C. Cabot. Cabot, because of both his solid family background and his earned position as professor of medicine at Harvard and chief of the west medical service at Massachusetts General, was able to express himself with a bluntness impossible for someone in a less secure position. His public statements comparing the private and hospital practice of medicine rankled many of his fellow physicians. In an address he sometimes gave and had published in the *American Magazine* in the spring of 1916, Cabot encouraged the middle classes to bring their ailments to the hospital. By avoiding independent private practitioners, he assured them, they would receive "Better Doctoring for Less Money." Though he credited the family doctor with doing "the best he knows how" and admired the results he obtained "considering the difficulties under which he works," Cabot labeled the medical system within which the general practitioner worked as inefficient. At a hospital a patient was studied by a group of specialists, subjected to indicated laboratory procedures, and probed if necessary by x-rays. Unless the patient in private practice had great enough wealth to visit numbers of specialists, his diagnosis and treatment depended on educated guesswork. In an age when no man could master all the complexities of a science, private medicine was second-class medicine.[66]

Cabot's critique of nonhospital medicine elicited complaints from doctors not in hospital practice. Physicians claimed that Cabot was undermining their practices by making them look bad to their patients. But another theme also ran through the criticisms of Cabot's remarks. Physicians stated that Cabot was trying to turn medicine either into a science or into a business. They found demeaning his contentions that medicine needed to follow the same division of labor used by industry and that patients should consider what they were purchasing and at what cost. Cabot's business metaphors missed the spiritual nature of the relationship between patient and physician. At the same time his contention that technology and laboratory procedures could supersede the physician's old-fashioned knowledge of his patient and his patient's "constitution" was objectionable. The x-ray, a powerful symbol of the might of scientific medicine for Cabot, was a bugbear to his opponents. Dr. J. W. Courtney accused the x-ray of revealing insoluble problems that both patient and physician would be better off not knowing. The traditional physician felt his helplessness uncovered because he could not compete with the "unerring penetration" of the x-ray or the overwhelming arsenal of the scientific hospital, and took refuge in an almost spiritual relationship with his patient that he would not let modern science or business invade. Cabot's less than tactful advocacy made him a target. Cabot's reply to a rebuke by the ethics committee of the Massachusetts Medical Society was characteristic: "Luckily, you cannot hurt me in the least." The answer reflected both his personal security and his conviction that the trends he represented were ascendent.[67]

The continued abuse directed against Cabot demonstrated a deepening gulf between scientific medicine and general practice. One general practitioner explained Cabot's seeming hostility toward the profession by noting what he misunderstood to be Cabot's excessive patient mortality. The Cabot Case Records were the reports of the weekly clinical pathological conference that Cabot had instituted at Massachusetts General, at which clinicians presented the records of patients dying during the previous week and tested their diagnoses against autopsy data. The angry practitioner associated Cabot's name with all the autopsies. What kind of physician is this, he asked, whose patients all die?[68]

Nonhospital physicians unhappy with Cabot were fighting a rear guard action. Henry Christian concluded:

Disease in man, except in its simpler forms, can be investigated increasingly by more and more types of instruments, which reduce to figures and formulae or graphic records suitable for comparison from day to day or from case to case data, which in the past had to be expressed largely in the form of impressions. Much of this apparatus is complicated and expensive. So it comes about that in many conditions diagnosis is best made where access to such apparatus can be had, and in its multiplicity it is, with few exceptions, the large hospital alone that can provide all of this type of apparatus that is needed.[69]

In an attempt to reassure general practitioners, hospital physicians pledged to cooperate with their nonhospital peers. Christian envisioned a program of mutual benefit in which practitioners would refer their difficult and therefore interesting cases to hospitals for diagnosis on a consulting basis. The Mayo Clinic pioneered this system in the United States. In 1916 Massachusetts General began a consultation clinic which offered diagnostic tests and specialist examinations to patients suffering obscure or complicated diseases. For a fee, the clinic accepted patients recommended by private practitioners and, after diagnosis, referred back all but very few cases for private treatment. The Boston Dispensary established the same kind of clinic in 1919.[70]

Hospitals offered to fight abuse by charging a fee. But whether they charged a fee or not, they could no longer be considered charities, because they now had something to offer to the nonpoor. In reports issued in the 1890s Children's Hospital recognized this new truth by refuting charges that it pauperized patients, asserting that it provided excellent medical care to patients regardless of their social background. Hesitant to challenge the established wisdom, however, it did not deny the possibility that medical charity could be abused, only that children could be accused of such abuse. Similar evidence led Richard Cabot to a more sweeping conclusion. In forwarding the outline of a speech he was to give on "the ideal of a modern hospital," Cabot penciled next to point one, "The most efficient diagnosis and treatment of patients possible, in the light of modern science," the note "abolishes 'hospital abuse.'"[71]

In an article in the *Boston Medical and Surgical Journal* in 1899, Dr. Agnes Vietor chronicled "The Passing of the 'Charity' Hospital and Dispensary." She concluded that, given the medical advances of which only hospitals were capable, it was anachronistic to organize them as charities. The relations of hospitals and dispensaries to the community had changed and hospitals needed to be readjusted to fit the new reality in which the nonpoor sought their unique medical benefits. One of Vietor's suggestions was that hospitals make available, for a charge, their laboratories and other technologies to patients who would not have to leave their homes. Those who remained at home would be spared the evil of parasitism while at the same time the integrity of the home itself would be protected as the family retained its responsibility for the care of the sick.[72] But this attempt to reconcile

science to the older moral order, implicit in a condemnation of charity abuse
and a defense of the home and family, was already doomed by social forces
operating in the metropolis. No longer was it "good medicine" to treat
the patient within his social context, in the home and among family. A new
medical style—reductionist in its reliance on medical specialities and laboratory data—proclaimed the superiority of the hospital.

# 5. Hospitalizing the
## Middle Classes

There was little in the medical science that had developed by early in the twentieth century that required hospitalization for the treatment of illness. Yet by that period hospitals had begun to attract substantial numbers of middle class patients. Contemporaries recognized that social factors—particularly the changing social ecology of the city—were responsible in part for the spread of hospitalization beyond the marginal. It is difficult to assess the relative significance of the social and medical forces, but it is clear that the changed pattern of hospital use forced hospitals to evolve further from the charity in which they had originated. New forms, practices, and procedures developed to accommodate the hospitalization of the affluent.

The natural constituency of hospitals had always included persons living by themselves. Doctors James Jackson and John Collins Warren had pointed to this group to demonstrate the need for Massachusetts General. The citizens of Cambridge had considered their "floating population of more than a thousand students" in deciding that their city needed a hospital.[1] About half of the adult patients entering Boston City Hospital in the 1860s and '70s were unattached individuals.[2] The visibility of the unattached in hospital wards was due partially to the overrepresentation of single adults in the population of Boston, a consequence of the imbalance in urban in-migration—both from the New England countryside and from foreign lands—which was weighted in favor of young adults entering the city on their own. But the disproportionate hospitalization of the unattached also resulted from the helplessness of individuals who were struck by illness or accident while living outside of home and family.

Until the late years of the nineteenth century, such unattached individuals had come largely from the lower and working classes. But in an urban world, a broader spectrum of the young tended to move out of the homes of their parents before marriage. If they did not marry, they continued to live alone, further swelling the totals.[3]

Many lived in lodging houses. Between 1880 and 1900, the number of boarding and lodging house keepers in Boston rose from 601 to 1,571. The increase more than kept up with population; in 1880 there had been one such keeper for each 604 inhabitants, in 1900 there was one for every 357. Major sections of the city were largely given over to this type of residence.[4] Newspaper features apprised Bostonians of the "great army" inhabiting the West and the South End and of their life-styles.[5]

Lodgers did not occupy the same positions as the boarders celebrated by Oliver Wendell Holmes. There was no shared breakfast table. What distinguished "The Lodging House Problem" was the absence of a sense of community or familiarity among the lodgers themselves. One observer noted the lack of family ties and the sadness of individuals "condemned to solitary living." The practice of lodging expanded as that of boarding declined. The Massachusetts census had found 15,938 boarders and 24,280 lodgers in Boston in 1885; in 1895 the figures were 9,496 and 44,926.[6]

Lodging differed from boarding in that common meals were not a part of the price of rent. The lodging house was made possible by the cafe, dining room, and restaurant. These eating places flourished in the South and the West End.[7] In his survey of the South End lodging house district in 1903, Albert Wolfe, a South End Settlement House resident, found other institutions also serving as corollaries to the lodging house. The 152 eating establishments were followed in prominence by 78 laundries, obviously necessitated by the condition of individuals living outside of family units.[8]

Most lodging houses provided little more than a place to sleep. The conditions Wolfe found in many—deficient sanitary facilities, poor ventilation, dampness, and the absence of heat during the day—added care in sickness to the functions for which residents had to go elsewhere. To the difficulties of illness in a lodging house would have to be added the need to secure food from the outside or to go out for meals while ill. Boardinghouses had at least been able to supply infirm residents with their meals. Neither the lodging nor the boardinghouse duplicated the traditional family in looking after and providing for other needs of the sick. Boston's diet kitchens offered meals to sick lodgers and boarders, but their services were limited; a spokeswoman for the South End Diet Kitchen bemoaned the expense borne by working girls in boardinghouses who were obliged to hire nurses to care for them and pay physicians for medical advice.[9]

The occupants of other new forms of residence faced much the same difficulties in illness as lodgers and boarders. The *Boston Transcript* carried its first advertisements for "Bachelor Apartments" in its classifieds in 1885. These differed from lodging and boardinghouses in that each occupant was provided with individual kitchen and bath facilities. In the more elaborate structures, a wing of the building might be turned over to servants' quarters and meals might be available in a dining room on the premises. Also differing from lodging and boardinghouses were single room tenements. Less elaborate than bachelor apartments, these housed "those of good habits and character, generally self-supporting,...living alone..." Surveying Boston in 1882, the Associated Charities found only one such building and called the attention of capitalists and builders to the need for more. The need was there; the YWCA and Industrial Union could not meet the demand for single rooms. Capitalists could expect good tenants and regular rents, with a higher return per square foot than larger tenements.[10] But the residents of bachelor apartments and single room tenements were as isolated in illness as lodgers or boarders.

As medical advances improved their image, hospitals emerged as corollary institutions for the city's unattached middle class individuals in much the same sense as the eating place or laundry. Examining the need for hospitals in New York City for the State Charities Aid Association in 1908, Phil Jacobs pointed to the "modern 'bachelor movement'" as "preparing a class of people...more and more dependent on the hospital." Jacobs was examining a relationship between increased hospital use and weakened family ties that had been pointed out in Dr. Walker Gill Wylie's 1876 study of hospitals. Wylie, who had won Harvard University's Boylston Prize for his essay, argued against expanding hospital facilities because he believed that the bonds of family would be destroyed were sick members taken out of the home for treatment and care. The family would be weakened as it gave up one of its traditional functions. Sharing a mid-nineteenth-century concept of hospitals as charities, Wylie believed that their indiscriminate use would encourage dependency and pauperization. Further, it would spread disease; in making health care available, hospitals would make people careless about avoiding illness and thus more vulnerable to disease. Jacobs, on the other hand, was not trying to protect the poor from themselves, but dealing with a phenomenon that had spread to the middle classes.[11]

Most middle class urban dwellers continued to live within the structure of the family, but even their life-styles were not unaffected. Families moving into apartments remained together, yet often had to curtail family functions that needed more space than their restricted new quarters provided.[12] The apartments even of the comfortable classes often did not provide sufficient room for the care of the sick. The New York hospital survery recommended that the city's growing apartment population be considered as creating a disproportionate need for hospitals.[13]

The apartment house represented a change in living style forced by the pressures of urban growth and consequent mounting property values. As cities grew, convenient and desirable residential land often became too expensive to allow a city lot to provide housing for just one family. The first apartment house, or French flat, in Boston was built in 1857. The middle and upper classes did not, at first, respond favorably. They associated flat living with the tenements built to house the poor. Moving into an apartment also meant certain sacrifices for families who had always had their own homes. Remembering the initial disfavor which greeted the apartment building and looking back from the vantage point of 1890, the real estate columnist of the *Transcript* noted:

Within the past ten years, however, the value of land has risen so much in the best parts of the residental portion of the city, and home rents have become so great, that, little by little, people have not only become reconciled to this mode of living, but it has become so popular that the majority of people prefer it to having an entire house. In fact, it is the fashion—we might say the rage. So that now suites in apartment houses in the most fashionable neighborhoods are as eagerly sought for by the wealthy as were those in the old tenement houses by those who were too poor to live elsewhere.[14]

Apartment houses went up in the Back Bay and other fashionable areas of the city and suburbs. The real estate columns noted, in 1890, that "though apartment houses continue to be built by the score, in town and out of town, the demand for family suites continues in proportion to the increase in the number of this class of dwellings."[15]

A new category of "Hotels and Family Suites" first appeared in the classifieds of the *Transcript* in the room, board, and real estate section in October 1883. The 1880s also witnessed a spate of newspaper accounts whose writers assumed that Bostonians were interested in finding out what they could about this new form of residence making great inroads in their community: "Old domestic citizens . . . ask information about the methods and ways of life in these apartment houses." In the columns of the *Transcript*, opinions were invited as to whether the advantages of apartment life outweighed the disadvantages. Discussed were questions of security, safety, health, crowding, privacy, the ability to entertain, cosiness, the burden of housekeeping, flexibility, and permanence. To counter the strangeness of the new residences, building owners tried to imbue them with a sense of familiarity by naming them. Henry Lee Higginson called one of his, on Commonwealth Avenue, the Hecla, after the copper mining investment that had done so much for Boston's fortunes.[16]

Contemporaries recognized that sickness was less likely to be cared for in an apartment with fewer and smaller rooms than in a private house. A 1907 article in *Charities and the Commons* pointed to "small rooms and contracted accommodations in large cities" as accounting for increased hospital use among a broader spectrum of the population. Presenting data derived from his study "Benevolent Hospitals in Metropolitan Boston" in 1913, William Mahoney explained that, in part, "the increased use of the hospitals can probably be attributed to congestion of population, an increasing proportion of which lives in apartments."[17] The trustees of Boston Lying-in explained their need for new and expanded hospital facilities by pointing to the number of relatively well-to-do women who were using them, "and with the rapid growth of the apartment house population, the number is fast multiplying." With the disappearance of guest rooms and spare rooms, a sickroom became close to an impossibility.[18] Presiding over the annual meeting of the American Hospital Association in 1912, Dr. Henry M. Hurd of Johns Hopkins explained: "The small house once tenanted by a single family, has given place to the tenement house and the apartment house where every inch of space is utilized and no room is to be found for the sick and injured. . . . The prospective mother, even, no longer finds needed privacy and quiet in her own home in childbirth and is too often compelled to resort to the lying-in department of a general hospital."[19] The lack of a sickroom made an illness more inconvenient for the unaffected family members, while in some cases its absence could threaten their health.

The sociologically extended family could not survive the transformation of the urban middle class into apartment dwellers. The mobility of urbanites also affected the quality of neighborliness—as did the spatial organization of the apartment house. Physical proximity to neighbors conduced to psychological distancing, a situation Wolfe recognized among lodgers whom he characterized as "oversolicitous" in protecting their personal privacy. The occupants of a French flat were left with fewer and less close relations with their neighbors. Servants were less likely to be kept by apartment dwellers.[20] All this, together with the increased employment of wives and mothers outside the home, left little likelihood of there being anyone within or near the home available for the care of the sick. A new urban social ecology thus broadened the class from which hospitals would draw their patients. And the psychic and emotional burdens of a sickness suffered in the modern home were not missed by contemporaries. Boston City Hospital noted, in its annual report for 1887, that the return of the still helpless sick to their homes would "add to the domestic burdens of a family already struggling under difficulties to maintain itself."[21]

The Sisters of St. Margaret provided Boston with an early solution to this difficulty by making available a suitable "home" for operations and other medical treatment for private patients. Members of a Protestant Evangelical order, the sisters had been invited from England in 1871 by a group of High Church Bostonians, among whom medical men were prominent, to provide nursing for the new Children's Hospital. At the request of doctors, when the sisters opened their new convent on Bowdoin Street near the Church of the Advent on the back side of Beacon Hill in 1877, they set aside two rooms as an infirmary. It was well received; "two lady patients came at once," and the rooms were seldom empty thereafter.[22]

In 1881 the convent enlarged its quarters. Following the Church of the Advent to the constricted respectability of the south slope of Beacon Hill,[23] the sisters moved into two adjoining houses on Louisburg Square. With the encouragement of the medical community, one of these houses was set aside as a hospital and the name St. Margaret's Hospital assumed. Soon both buildings were providing accommodations for fifteen private patients. By early in the twentieth century, St. Margaret's had opened two more houses at the other end of the square for hospital use.[24]

St. Margaret's was the city's first private hospital. Patients were admitted under the care of their personal physicians, for whose fees they were responsible. In addition, patients paid for their room and board at rates of $10 to $40 per week (in 1891). Patients were both Bostonians and nonresidents; the hospital records list patients from Nova Scotia, Providence, and New Hampshire, as well as the nearby towns of Waltham and Nahant.[25]

Previously, many patients coming to the city for private treatment had stayed in boardinghouses or hotels. A physician might attend a patient in rooms engaged by the patient himself,[26] or the patient might be directed to a boardinghouse with which the doctor had prior arrangements.[27] Practitioners advertised for rooms in which to board patients coming to see them.[28] Some boarding and lodging house keepers specialized in providing this quasi-medical sevice and advertised their rooms to the medical profession.[29] This willingness to assume the additional responsibilities entailed in caring for the sick no doubt stemmed from the straitened financial circumstances in which Albert Wolfe found many lodging house keepers. Operating on a narrow margin of profit, they often sought other activities to supplement their incomes.[30] Boston's medical community was shocked and split in 1876 by a coroner's inquest into an apparent abortion performed by a reputable physician in one of the city's most respectable boardinghouse lying-ins.[31]

St. Margaret's limited "medical" facilities suggest that in-town-patients came because of the deficiency of their own homes or a lack of family to look after them. In his memoirs, John Collins Warren remembered that surgeons would use St. Margaret's for their private patients "when for one reason or another it was not possible to set the stage in a private home for the complex ritual of an operation." There was apparently no fixed room especially fitted for surgery, any more than in an ordinary home. When the records indicate where operations were performed, they mention such locations as the parlor, reception room, the visitors' sitting room, or a patient's room: "Dr. Strong operated on Miss Humphreys up two flights in [room] 17"; "Dr. Eliot operated on Miss [blank] in Miss Oliver's room." After surgery, a patient might be carried up several flights to the room she would occupy for her recuperation. Besides not being especially equipped as a hospital, St. Margaret's was not rigidly defined as one. It is sometimes difficult to separate its hospital function from the hospitality of the convent. Guests of the order visiting Boston stayed in rooms otherwise used for patients.[32]

Though in many ways like a home, St. Margaret's helped introduce the comfortable classes to receiving care outside of their own homes. Physicians and surgeons, reluctant to have their private patients enter general hospitals, encouraged the use of St. Margaret's; it allowed them to begin to centralize their private practices. Dr. John Homans, who did much of the early surgery at St. Margaret's, treated patients in "his own room" there. When Homans tried the fad of electrical treatments in the late 1880s, he had his patients come to St. Margaret's "to be electrified." The convent records noted that "Dr. Homans had *five* patients for electricity this afternoon!" and nine patients another day.[33]

On a more limited scale, a similar situation existed at Carney Hospital. Though a charity, it made some rooms available to favored doctors for their private patients. In the case of Dr. Homans, the sister superior went further, "sending all cases of ovariotomy [applying at the hospital] to see Dr. Homans

at his office," enabling Homans to enter them as his private patients at
Carney.[34] Homans's special status was probably a reward; his pioneering
surgical work had built a reputation for Carney and helped put the Catholic
hospital in the good graces of charitably inclined Back Bay Protestants.

Other private hospitals followed, challenging St. Margaret's as "the home
of private surgery in Boston," and gradually replacing the patient's home as
the site of private surgery. Surgeon John Finney remembered assisting surgeons in the late 1880s: "In the early years of my practice, the question as to
where an operation was to be done in the hospital or in the home was always
uppermost and was usually settled by the patient or his family insisting upon
having it done at home."[35] Proprietary hospitals, first appearing in numbers
in Boston in the 1890s, made hospital surgery an increasingly more likely
choice. Like St. Margaret's, these institutions catered to the comfortable
classes and were a response both to the needs of physicians and surgeons and
to the changing nature of the urban home. They were smaller than Boston's
major charitable hospitals. Unlike St. Margaret's, most were operated for
profit.

The most successful such hospital was the L. C. Elliot Private Hospital.
With St. Margaret's, it was favored by Massachusetts General staff members.
It opened in the early 1890s around the corner from St. Margaret's on
Beacon Hill. In 1893 it moved to a pleasant block on Commonwealth
Avenue, near the Public Garden, in the fashionable Back Bay. Most of the
other private hospitals opening in the 1890s were less prosperous. Some, like
the Pirlot Private Hospital, the F. A. Reinhard Hospital, the Laing Dispen-
sary, and Dr. Phillips Private Hospital, appeared in the city directory for a
year or two and then vanished. They were marginal operations, depending on
the good will and continued patronage of active surgeons. Boothby Surgical
Hospital, a homeopathic institution located near Boston City on Worcester
Square in the South End, duplicated the success of Elliot Hospital.[36]

By the early twentieth century, a growing patient clientele made the
operation of such hospitals on a more permanent footing possible. A survey
performed for Massachusetts General in 1911 found forty-three private
hospitals, with a capacity of about a thousand beds, scattered through
Boston, Brookline, and Cambridge. Excluding the six which mixed charity
and private patients left thirty-seven private hospitals with 797 beds. Those
examined in detail charged up to $75 a week for room and board. These
small private hospitals fell into two groups: those run by nonprofessionals,
mainly businesswomen, to profit on payments for room and board, and those
owned by physicians, either as individuals or in groups. The latter did not
have to provide an adequate return on invested capital to be profitable, as
the practitioners involved benefited from their professional fees.

The data presented for one unnamed institution showed a plant of $150,000
with twenty-nine beds, managed by physicians and returning less than the
acceptable six percent per year.[37] This was the Corey Hill Hospital, opened in

Brookline in 1904. Organized by fifteen practitioners, chiefly surgeons from Boston's medical elite, it offered private patients pleasant suburban surroundings, "an abundance of fresh air," and experienced nursing. Surgeon Charles B. Porter reported that many of his patients who balked at entering a general hospital because of the taint of charity did not refuse private hospitalization. Informed that his son had recuperated successfully from an appendicitis operation, Harvard Medical School's former Dean Henry P. Bowditch joked with his wife: "I wrote to Dr. Richardson yesterday suggesting that he should have a ward in his Corey Hill Hospital called the 'Bowditch Ward' trusting to the Bowditch family to supply all patients."[38]

Corey Hill prospered because of the social changes that made hospitalization an attractive alternative to home care. No overriding medical imperative forced patients out of their homes and into the medically primitive St. Margaret's, Corey Hill, or Boston's other private hospitals, most of which were little more than boardinghouses. Using data devloped by the Massachusetts General survey, a group of physicians concluded that "none of the existing private hospitals in Boston has an adequate laboratory, X-ray or radium plant, electrical treatment room, hydrotherapy room, or place for gymnastic treatment. The small private hospitals cannot afford to provide these things."[39] Private hospitals were medically safe and more comfortable and convenient for illness or operation than many urban homes. Corey Hill and institutions like it made the comfortable classes consider hospitals in a more favorable light.

A wide range of other institutions began to accustom the well-to-do to accept health care outside of the natural setting of home and family. Historians of nineteenth-century psychiatry have demonstrated that the use of the insane asylum was motivated alternatively by hope of cure and by despair.[40] Boston's finest families entrusted their mentally ill to the McLean Asylum fcr the Insane, a separate department of Massachusetts General. By 1865, only a small proportion of the patients at McLean's could be considered poor, and patient fees enabled it to be self-supporting. Operating under a charter that defined their trust as a charity, the Massachusetts General trustees found it necessary to resort to the public press in 1895 to correct "a mistaken impression" that McLean's catered only to the very wealthy. This popular impression, no doubt, owed something to the construction of mansion-like "cottages," each designed to house an individual patient and his servants and attendants.[41]

Desperation led to the institutionalization of other patients regarded as hopeless. Quacks promised successful treatment of "ALL DISEASES," including specifically tuberculosis, paralysis, and cancer "without knife, caustic or poison."[42] If the irregular practitioner was in a distant city, the patient might stay at a hotel.[43] Quacks also established hotellike hospitals. Newspaper advertising invited Bostonians to the Invalids' Hotel in Buffalo, New York. In pleasant surroundings, patients would be treated by the specialists of the World's Dispensary Medical Association of Buffalo, a part of the pill empire of R. V. Pierce, M.D. Dr. Pierce stood ready to provide Pleasant Purgative Pellets and "Extract of Smart-Weed, a magical remedy for Pain, Bowel Complaints and an unequalled Linament for both human and horse flesh." Bostonians could stay in their own city and patronize the Hotel Flower, a "Palace for Invalids" opened in 1889. Operated by Dr. R. C. Flower of the patent medicine family, the institution specialized in incurable afflictions and promised successful treatment for "cancer, tumor, consumption, paralysis and nerve trouble in a most marvelous manner." Promotional articles described the gold and silver burnished walls and ceilings, "costly pictures on the wall," and "elegantly furnished" rooms. A "triumph of the designer's art," the "health palace" was characterized as a "fairyland."[44]

Quack institutions specialized in the chronic and incurable; here lay the major reason for their acceptance and profitability. Flower promised to end long-term incapacities. Testimonials for late-nineteenth-century quack remedies generally began with the long duration of the patient's infirmity. Modern physicians studying developing countries have noted that the sick abandon traditional folk or primitive medicine in extreme conditions, "where there is little that can be done to help them, or when they can be saved only by heroic effort."[45] Similarly, recourse to the quack hospital comes after the perceived failure of traditional home care. This perception of failure probably develops after an extended, debilitating, and unrelieved illness. Those who resorted to quacks were not necessarily the poor; luxurious institutions appealed to those whose means made them attractive targets for irregular practitioners. Quackery thus may have provided part of the complex of institutions and practices which served to initiate the comfortably settled to the notion of going among strangers when ill.

Some treatments favored by respected medical practitioners could be had only at a distance and therefore required leaving home and family and perhaps entering an institution. Sanatorium treatment of tuberculosis provided one such instance. The tuberculosis sanatorium movement in the United States began with the institution established by Dr. Edward L. Trudeau at Saranac Lake, New York, in 1885. But even when Trudeau arrived in the Adirondacks to cope with his own tuberculosis in 1873, he found that other invalids had preceded him. Trudeau's contribution was to extend the possibilities of the wilderness cure to patients who could not afford renting houses and hiring servants, or paying for an extended hotel stay.[46] The wilderness cure was a form of the climatological treatment popular in the 1870s. Both the medical press and general newspapers in Boston carried articles on the advantages of treatment at the spas, springs, baths, and resorts in the different climates of the distant south and west.[47] Special institutions for nervous diseases and drug addictions also proliferated. These suggested the value of a change of scene and a rest from the normal activities of home life in treatment and recuperation. Bostonians could secure such treatment at local as well as distant institutions.[48] Lunatic asylums, quack institutions, climatic resorts, and specialized sanatoria contributed to the familiarity with which the comfortably settled greeted private medical hospitals at the turn of the century, and helped assure their success.

The comfortably settled were thus newly disposed to consider hospitalization. But the older hospitals, organized to care for charity patients, did not know quite what to make of them. A major question was should they be charged doctor's fees. Throughout the nineteenth century, formal statute at Boston City prohibited professional fees.[49] Answering a complaint made to the city council by a Montreal resident charged a professional fee in addition to his hospital bill, the Boston City trustees acknowledged in 1868 that 32 of 4,838 patients so far admitted had "by fee, gift or otherwise" remunerated their physicians.[50] The trustees hastened to add that none of the patients had been Boston residents, and further that all had occupied private rooms. While providing a welcome source of revenue, private patients had never been so numerous as to raise serious questions about the hospital's charitable role.

Private patients at Massachusetts General paid the established rate of board for the rooms they occupied, in the same manner that ward patients were expected to contribute what they could. But the matter of professional fees was, for some time, more ambiguous. The trustees decided in 1844 that private room patients were to pay $3.00 weekly beyond their hospital bills for professional attendance. Such patients were also to pay for surgical operations at a rate two-thirds that indicated on the "Fee-table of the Physicians and Surgeons of Boston." These fees were to go to the hospital to underwrite the care of poorer patients.[51] A case arising in 1880 required the trustees to reexamine hospital policy. A visiting surgeon, uncertain of what to do with a professional fee of $100, forwarded the check to the trustees and asked their advice. At the same time, the hospital's chief administrator, resident physician J. J. Whittemore, requested a clarification of policy, noting that "there is often some difference of opinion amongst the surgeons on this matter of receiving fees." After a poll of the visiting staff disclosed that they opposed accepting fees by a vote of fifteen to three, the trustees voted that "fees are not to be paid or received."[52] The staff had little economic stake in private patients from out of town whom chance had seen fit to deposit in the hospital.

This was not the case, however, with those who came to Boston specifically for medical treatment. Boston had early developed as a medical center for New England and many of its prominent physicians and surgeons enjoyed a consulting practice that requird extensive travels throughout the region and to cities as far distant as Albany.[53] The city's reputation drew poor patients with "perplexing cases" from New England and the Canadian maritime provinces to local hospitals, while the more affluent came bearing referrals from hometown doctors to specific practitioners.[54] This latter group could be expected to resist hospitalization. With charitable hospitals refusing their staff members permission to collect fees from hospital patients, doctors opposed the hospitalization of these private patients.[55]

Physicians protested when patients in this latter category entered Massachusetts General. With arrangements made for nonhospital care or surgery and with a fee agreed upon, the patient might discover that the same medical attention could be had gratis in the pay ward of the hospital. The prospect of this economy might outweigh fear of hospitalization. Paying only hospital charges for room and board, the patient deprived the practitioner of his livelihood.[56] Surgeon Maurice Howe Richardson recounted a poignant example of this injustice. He had been treating the wife of a wealthy New York attorney as his private patient for more than a year. Requiring surgery, she informed Richardson that she would enter Massachusetts General where she could have his services for free. "Her husband thought that, in the present hard time, it was a good chance for her to economize." For the $21.00 she paid the hospital for several days board, the patient had her surgery. Richardson noted that the operation required considerable skill; it was "one which these people had no business in the world to have done for nothing." Richardson performed the operation but received no fee. Such cases forced a reconsideration of hospital policy. Some members of the Massachusetts General visiting staff, particularly surgeons, pressed for an end to the prohibition against collecting professional fees from private room patients.[57]

The issue came to a head in 1886. Support for the policy change seems to have been limited, probably because the kind of case in question was still the exception. Leading the opposition to change was surgeon Henry J. Bigelow. Bigelow, perhaps the most illustrious member of the staff, defended the hospital as a charity and warned that allowing professional fees would threaten its purpose and destroy its reputation by transforming it into an institution which served and enriched its medical staff. On the advice of Chairman Samuel Eliot, he offered his resignation to elicit a vote of confidence in his position. To his surprise his resignation was accepted. Bigelow refused the promotion to surgeon emeritus and the honorary position of consulting surgeon offered him by the trustees to mask the acceptance of his resignation. Continuing his crusade against professional fees, Bigelow grew increasingly estranged from the hospital's management; asked for his portrait by the trustees, he first acceded but later refused. At his death in 1891, the trustees renamed their operating room for Bigelow, but when they asked his son for a portrait they were informed that the deceased had precluded that in his last will. Henry J. Bigelow carried to the grave his bitterness at what he considered his shabby treatment. Nonetheless, he had made his case effectively. Bigelow's determination and his commitment to the stewardship role forced the question of professional fees to be considered on moral grounds. The trustees took what even he conceded to be "vigorous action" in reaffirming their rules against hospital officers' or employees' accepting fees or gifts from patients.[58]

Meanwhile, private hospitals were increasingly drawing off patients who might otherwise have found their way into Massachusetts General. When Ward B, the hospital's eight-room ward for private patients, reopened after alterations late in 1893, it was able to attract only one patient in more than three months. At the same time, steadily rising expenses put the hospital in financial difficulty. Seeking additional revenue, the trustees sought the advice of the visiting staff as to whether Ward B could be made "a source of larger income" as well as more useful to the public. One alternative was to lower the rates, since the ward had suffered a noticeable drop in patients when its charges had been raised in 1891 from a range of $14 to $35 per week to one of $50 to $70 per week. Other possibilities were remaking the structure into an open ward or allowing practitioners to collect professional fees so that they would be more likely to encourage their private patients to enter.[59]

Several respondents suggested why there were so few patients in the ward. Implicitly assuming the ward held no attraction for patients living in Boston, Reginald Heber Fitz explained that doctors had not been sending their out-of-town patients because only in the rarest cases did Massachusetts General offer better care than a private hospital, hotel, or boardinghouse. Further, patients sent would have represented income lost to the physician. Maurice Howe Richardson echoed this latter plaint, explaining, "I cannot afford to send my private patients into Ward B, as I am entirely dependent upon my practice for a living." John Homans stated simply that the ward would pay if surgeons sent their private patients, but they did not.[60]

As to what to do in the future, Frederick C. Shattuck insisted that Ward B had been a mistake originally. The hospital was a charity and should confine its ministrations to the poor. Patients in "comfortable circumstances" should go to St. Margaret's or to the Elliot Private Hospital. Should the Massachusetts General staff charge patients, they would be doing an injustice to the rest of the profession by unfairly using hospital positions to their direct advantage. Should they not charge these private patients, they did themselves an injustice by treating free those who were not legitimate objects of charity. Fitz warned the trustees that professional fees would create "a lamentable distinction" between charity and pay patients, while John Collins Warren remarked that the existence of a ward of private rooms had established too much of a class system already. On the narrow issue of the disposition of Ward B, all replies recommended that the trustees either turn it into an open ward or lower its rates. Even with this latter course, Henry Beach cautioned, many patients would continue to choose St. Margaret's. Charging professional fees in Ward B was rejected by the visiting staff.[61]

Gone in large measure from this discussion, however, was the absolute argument made against professional fees in the 1880s. Few responses were as rigid as Shattuck's in arguing from the premise that the hospital was a charity and its charitable purpose was not to be tampered with. Only Homans's answer was as direct. Many of the replies linked disapproval of the proposal to its inadvisability in a facility as small as Ward B. With only eight private rooms divided among the visiting staff, each staff member could expect no more than one or two private patients in the hospital at a time. To attend them when he was not on his short annual term of service would be inconvenient. Were there more room in the private ward and each practitioner assured sufficient accommodations for his patients, the prospect of collecting professional fees from private patients would be more attractive. Charles Porter noted that allowing fees in Ward B might endanger the marginal private hospitals. Were the hospital to decide on this course, therefore, he advised a large facility, since if Massachusetts General provided sufficient private accommodations, the survival of the small private hospitals would no longer be important.[62]

The trustees decided to keep Ward B as it was, but lowered its rates.[63] This could be no more than a temporary solution, however. Social and medical realities were leading to "the gradual but inevitable disappearance of prejudice regarding treatment in hospitals for all classes,"[64] and hospitals were emerging as an alternative to home and family care in illness. The debate at Massachusetts General in 1894 showed that pragmatic arguments were replacing the moral positions of the 1880s as private patients became more inclined to use hospitals. In another survey undertaken in 1894, Massachusetts General Superintendent John Pratt sent questionnaires to hospital superintendents in Boston and Philadelphia, while John Collins Warren wrote to hospital physicians in New York, Chicago, and Philadelphia. They inquired what accommodations other, originally charitable, hospitals had for private patients and whether staff members were permitted to charge professional fees. Replies indicated that Philadelphia's Orthopedic Hospital, Methodist Episcopal Hospital, and University of Pennsylvania Hospital permitted fees, as did New York's St. Luke's, Roosevelt, and New York Hospital. Dr. Nicholas Senn informed Warren that he had a continuous (year-round) service at St. Joseph's and Presbyterian Hospital in Chicago and charged fees at both: "It is here I earn my daily bread because I have not the time to operate in private houses." Warren was impressed. He forwarded Dr. Senn's letter to trustee Dwight, noting, "Dr. Senn is one of the most prominent men in the country. He told me recently he 'paid no visits'—He is said to have an income of $75,000.00 a year."[65]

Among the institutions responding to requests for information, only Pennsylvania Hospital and Boston City Hospital forbade professional fees. But at Pennsylvania, the practice of charging professional fees had nonetheless developed somewhat and had only recently been squelched by the board of managers. As for Boston City, Superintendent George H. M. Rowe reported that although in theory physicians and surgeons received no fees from patients in the thirty-four private rooms, and that "Officially the Trustees or myself do not know that any member of the Visiting Staff does receive pay from paying patients in private rooms," nevertheless "it is an open secret, however, that they do." Were the issue to be "categorically submitted to the Trustees," Rowe felt "their answer would be that no fees should be received

by the Visiting Physicians and Surgeons." Rowe's strained interpretation of
the hospital rules allowed the practice to continue. The rules forbade any
officer or employee to accept payment from any patient. Though visiting
staff were considered hospital officers in the then current usage of the term,
Rowe interpreted the absence of a specific prohibition in their case as con-
doning their practice. He rationalized his interpretation by citing the
emerging consensus that "people who are able to pay for the same physician
or surgeon in a hotel should reasonably render something more than the
small fees they pay for their support in the Hospital." Even the trustees
acknowledged the justice of this arrangement. Rowe further argued that the
hospital benefited by accommodating to the new pattern of use. He noted
that "well-to-do patients" were forsaking their homes, "seeking the hospitals, and will, in the future, to a much greater degree." If they were
excluded from the large public institutions, this class would "inevitably"
enter small private hospitals. General hospitals in other cities allowed staff
members to collect professional fees: "Just how far the large number of
private hospitals that have sprung up in this community can be accounted for
by the fact that hospitals maintain a different attitude here in Boston, is an
interesting question worth finding out." Public hospitals could not afford
the loss of revenue represented by private hospitals. In 1906, Boston City
Hospital modified its rules to conform with actual practice. Private rooms in
two wards were set aside for private paying patients "to whom the members
of the Staff may give their services in return for professional compensation,
in a manner heretofore not provided by the Hospital rules."[66]

No informal arrangement permitted professional fees at Massachusetts
General. The hospital was part of a complex of local institutions stewardship
over which was still important to the self-definition of certain families.
Trustees and physicians alike resisted any informal arrangements that might
threaten the hospital's role in the traditional scheme of things, or impugn its
integrity. The outcome of the discussion in 1894 did not mean that there
would be no facilities for private patients, but rather that any future change
in that direction would have to be carefully thought out and justified.

In 1905, the Massachusetts Medical Society considered the "Abuse of
Medical Charity," explicitly focusing on the policy of the Massachusetts
General trustees. The *Boston Medical and Surgical Journal* devoted an entire
issue to the discussion.[67] By this time, the "abuse of medical charity" had
taken on a new meaning. It no longer meant simply the dishonest use of the
community's charitable medical facilities by those whose economic status
was relatively secure. Though discussants paid lip service to this older form
of abuse—as in the case of applicants for outpatient care who could afford to
pay for the services of a private physician—the real issue was new. Increasing
numbers of relatively affluent patients, making no attempt to disguise their
finances, were paying the hospital its going rate for the private rooms they
occupied and denying the attending practitioner the opportunity to collect
for his professional service. When the number of such cases had been small,

the problem had been minor. But by 1905 the practice had grown to the extent that the medical profession perceived it as a threat. George Gay, senior surgeon at Boston City Hospital and the meeting's main speaker, announced that Massachusetts General had collected about $75,000, nearly one third its operating budget in 1904, from its patients. He did not deny the hospital the right to serve nonpoor patients or to charge them for what had once been a charity. What was of concern was the injustice of allowing patients to pay from $21 to $35 weekly for board and nursing in private rooms and escape professional fees. Gay's own institution was immune to such criticism because of the prevailing informal practice of charging fees of private room patients.[68]

Massachusetts General was the villain; by the end of the meeting, its assistant superintendent, Dr. Frederic Washburn, felt called upon to defend its practices. Its most vociferous public critics were not the imposed-upon members of its own staff, but outside physicians.[69] Free care of the relatively affluent was, after all, not entirely to the disadvantage of staff members, who might expect some "freely" treated hospital patients to swell their private practices for aftercare, or for other treatment after discharge. But outside doctors, who lost paying patients to Massachusetts General, gained nothing and reacted in alarm to a force they perceived to be undermining their practices. A new twist emerged to the old story of the private patient who, with the preparations for home or boardinghouse surgery completed, deserted to the free professional care available at Massachusetts General. Two speakers recounted experiences with patients set for care in private hospitals entering Massachusetts General at the last moment instead.[70]

It was the sense of the meeting that Massachusetts General needed to change its policies. In a variation on a traditional theme, surgeon J. W. Elliot insisted that patients who could pay for care at the rate of $20 per week had no business in a public hospital. The hospital should close its luxurious facilities and allow such cases to seek care in private hospitals established for patients of their social class. Majority sentiment, however, seemed to echo George Gay: in theory the argument against any private accommodations in public hospitals "is all right," but "the private rooms are here and here to stay." Massachusetts General should follow the lead of other hospitals in Boston and elsewhere and operate private facilities in which physicians could and should charge. Entirely private hospitals could coexist with private wards in public hospitals. Dr. Farrar Cobb of the Masschusetts Eye and Ear Infirmary went further: "The establishment of private pavilions or wards . . . is necessary. The proper place for a private hospital is under the wing of a large charitable hospital."[71]

Probably influenced by the Massachusetts Medical Society,[72] the hospital trustees reconsidered the matter of private patients and professional fees. The inability of the recently opened private Corey Hill Hospital to accommodate all the patients seeking admission no doubt also influenced the trustees. By January 1906, Superintendent H. B. Howard was considering a proposal for a private ward submitted by trustee Charles H. W. Foster.[73] Foster, a private trustee whose profession was to invest and manage the capital of the heirs of Boston's mercantile and manufacturing fortunes,[74] would become a driving force behind the establishment of the private ward.

The first imperative was to make it clear that funds entrusted to Massachusetts General for its stewardship of the poor were not being used in this new venture. An early suggestion to amend Foster's plan addressed such fears. The facility to be established by the "Massachusetts General Hospital Pay Ward Fund" was to have "a distinct name as distinct as the McLean Hospital." McLean's provided a model for the trustees to a draw upon in extending general hospital care beyond the poorer classes, demonstrating the significance of a separate name and a location at some remove from the general hospital itself in order to emphasize the distinction between the institutions and the classes they served. The proposal for the private hospital originally suggested a location in Belmont, near McLean's. When staff members noted that Belmont was too far away, Superintendent Howard proposed a site in Cambridge, directly across the Charles River from the general hospital, that offered proximity, a good view, and good air.[75]

By 1908 or 1909, Charles Foster had drawn up a proposed circular for what he called the "Warren Hospital Fund" of Massachusetts General. At this point, the trustees had overcome their fears. In their annual report for 1910, they announced their support for "a private hospital *close at hand* [emphasis added] for the accommodation of those who are able to pay their own surgeon or physician, but wish the advantages which only a hospital čan supply." The McLean's model proved fragile, however, and the trustees quickly lost their conviction that the Warren Hospital would not be seen as a perversion of their charitable trust. The public outcry over Harvard's "theft" of the Brigham trust, meant for the poor of Suffolk County, may have influenced the trustees to retreat from their 1910 announcement. C. H. W. Foster informed Dr. Frederick C. Shattuck in 1911 that the trustees no longer sought a donation to build the private hospital, but instead preferred funds for a new administration building. Foster wrote that "the fundamental financial principles of the Private Hospital are based on profit; those of the MGH are based on charity, and it seems as though it would be difficult to mix the two with entire justice to each principle." It seemed fairer for the obviously necessary private hospital to be independent.[76]

When the trustees pulled back from direct involvement, planning continued for a completely independent hospital. The principals in the scheme were fourteen physicians, of whom a majority were connected with Massachusetts General, and ten prominent businessmen, among whom were Massachusetts General trustees Foster and F. L. Higginson.[77] A circular for a "Proposed Private Hospital," dated May 1, 1911, was issued over the names of the group, and plans for a "Hospital on New Lines" were announced in the public press. The proposal called for a corporation, with 4,975 shares of preferred stock to be sold to the general public at $100 each and 25 shares of common stock to be apportioned among the founders of the corporation. The preferred stock would pay an expected dividend of five percent and, if held in lots of 50 shares (the optimal holding), would confer certain privileges in the use of the hospital but no voice in management. The common stock would not pay dividends, but would vest its holders—a self-perpetuating body—with control of the institution. In form, the proposed corporation was a variation on earlier Massachusetts corporations that maintained a limited profit orientation and business structure while defining themselves as beneficially serving some larger public interest.[78]

The "proposed private hospital" was to offer the highly specialized laboraties and apparatus that medical science had brought to larger general hospitals, but which the area's private hospitals uniformly lacked. It would have perhaps one-hundred-fifty to two-hundred beds. Its location was still uncertain in late 1911, but when discussed at a directors' meeting "the Back Bay region, in the vicinity of the Medical School, seemed to be preferred." Planning was quite advanced by this time; the directors had drawn up contracts, printed subscription forms, and charted the institution's finances.[79]

Then planning stopped. Some directors feared that their goal of a comfortable duplication of the facilities of Massachusetts General was prohibitively expensive. Reginald Heber Fitz suggested that "with a much lower standard—e.g., the Deaconess or Vincent Hospital somewhat bettered, the enterprise is [more] likely to be successful." But as planned, construction costs would be at least $15,000 per bed. With other fixed costs, the hospital would price itself out of the market and be unable to compete successfully for patients with prominent medical men practicing in "second rate boardinghouses."[80] An institution connected with the Massachusetts General Hospital would have less difficulty raising capital and would be able to escape some duplication and thus expense.

For their part, the Massachusetts General trustees recognized the folly of forcing this de facto branch of the general hospital to be organized and located elsewhere. Charles Foster, in a note dated 1948, remembered that at this point in the proceedings all concerned pulled back from a plan that "would have divided the time and interest of the doctors between the two hospitals." Massachusetts General had realized that, in a teaching hospital, a physician's practice would henceforth center on the hospital itself, that the visiting staff would no longer "visit" on a part-of-the-year, part-time basis. It had already taken the first tentative steps toward reorganization by placing two of the visiting physicians on continuous year-round service in 1908 and by placing the chief of the newly established children's medical service on continuous service in 1910. With a private facility on the grounds of the general hospital, staff members could further centralize their activities. A private facility would thus contribute to hospital reorganization—to bringing Massachusetts General in line with the demands made by scientific medicine. One complaint made against a hospital pay ward in 1894—that it would force practitioners to make incovenient visits to the hospital while not serving their terms—was no longer relevant. Planning on the separate private hospital "was halted for a further attempt at harmonizing the law and the spirit of charity."[81]

Finally, in December 1913, the trustees voted to expand their definition of charity and to build a pay facility. While serving the poor, they announced, the hospital had developed the power to do good for all mankind. In limited form, this had been hospital doctrine from the beginning; by training practitioners, the hospital had benefited the entire community. Without stinting in their commitment to the poor, the trustees now decided that they could make available to the entire community knowledge and facilities beyond the individual means of even its wealthiest member. The concept of stewardship could be updated to apply to science and expanded to include the service of all. In arguing for Massachusetts General involvement in a private hospital in 1911, trustee Foster had struck this theme: "Does it not seem wise that the first one to be started on an enlarged scale should be conducted by the very best medical men we have, in order that the proper relations between the public and a medical institution, run for profit, should be set up for the benefit of the whole community?" "Taking a larger view of their charitable trust," the trustees voted to turn what had once been simply a charity into a public trust.[82]

Massachusetts General offered several other reasons in support of its radical new departure. In its relatively new role as a research center seeking the same recognition as other major teaching hospitals, it had to offer attractive terms to compete for practitioner-scientists. A Rockefeller Foundation grant enabled Johns Hopkins to salary its staff,[83] while some institutions allowed staff members to collect professional fees from the hospital beds put at their disposal. The Massachusetts General trustees explained that the pay ward would enable them to offer an inducement to keep the hospital's "eminent men."[84]

Besides keeping good doctors at the hospital, the pay ward would also attract affluent patients. Like McLean's, it would pay for itself. But the hope was also that, like McLean's, the new ward would rouse a sense of obligation in its well-to-do patients and their families, creating "a rapidly increasing circle of friends for the Massachusetts General Hospital," which would translate into subtantial donations for the hospital's charitable and research work. This hope was apparently well founded. At an early meeting of the private ward's managing body, "Mr. Foster stated that the returns from the Free Bed appeals show that the Phillips House [the private ward, see below] had helped the increase in the number of Free Bed subscriptions."[85]

The private ward opened in May 1917. It was an eight-story structure, overlooking the Charles, with room for 102 patients. Appropriately enough, its first patient was John Collins Warren, grandson of the original cofounder and himself long connected with Massachusetts General professionally.[86] He was a symbol of change as well as continuity, however. As a member of a distinguished Brahmin family, Warren was very different from the patients whom his grandfather had had in mind and with whom Massachusetts General had been associated. Symbolically, their first private ward patient was all that the trustees could have hoped for.

Though the private ward was on the grounds of the general hospital and shared its laboratories and staff, every effort was made to emphasize that the facilities were distinct and separate. Telephone service was not through the central exchange, but through a separate number prominently displayed. Even its name was distinctive: Phillips House, in honor of one of the Commonwealth's first families and more specifically of William Phillips, twelve-term lieutenant governor of Massachusetts in the early nineteenth century, president of the Massachusetts Bank, Massachusetts General Hospital, and first president of the Massachusetts Hospital Life Insurance Company. The separate name not only made it clear that funds entrusted to the charitable purposes of the hospital were not underwriting the care of the wealthy, but by its connection with Phillips Exeter and Phillips Andover academies also assured prospective patients that they were not in danger of mixing with the common classes.[87]

Before the private ward acquired its name, Charles Foster informed a meeting of the managers that a patient, believing it to be part of the general hospital, had refused to follow a physician's advice to enter. The patient need not have worried. There was little relation between conditions in the general hospital and those in the private ward. The new facility attained what Reginald Heber Fitz had in 1911 set as almost prohibitively high, yet necessary, standards: "Cookery, service, and table furnishings should be as good as if not better than those provided by the best hotels. Rooms must be attractive in size, situation and proportion. Quiet and accessibility are needed, seclusion and space are important. Rooms for relatives are needed." Meals were served with silver and on fine china. The large rooms could be formed into even larger suites by opening connecting doors. Advance booking was thus more complicated than in the general hospital, where the average patient required simply a bed in the proper ward. To learn how to handle requests for specific views and combinations of rooms, Charles Foster turned to the most appropriate models available. After visiting the Hotels Touraine and Copley Plaza, among Boston's most distinguished, Foster reported that their reservations policies were essentially the same as those of the private ward, except that advance reservations for specific hospital rooms were discouraged by requiring payment from patients from the time of booking. Since policies of the hotels and the ward agreed, the private ward executive committee decided to continue its then current practices.[88]

Though modeled on those of exclusive hotels, the ward's rooms were homelike. Yet the Phillips House was definitely a modern hospital, lavishly equipped as well as luxuriously furnished. Each patient room was connected with an electrocardiograph, the advantages of which one young staff physician, Paul Dudley White, had been sent to Europe to study. The trustees boasted that the facility "might save a valuable life," but implicit was a judgment as to whose life might be considered valuable. Within half a year of its opening, its managing body raised the price of its cheapest rooms from five to six dollars a day. They gave as their reason the fact that some of the paying general hospital patients had heard of the availability of like-priced rooms in the private ward and requested transfer. The ward's executive committee concluded "that it would be better for this reason, as some were not desirable, to change the price." To help assure a steady supply of "desirable" patients, the committee sent notices "to principal hotels in Boston for the attention of their guests" and to principles of private schools in the area.[89]

The hospital also restricted the privilege of practice in the Phillips House to Massachusetts General staff members and staff alumni. This was a complete turnabout from the proposed private hospital of 1911, in which the lack of established institutional support was to be overcome by giving hospital privileges to all medical society members. Once the Phillips House opened, its executive committee granted privileges to a limited number of outside practitioners in order to expand the patient clientele. The trustees approved the discretion with which these selections were made. The trustees also monitored certain aspects of medical practice, particularly fees. The board, for example, reprimanded a surgeon who charged $10,000 for an operation in 1924, and instructed the surgeon to lower his fee or "be debarred from further use of the Phillips House." Even a fee of $5,000 was considered inappropriate. Exorbitant fees, the trustees feared, would damage the reputation of the hospital.[90]

Because of the dislocations of wartime, as well as the novelty of a hospital for the affluent, patients did not immediately fill the private ward. The war, however, provided the hospital with the opportunity to expand its services and encourage use of the new ward. Asked by a staff member to allow caesarian sections and normal obstetrical cases in the private ward because of war-caused shortages of obstetricians in the area, the private ward executive committee opened its facility to caesarian section cases in May 1917. By September the committee, motivated by its desire to fill the ward, decided to admit normal obstetrical cases also, "at least until all rooms were required for general surgical and medical cases." They set aside an entire floor for lying-in cases, a category never before admitted to the hospital. Though forced in this direction by necessity, the private ward management was recognizing a new readiness on the part of affluent women to leave the home and enter hospitals for childbirth. The trustees of Boston Lying-in also responded to the same phenomenon. In planning to move from the neighborhood of Massachusetts General to the vicinity of Harvard Medical School, the trustees decided to include a private hospital in their plans. Like the Phillips House, it would be distinguished by a separate name—Richardson House—and have a separate entrance.[91]

Hospitalization for childbirth was linked to the rise of the obstetrician. According to Francis E. Kobrin, middle- and upper-class women became more disposed to use obstetricians as the movement toward the limitation of family size accelerated early in the twentieth century. With the decrease in the number of births, pregnancy grew sufficiently rare to be equated with surgery and other forms of medical care requiring a professional. This shift in attitude was paralleled by an increasing consciousness in women of their own welfare as women. "With 'womanhood' no longer rooted in the domestic, 'natural' environment, or perhaps reflecting the struggle for release from such roots, the 'natural' way of doing things was losing its appeal for the many emerging American women, and the obstetrician was increasingly there to reap the results of a growing anxiety about childbirth."[92] Redefining childbirth as unnatural facilitated its transfer out of the home and to the unnatural setting of the hospital. Hospitals provided the obstetrician with the best location to practice his increasingly complex and scientific art, including the resources to cope with difficult childbirths. Boston Lying-in performed its first caesarian section in 1894, and in the following years the once rare procedure became relatively more common. By 1903 fifty had been performed, and twenty cases in 1907 brought the total to over one hundred. Meanwhile, the home became an increasingly inconvenient site for childbirth in general. The Boston Lying-in trustees recognized this: "There are hundreds, of limited means, who are able and anxious to pay moderately for a bed in a semi-private ward, and with the rapid growth of the apartment house population, the number is fast multiplying. The well-to-do patient desires a private room in a separate private ward."[93]

Boston Lying-in opened Richardson House in 1930. By then, the nature of the hospital population had already changed significantly. This can be demonstrated by using the percentage of unwed mothers to total lying-in admissions as a rough indicator of the social class of the constituency of use. It is not unrealistic to assume that higher percentages of publicly acknowledged illegitimacy correlate with lower class status in late Victorian and early-twentieth-century America. In every decade from the 1870s to the 1920s, the percentage of mothers admitted to Boston Lying-in for illegitimate births fell. From 1873 to 1879, fifty-two percent of the patients were unmarried; from 1880 to 1889 forty-nine percent were; in the 1890s, thirty-seven percent; from 1900 to 1909, 18 percent; between 1910 and 1919, eleven percent; and in the 1920s, three percent.[94]

The figures for the nativity of patients show the shift less clearly. The foreign born retained a slight plurality in every decade through 1919. The first twentieth-century year showing a native born majority was 1923. The size and suddenness of the shift—in 1922 fifty-two percent were immigrants, while in 1923 forty-two percent were foreign born—suggests that it was due not to immigration restriction, but to the relocation of the hospital.[95] Boston Lying-in abandoned its site within the overwhelmingly immigrant West End and near the immigrant North End in 1923 and moved to the Harvard Medical School area. As indicated by the data on marital status, the patient population changed even while the institution remained in the immigrant neighborhoods. With the move into a new plant in an area less convenient to the concentrations of foreign born, increasing numbers of native born Americans entered.

Gross data derived from the nativity of Massachusetts General patients obscure any shift that might have occurred in the social classes from which it drew its patients. To be sure, the percentage of patients born abroad dropped: fifty-three percent in the 1870s; forty-seven percent in the 1880s and '90s forty-eight percent from 1900 to 1910; forty-six percent from 1910 to 1919; and forty-one percent in the 1920s. It is difficult to assess the significance of this drop, however, for while the percentage of foreign born in Boston remained fairly constant at thirty to thirty-five percent, the proportion of Massachusetts General patients who were residents of Boston dropped steadily from forty-three percent in the 1870s to twenty percent in the 1920s.[96] In contrast, the proportion of city residents among Boston Lying-in patients remained high, at least through 1922. From 1873 to 1922, eighty-one percent were Boston residents, while from 1923 through 1930, seventy-two percent were.[97]

At Boston City, which of all these hospitals was least free to refuse patients because of their nativity and which theoretically was open only to Boston residents, the data most clearly show the shift in the national origin of patients. At the beginning of the period, immigrants were substantially overrepresented among city hospital patients; their presence was double their percentage of the city population. By the 1920s, the proportion of foreign born among the patient population nearly duplicated that for the city as a whole. In 1870/71, sixty-eight percent of Boston City patients were foreign born; this dropped to sixty-one percent in 1880/81; to fifty-seven percent in 1890; fifty-five percent in 1900/1901; forty-nine percent in 1910/11; thirty-six percent in 1920/21; and twenty-eight percent in 1930.[98] These quantitative data support the contention, developed from qualitative sources, that by the 1920s hospital patients no longer came disproportionately from one segment of the population. Certainly they were no longer overwhelmingly foreign born.

One further set of qualitative social data meticulously collected and published by Boston's hospitals needs to be examined. Indications of socioeconomic status of Boston City Hospital patients can be derived from published data on patient occupations. This information is available only from the founding of the hospital through the annual report for 1901/02. Publication ceased presumably because the patient was no longer understood in the context of his larger environment, but was perceived as a more purely physiological entity. Such social information was no longer considered medically significant. Even in the short period for which the data are available, however, the increased use of the institution beyond its original patient population is evident.[99] Between 1880 and 1900, the percentage of male Bostonians in white collar positions rose only from 32 to 38 percent. Among city hospital patients, this percentage jumped from 8.2 percent in 1870 and 10.5 percent in 1880/81 to 19.6 percent by 1900/1901. The redistribution among socioeconomic levels of the remaining patients, all of them blue collar, is even more dramatic. While the census showed Boston's unskilled and menial service workers declining only from 15 percent to 12 percent, that same group, heavily overrepresented in the patient population at the beginning, fell from 43.5 percent in 1870/71 and 36.1 percent in 1880/81 to 24.1 percent in 1900/1901.[100] These socioeconomic data show that the city hospital's patients were coming to approximate a cross section of the city population at the beginning of the twentieth century. But, as might be expected, blue collar workers in general and unskilled laborers in particular were still found in disproportionate numbers.

Published occupational data for Massachusetts General male patients are available through 1919, when it would be expected that their socioeconomic status would more nearly parallel that of the general population.[101] In 1870 and 1880, white collar occupations were underrepresented, accounting for 16.9 percent and 18.1 percent of patients, while in 1900 that figure fell to 15.1 percent. In 1910 and 1920, data derived from the census show Boston's male white collar population to be 35 percent and 32 percent, while among patients the percentage climbs to 22.4 percent in 1910 and 27.1 percent in 1919. In fact, the Massachusetts General figures for 1919 are startling in their similarity to statistics derived from the 1920 census. The census identified five percent as professionals, hospital records 4.1 percent; other white collar occupations accounted for 27 percent locally and 23.0 percent at the hospital; for skilled laborers, the figures were 27 percent and 28.2 percent; for semiskilled and service workers, 31 percent and 30.1 percent; and the census counted 10 percent as unskilled labor and menial service, while the hospital treated 14.6 percent of its male patients from that category.[102]

Hospitalization by the 1920s was no longer an experience reserved for the socially marginal. The changed pattern of use to include a broad spectrum of the population could not have evolved independently of medical progress. But medical science alone did not compel hospitalization; the changing social ecology of urban life led many middle class Bostonians to depend on hospitals before they provided medical services not available elsewhere. The private hospitals to which many Bostonians resorted in the early twentieth century were little more than boardinghouses.

This new readiness of the fortunate classes to forego the comfort of home and family in illness helps explain institutional adjustments in hospitals and the medical profession. With more acceptance of hospitalization, physicians found a greater proportion of their practice within hospital walls. They had to rework their relationship with their hospitals. No longer could they identify their work there as a peripheral interest, absorbing only a fraction of their professional time. By the 1920s, physicians were directly deriving income from what had once been charitable work; hospitals were on their way to dominating both the economics of medical practice and modern diagnosis and therapeutics. Hospitals moved to the center of medical practice and came to dominate the experience of the public in severe illness.

# 6. The Burden of
   Hospital Support

After operating a system of free beds for almost a century, the trustees of
Massachusetts General formally organized an actual free bed fund in the
early 1920s. They established a distinct account for moneys received as
annual free bed subscriptions and for the interest generated by free bed
endowments. The hospital then drew on this account to pay the bills of free
bed patients. Donors endowing permanent beds agreed to the stipulation
that their contributions could support free patients only to the extent of
investment earnings. The hospital informed annual contributors that their
$100 gifts actually paid for less than three weeks of patient care. In effect,
the trustees challenged the notion—which by the 1920s may have been more
widespread than the practice—that the free bed donor could keep "his" bed
occupied year-round. At Boston City Hospital, where politicians had dispensed the privilege of free care, the same change occurred. Officeholders
and ward leaders found their requests for free care for constituents rejected.[1]

The new regulations governing the free bed funds at Massachusetts
General were more than simple accounting procedures. On one level, they
reflect a sharpening of the early-twentieth-century crisis in hospital costs. By
discouraging donors from nominating patients for free beds, the trustees
hoped to perpetuate a nineteenth-century charitable tradition—the free
bed—while accomodating it to the financial exigencies of modern hospitals.
They hoped to minimize the drain on hospital revenues represented by free
care without alienating long-time contributors. But rising costs outstripped
contributions from traditional supporters and hospitals had to seek new
sources of funding. They turned to patients. In 1904 the Massachusetts
General trustees raised outpatient rates and instituted an operating room
fee, not to discourage the use of hospital facilities but to raise revenues. They
extended this principle in 1907 when they reached a policy decision to meet
the deficit by raising patient charges. In 1870 patients had contributed
$12,000 toward operating expenses of $67,000; in 1910 they paid $151,000 of
$350,000.[2]

The transformation of the free bed signaled the end of the hospital as a
charitable institution. While an ever-decreasing minority of patients might
continue to receive free care, patient care ceased to be a legitimate object of
charitable benevolence. No longer would it be common practice to earmark
donations for free care; no longer would patients expect free care. In the
twentieth century, hospital patients would give as well as receive.

Illness and accident impair the ability of the stricken to pay for hospital care. Because of this, the principal means by which most patients handled their bills would ultimately be prepayment, or third-party payment, through some sort of health insurance program. In the late nineteenth century, for example, some benevolent societies and fraternal organizations, financed by dues, secured medical attention for their members.[3] Dr. George Galvin's Wage Earners' Emergency and General Cooperative Hospital Association, embodying the same principle, cared for members in return for an annual contribution of one dollar per person. By 1910, Galvin's institution had failed; Dr. Richard C. Cabot endorsed a scheme to purchase and conduct it as a cooperative hospital financed by the subscriptions of members. Cabot's plan progressed no further than a prospectus.[4] But the first major program in Massachusetts for third-party payment of medical care soon followed.

The Massachusetts legislature passed the Workingmen's Compensation Act in 1911. The law took effect in 1912. Recognizing that "the cost of injuries [is] incidental to modern industry [and] should be treated as part of the cost of production," the statute provided employers with elective insurance for the compensation and care of employees injured at work.[5] Though workmen's compensation provided only limited benefits to employees—Roy Lubove has noted that the benefits were too small to shift the burden of industrial accident away from the worker[6]—it wrought large changes in hospitals.

As a result of workmen's compensation, a powerful outside force was aggressively concerned about the nature of hospital treatment. To minimize their costs and secure the employee's quick return to his work, the private insurance companies administering the program supported and encouraged the efforts of scientifically oriented practitioners in following up cases and measuring the efficacy of treatment by the results obtained.[7] This development was not entirely unanticipated. A physician noted that "when the compensation law became effective four years ago, a considerable number of surgeons, who were engaged in a movement to elevate the standard of surgery, were apparently hopeful that the centralized power, lodged in the hands of the insurance companies, would be used in a way to aid their movement."[8]

The power of the insurance companied derived from the money they paid hospitals for the care of patients. How workmen's compensation would affect the nonprofit hospitals was, at first, unclear. Soon after the compensation program began, a local medical society complained that Boston City Hospital did not charge insurance companies for outpatient care and that insurance companies were diverting injured workers there for no cost treatment, depriving outside practitioners of their fees. With inpatient care, however, hospitals quickly took advantage of the law. The trustees of both Massachusetts General and Boston City Hospital ordered their superintendents to charge the insurance companies for all inpatient workmen's compensation cases. Consequently, many patients who had hitherto received free treatment now payed for their hospital care, indirectly at least, through third-party payment.[9]

Not only did more patients pay for hospital care, but workmen's compensation indirectly raised hospital charges for all patients. The Industrial Accident Board, which administered the program, found many hospitals and practitioners raising their charges for insurance cases. The Boston City Hospital trustees, for example, set $3.00 per day as the rate for workmen's compensation cases, leaving the regular rate for paying patients at $7.00 per week. The board insisted that these new rates were unwarranted. It ordered that no more be charged "for an injured workman whose employer is insured than [for] a man in his walk in life whose employer was not insured." Finally, the city hospital and the board negotiated a rate of $10.00 a week in 1915. But in 1917 the board returned to its earlier ruling, deciding that insurance companies were liable only for the same rates paid by the public, even if those rates were below cost. Rather than lower its compensation rate, the city hospital raised its public rate to $10.00 per week.[10]

Massachusetts General also took advantage of workmen's compensation. Presented with the opportunity to bill insurance companies, the trustees simply raised the general ward rate from $10.50 per week to $15.00 per week. In 1917, when the hospital raised the rate for insurance companies and ward patients who could pay to $17.50 and insurance companies protested that this was higher than the $15.00-per-week maximum approved by the Industrial Accident Board, the board upheld the hospital, finding that "this is not a discriminatory rate, but is the standard rate charged by the hospital for all patients who are able to pay."[11]

Boston City Hospital cited the rates paid by workmen's compensation in trying to extract higher payments for patient care from state and local governments. The compensation board ruled that insurance companies would pay up to the actual cost of hospital care. In contrast, the legislated rate for state settled patients was too low to meet costs, the hospital trustees complained—$5.00 per week in 1913 and $7.00 in 1915. When the federal government asked the hospital to care for its injured workers, the trustees, unfettered by state statute, set a rate of $15.00 per week. The ultimate goal of the hospital was to set all of its rates at actual cost. Payment at cost, even when it came from the State Board of Charity, was not charity; workmen's compensation thus led to a cost related rate structure which made the hospital less dependent on charity. As more patients came under the scope of the workmen's compensation law—the first of many industrial diseases was redefined as a covered injury in 1915—the hospital was able to recover its costs for more of its patients.[12]

Practitioners did not derive unmixed benefits from workmen's compensation. Medical journals carried frequent complaints that insurance companies directed injured workers to physicians and hospitals with whom the insurers had prior arrangements. Patients were thus deprived of their free choice of doctors, and physicians without insurance contracts lost potential paying patients.[13]

Another major problem centered on the payment of doctors for hospital care. Generally, staff physicians in hospitals that were organized as charities—including both voluntary and city hospitals—treated workmen's compensation cases as ordinary ward cases. Though insurance paid for the worker's hospital care, it did not cover professional fees. This led to complaints that insurance companies, not patients, benefited from charitably given professional care. But the practice was defended because it kept staff members from profiting unfairly—to the detriment of outside doctors—from their hospital positions. Staff members in private hospitals did receive fees for the care of insured patients. Observers noted that some practitioners were quick to exploit this opportunity for profit. One noted that "there is springing up at present a type of so-called emergency hospitals, which are masquerading under the guise of charitable institutions, but really are preying on industrial cases." Another physician, labeling these "patch-'em-up hospitals," observed that they discharged patients after providing the exactly two weeks' paid care covered by the law and the insurers. Established private hospitals also took advantage of workmen's compensation. By 1921, Corey Hill Hospital had devoted two of its wards to the treatment of industrial accidents.[14]

Under certain circumstances, even physicians in voluntary or city hospitals could charge for professional attention to workmen's compensation cases. When these patients were admitted to private or semiprivate wards, physicians could receive whatever fees "the custom or rule of the hospital" allowed. Except for teaching institutions, most of the charitable hospitals in Massachusetts classified compensation patients as private or semiprivate cases by the 1920s. At Massachusetts General, however, injured workmen were not considered suitable for the Phillips House, the only private accommodation at the hospital. Pressure mounted, therefore, for a semiprivate ward where practitioners could charge professional fees. But staff physicians did not have to wait until Baker Memorial opened in 1930 before they were able to take advantage of insurance fees. In 1921 the trustees approved the assignment of individual compensation patients to specific staff members who retained responsibility for follow-up treatment after discharge. Insurance companies paid Massachusetts General doctors for aftercare and thus indirectly for hospital treatment. The insurance companies accepted this arrangement because it reduced their expenses; with high quality, integrated care, patients were likely to return to work more quickly.[15] Workmen's compensation thus helped spell the end of much of the free professional care traditionally given in Boston's hospitals. By paying for the treatment of a significant part of the hospital population, workmen's compensation removed these patients from the realm of charity.

Workmen's compensation also affected another aspect of hospital charity; the free bed system. Employers had underwritten free beds at hospitals for the use of injured employees.[16] Massachusetts General had solicited annual contributions to its free bed fund from railroads and other corporations. It was understood that these were not simply charitable contributions, but purchased a service. But the tradition of charity kept the hospital and the purchasers from rationally negotiating a price for these services. The trustees several times debated the proper charge for a free bed, but deferred action as often as they took it. Most corporate free beds remained at $100 annually. Even the Boston and Maine Railroad, which contributed more than any other corporation—its rates ultimately mounted from $100 to $1,600—paid for care at less than the standard ward rate. Corporate free beds disappeared when workmen's compensation began; the Massachusetts General trustees decided in 1912 to abolish free beds underwritten by companies for their employees. Henceforth, the hospital charged corporations the going ward rate when they paid for their employees.[17]

Third-party payment did not become the norm, of course, until after the Blue Cross–Blue Shield program developed in the 1930s. Yet workmen's compensation prefigured the end of patient care as a legitimate object of voluntary charity. Hospitals continued to solicit contributions, but they asked money for capital expenditures and research, not for patient care.

Some funds had been proffered Massachusetts General for medical research in the late nineteenth century. The first such gift had come from the Samuel Cabot family in 1888 and the second from the Dalton family in 1891. Both were for $10,000 and came from families of practitioners connected with the hospital. With the turn of the century, the hospial enlisted new donors, directing their contributions as well as those of long-time supporters into areas other than patient care. When Peter Bent Brigham Hospital began to ask for money, its trustees assured potential donors that gifts would not be used for care of the poor, but for research and construction.[18]

Massachusetts General received its first foundation grant in 1898. The gift of $20,000 endowed research in pathology. In the following years, various donors—including businesses and foundations as well as individuals—gave the hospital funds to equip and support laboratories. Corporate gifts, previously used for employee free beds, sometimes went into research that might benefit the corporation. In 1916, for example, the United Fruit Company contributed $2,500 for the study of tropical diseases. The Industrial Clinic benefited especially from corporate donations. Although not formally organized until 1916, the clinic grew out of research in lead poisoning begun in 1908. When the workmen's compensation program ended the traditional justification for corporate giving, the Massachusetts General trustees immediately cited the clinic for "the first systematic work on Industrial Disease taken up by any American hospital." In 1920 the clinic received a $500 gift from Pacific Mills; the previous year the clinic had begun "a special and prolonged study of a particular factory in which an extremely interesting disturbance of health is present, and which the owners desire investigated at length so that they may attempt to control the condition." The textile industry continued its contributions in 1921, with American Felt and Bigelow Hartford Carpet each donating $500. Corporate gifts also served as public relations gestures. S. S. Pierce Company contributed $100 to the free bed fund in 1917 with the stipulation that it was "not for employees." Other retailers, including Jordan Marsh and R. H. Stearns, contributed to the free bed fund on the same terms. [19]

This new pattern of donations at Massachusetts General crystallized in 1904. As noted previously, the trustees adopted several strategies in that year to increase the proportion of operating costs borne by patients, but they also established a new department of scientific research and authorized, for the first time, a newspaper advertisement "reciting the financial needs of the Hospital, and soliciting bequests and donations." Subsequent pleas for funds noted that the department of scientific research was "one of the most interesting and important of the whole institution" and explained that "those who give money to the Hospital may well feel that they are aiding most intelligent and painstaking efforts to find new agencies to repress and cure disease and pain." [20] Massachusetts General specifically directed these pleas toward a much larger public than ever before. Hospitals began to ask for money as participants in a democratic conquest of disease; they retreated from their image as an expression of aristocratic stewardship.

Two fund raising campaigns during the 1920s marked the culmination of these efforts. In 1923 the hospital began a major drive to rebuild its original structure, the Bulfinch Building, remodeling its wards and upgrading and expanding its laboratory facilities. After the Rockefeller Foundation's General Education Board donated $100,000 for the project. Massachusetts General approached the public for the remaining $200,000 necessary. Local banks contributed newspaper advertising; 850 contributors responded. There were only two gifts of $10,000, both from trustees; a variety of donors gave the balance in the successful campaign. Donors included department stores and a sprinkling of contributors recognizable as Armenian, Irish, Jewish, and Italian. The appearance of a number of ethnic names continued a pattern that began around 1920 with a concerted effort to increase the hospital endowment. As part of the 1923–24 campaign, the annual report in 1924 began to include, after the names of the trustees, an additional list of "other members of the corporation." These names came from the same social strata as the trustees. [21]

Building upon this background, the trustees launched their 1926 Fund, a drive for unrestricted donations with an original goal of over $2 million. They asked a large and diverse group of citizens to lend their names to the effort as an advisory board. Brahmins, like Charles Francis Adams, were joined by a Greek Orthodox bishop, a rabbi, Italian, Irish, and Jewish businessmen, politicians, and women, though the women were alphabetized separately. The selection of these individuals revealed a conscious effort to broaden the hospital's constituency of support. The campaign hired a professional fund raiser at a salary of $7,500 per year and issued a promotional pamphlet.[22]

The campaign attracted 3,275 donations and raised $1.2 million. But many of the gifts listed as single donations were actually collective contributions. Many gifts came from individuals with apparently very little money to spare, and most came from donors and groups who had never given to the hospital before. Employee groups gave, while company donations had come only from employers in 1923. Forty-six employee groups each contributed $10 or less, and 102 groups gave more than $10 each. The largest such gift, from employees of the Boston Postal District, was more than $1,300. A number of labor unions, contributing from $3.75 to $500, gave a total of $2,100. Church and synagogue groups and ethnic societies subscribed, as did such clearly ethnic businesses as Sadie Kelly's Spa ($50) and the Lithuanian Furniture Company ($10). Though all 14 gifts of $10,000 or more came from Boston's Protestant upper class—the largest, clearly ethnic individual donation was $2,000—the campaign successfuly attracted small donors. An anonymous gift of $50 that summed up the spirit of the drive came from "a man who can't afford an automobile." Having secured "a large group of new friends," the trustees determined to encourage annual donations from these people as they had secured annual donations from old friends for the free bed fund in the nineteenth century. By 1927, however, the purpose of a continued gift was stated differently: "It will insure, beside the best care of the patients, that scientific work in the clinics and laboratories upon which the future service of the Hospital so largely depends."[23]

Annual donations from new financial supporters predated the 1926 campaign. The Italian community of Boston organized the Italian Free Bed Fund in 1920 to show its appreciation for the Brahmin founded hospital located in its midst. This fund differed from an earlier unsuccessful effort in 1914 to solicit contributions for the care of Italian patients. The Italian Free Bed Fund began its annual gifts to the hospital in 1920, "in recognition of the service rendered" by the institution "to this community." Dr. Gerrado Balboni, the first Italian physician on the Massachusetts General staff, forwarded the gifts to the trustees. Individuals and business, fraternal, and religious organizations contributed. The fund raised over $5,000 from 106 donors in 1920; the largest contribution was $250, the smallest, $5. Balboni himself gave $100, the Franciscan Brothers $200, and three spaghetti companies a total of $170. In 1926, 219 gifts totaled $7,000. The Boston Fruit Auction Buyers Association gave the largest gift—almost $1,700. Recorded gifts ranged downward to 20¢ and included several collective contributions from groups organized according to village of origin in Italy. Along the same lines, the hospital in 1919 began to receive an annual gift of several hundred dollars from the estate of Photius Fisk, "to aid and assist poor and needy colored people."[24]

Traditional recipient groups not only undertook the support of existing hospitals, but also committed themselves to maintain their own distinctly ethnic institutions, hoping, perhaps, to avoid the stigma of being thought of as unable to care for their own. Dr. David Cheever expressed the sentiments of those who felt their good will overly presumed upon by Boston's immigrants. In his memory, "hospital patients were mostly Irish." Before their arrival "poor people used to have a self-respect, they preferred to stay at home" when ill. The situation deteriorated further by the end of the century: "Since the Slav and Latin nations have come in, they always expect to be hospital patients; they never mean to employ a doctor in any other way."[25] Underlying this hostile attitude was the unstated criticism that immigrants were using institutions established and supported by earlier residents.

An ethnically or religiously organized hospital presented obvious evidence that a group was aware of its obligations and was assuming a responsible role in the larger community. At a banquet in 1914 celebrating the successful fund raising for a new and expanded St. Elizabeth's Hospital, former mayor John Fitzgerald pointed to the benefits that Boston as a whole derived from this effort by its Roman Catholic citizens. He was proud that "a new impression will be gained of the strength of the Catholic element of the population by many of those who have been prone to belittle their ability." St. Elizabeth's had previously adopted the policy of admitting patients of all religions. Among other ethnic hospitals, Carney early announced that it accepted patients of any class, creed, or color; while Mt. Sinai proclaimed that it did not limit its services to Jewish applicants.[26]

The major function of such institutions, however, was not to project an image to the entire community but to serve quite specific needs within their own communities. They were organized and supported both out of fear and mistrust of the larger society, and because of special services they offered their own people. Like churches and fraternal organizations, hospitals were agencies of identification for uprooted immigrants, promoting group cohesiveness. Sociologist William Glaser points out that in countries with competing religions, denominations hold onto their hospitals, resisting nationalization. Maintaining a hospital is a way of maintaining religion and religious identity in the face of competition.[27] In addition, hospital patients are physically weak, perhaps facing death and almost certainly undergoing personal crisis; non-Protestant Americans feared, even into the twentieth century, that in hospitals under rival auspices they might be subjected to conversion. Even were such pressures not applied, they might be denied benefit of their own clergy. Relying on the hospitals of others abandoned the weak to perhaps hostile strangers.

These fears were not unfounded. Prosletyzers had long recognized the value of medical institutions in their work. Boston offered ample evidence to stimulate the anxieties of Jews and Catholics. Not until 1883 did the city's corporation counsel rule against compelling the attendance of the city's institutionalized juvenile wards at Protestant religious services. The rising political power of immigrant groups undoubtedly contributed to that ruling as well as to the decision of the Boston City Hospital trustees to bar missionaries from the wards. Nongovernmental institutions, however, were not so restricted. The Epworth League, a settlement house, operated a "medical mission" in the North End, working "chiefly among the Jews and Italians." Evaluating the efforts of the league, Robert A. Woods noted that "no aggressive attempt is made at proselytism," but that "there is a distinctly religious atmosphere about all the work of this settlement." The Cullis Home for Consumptives was less restrained. Explaining the services it offered, a supporter noted, "[Patients] are cared for and comforted, and many of them are converted."[28] The aggressive evangelical Protestantism of Cullis caused a furor among Roman Catholics. Its policy was to refuse priests entry to administer the last rites. One account reported an instance in which a patient had to drag himself off his deathbed and out onto the street, where a priest heard his confession and administered the sacrament in a carriage. Reacting to this hostility toward Catholics, a Catholic group established the Free Hospital for Consumptives in Dorchester.[29]

Denominational hospitals offered group members a nonalien environment and security from religious intolerance, and they expressed their special nature most distinctively when they did not depend on the larger community for support. From its founding in 1868, St. Elizabeth's had been somewhat marginal, supported by haphazard fund raising by the sisters; reflecting the need for non-Catholic support, its early medical staff had been heavily Protestant. The hospital was part of the larger Catholic community, however, and it was affected by the shift in the orientation of the archdiocese in 1907 following the replacement of John J. Williams by William O'Connell as archbishop of Boston. Williams, a student of Boston Catholicism has noted, "clung to a utopian desire for Catholic insignificance." O'Connell, though, demanded a more aggressive assertion of Catholicism, and to that end, he centralized control of Catholic institutions in his office. When its control was transferred from the Franciscan order to the archdiocese of Boston in 1911, St. Elizabeth's began aggressively to articulate its Catholicism, striving at the same time for the status of a major institution with a modern physical plant. It embarked on a carefully organized fund raising campaign among Boston area parishes, and a commitment to Catholic support became a matter of doctrinal policy. In the same spirit, the hospital board proclaimed its belief "that the practices and methods of treatment carried out in a hospital Catholic in its administration and control should be in accordance with the principles of Catholic morals and ethics." "Based on the above belief," the board announced a new, overwhelmingly Catholic medical staff. Catholic practitioners participated in and benefited from this new group self-awareness. They came together in 1910 under the auspices of William Cardinal O'Connell in St. Luke's Guild, a Catholic medical society.[30]

Carney Hospital did not break so radically with its past. It changed more gradually, in part because its professional staff early included prominent Catholic converts from among Boston's first families. Also, its Harvard affiliation in the twentieth century put certain of its key medical positions under the control of the medical school. A growing Catholic commitment eclipsed Protestant financial support by the end of the nineteenth century, but the Back Bay continued to play a significant role. The roster of the Ladies Aid Association, organized in 1894, contained a heavy representation of Brahmin names. Its officers lived in the fashionable Back Bay and on Beacon Hill. To work for Carney, Irish Catholic women from South Boston and other less fashionable areas of the city formed the Ladies of Charity in 1897.[31] Continuing Protestant involvement did not obscure the Catholicism of Carney Hospital.

Boston's Jews, because of language and prescribed diet, encountered even more difficulty than the city's Irish at Protestant hospitals. One Jewish response was to try to influence the policy of the democratic Boston City Hospital. They made an unsuccessful attempt in 1911 to establish separate wards at the city hospital for Jewish patients, where they might have available "nurses of their own race and food prepared according to the prescriptions of their religion." At the same time, a Jewish women's group requested permission to visit Jewish patients at the hospital. Communal leaders asked the city hospital trustees to allow the Passover distribution of "unleavened bread to convalescent patients of the Jewish faith."[32] Like the Irish, though, Boston's Jews directed their major effort toward the maintenance of separate institutions.

Mt. Sinai Hospital opened in the West End in 1902. It provided only outpatient care and a home lying-in service. A bilingual institution, the hospital distributed literature in both English and Yiddish on child feeding, tuberculosis, and sanitation. The labels of medicine bottles were printed in both languages. Supporters explained that the hospital was needed because Boston was a leading port of entry for non-English-speaking Jewish immigrants.[33] The language barrier seriously hampered the efforts of these patients to secure medical care at other institutions. In 1907 a Jewish Harvard medical student studied a series of fifty-one Jewish patients seen at Massachusetts General. All had been diagnosed as "Hebraic debility," but he found that their complaints had generally been misunderstood. Patients were unable to explain their pains.

> It has been supposed by some that the adjectives "*brennend*" and "*stechend*" are peculiar to the symptoms of these Jewish patients, that people of other races do not describe their pain sensations in such terms. I find, however, that they are used idiomatically in Yiddish. Moreover, I have heard not infrequently others than Jews describe their sensations of pain as "burning" or "cutting." Another error due to misinterpretation comes in the localization of the pain. The great majority of these patients speak of "pain in the heart,"—"*es brennt mich, es stecht mich ins Herzen.*" Often this may be translated literally into "heartburn." Much more frequently, however, the term "heart" covers a larger region, including the whole chest and upper abdomen.[34]

The student concluded that the problems which had been treated symptomatically stemmed from the dislocations of the immigration experience.

Cared for in a strange institution where he could not understand others or make himself understood, an immigrant patient might have his problem not only misdiagnosed but actually compounded.

Since Mt. Sinai was really only a dispensary, Jews still lacked a proper hospital of their own. From its beginning, Mt. Sinai had been intended to develop into a complete hospital; its annual report periodically repeated this intention. Differences within the Jewish community, however, stalled efforts to raise the necessary funds. The more assimilated and well-to-do German Jews were wary of the venture. Some opposed a hospital because they feared it would create unnecessary visibility and increase discrimination against Jewish patients and practitioners in existing hospitals by antagonizing their medical and lay sponsors. This view predominated among the leaders of the Federated Jewish Charities, which used its considerable influence to block activity on behalf of a new hospital. In their annual report for 1911, Mt. Sinai's directors pledged their support to a community-wide effort for a new hospital, but they were soon forced to renege. Indebted to the federation for the major portion of its operating revenue, the dispensary had to defend the federation position that the time was not right for such a project. The community should postpone the undertaking until it was certain of a level of support that would make possible a major modern institution; any other kind would reflect unfavorably on Boston's Jews. The immediate need was a new dispensary. [35]

Rival groups continued to press for an inpatient facility. Founded in 1911, the Beth Israel Hospital Association countered arguments that Boston had all the hospitals it needed by pointing to the special requirements of the less assimilated for kosher food and an unthreatening atmosphere. The association raised money through small contributions until by 1915 it had $8,000 and purchased a site in Roxbury. After the fire department condemned the building housing Mt. Sinai, the federation withdrew its support, thus closing the dispensary in 1916 and leaving Beth Israel without any competition in the community. The dispensary's furnishings were turned over to Beth Israel Hospital, which opened in 1917 in a converted house. It had forty-five beds, provided kosher food only, and copied Mt. Sinai in making patients unfamiliar with American customs and the English language comfortable. The hospital directors took pride in reading letters from former patients indicating "how happy they were to have been in a hospital among their own people." As the Irish hospitals had done for Catholic practitioners, Beth Israel offered Jewish doctors opportunities for hospital affiliation otherwise generally denied them. And soon after it opened, Beth Israel began a nurses training school, opening to Jewish girls a career from which they had been excluded. [36]

These ethnic institutions provided Boston's Jews and Catholics a sense of control over their own lives and a fuller sense of participation in the affairs of the city. Lukewarm approval of Beth Israel by German Jews gave way to active participation and support as the institution began to plan in the early 1920s a large modern hospital in the vicinity of Harvard Medical School. The Federated Jewish Charities, still controlled by the more assimilated, German Jews, made its first contribution to Beth Israel in 1920 and increased its support as plans for the new hospital progressed. German Jews and newer immigrants continued to disagree over fund raising, however. The federation, apparently fearing that campaign might appear too distinctively "Jewish," asked that a joint federation-hospital committee handle fund raising. Perhaps manipulating the fears of German Jews, the hospital won its first increase in support from the federation by suggesting it would hold a fund raising "Purim Ball" were the increase not granted. The ball was not held. The new hospital that opened in 1928 forsook the heaviest concentration of Jewish settlement, inconveniencing many patients, but the move into the city's "hospital area" signaled the commitment of Boston's Jews to a project that compared favorably with Boston's best hospitals.[37] The new hospital refuted gentile skeptics and assured affiliation and training for Jewish doctors and medical students in a period when major institutions were embracing exclusionary quotas.[38]

In his jubilation at the successful campaign for a new St. Elizabeth's, ex-mayor Fitzgerald expressed the sentiments of Boston's Catholics, and probably reflected those of its Jews:

> No community can rise to its proper place when the powerful group financially keeps its foot on the neck of the majority struggling to rise, smothering their ambition and dampening their ardor. When there comes due recognition, mutual confidence and good will, a true fellowship among all people of this great community, then we see its true proportions.
>
> If on the other hand, we witness a city where a few with the power and wealth of the community largely in their own hands look down in a patronizing manner on the great majority silently submissive, we see a declining community. Therefore, the raising of $2,000,000 and a goodly sum to spare in ten days marks a new era.[39]

Ethnic hospitals democratized hospital support, continuing what the city hospital had begun. In a society marked by schisms between rich and poor, old families and new immigrants, a city hospital was imperfectly democratic. The taxes of the wealthy carried a disproportionate burden of its support; the poor disproportionately filled its wards. But in the case of an ethnic hospital like St. Elizabeth's or Beth Israel, Catholics and Jews making only small contributions or none at all could share the pride of having their own hospital. At a time when the fact of hospitalization no longer involved invidious class distinctions, these new ethnic hospitals further erased the stigma of hospitals' original patient populations. Boston's immigrants would not be patronized in their own hospitals. Nor would they, as patients, be automatically identified as charity recipients when they entered the city's other hospitals.

In the twentieth century, as traditional charity proved incapable of meeting the mounting expenses of scientific hospitals, Boston's general hospitals ceased to be charities. In seeking new sources of income, hospitals altered their relationship with both historic donor class and patients. The expansion of the patient population into the middle classes and the workmen's compensation insurance program meant that patients were no longer simply the recipients of institutional largesse. As they paid for their own care at prices ever more directly related to hospital costs, patients contributed to the redefinition and redirection of hospitals. The free bed and the charitable impulse that it implied became an anachronism.

Hospitals continued to receive donations, not simply for patient care and building costs as in the past, but for scientific research. As significant as the reallocation of contributions was the shift in their origin. Established voluntary hospitals looked beyond the upper classes for money. They asked for the support of Boston's working class and ethnic residents. These same groups undertook to finance newly prominent Catholic and Jewish hospitals. No longer would hospital support be an expression of merely upper class stewardship; it became democratized as a community responsibility.

# Epilogue

For most of the twentieth century, the American hospital has been perceived as a triumph of modern medical science, a monument to man's knowledge and his best instincts. As medical science evolved into the most completely fulfilled of the promises of the twentieth century, the hospital seemed the inevitable, the only logical setting for the provision of health services. While some physicians complained that the institution undermined the therapeutic relationship, and some patients avoided it, there has until the recent past been little sense of alternative possibility as the hospital moved inexorably to the center of medical practice. But in the last decade or so, the ready identification of the hospital with beneficent progress has been widely questioned. As the claims of science and medicine have been challenged, the hospital—one of the most visible and expensive artifacts of the modern technological order—has come under scrutiny.

Today the hospital stands accused of embodying the most unfortunate features of modern medicine. It dehumanizes its patients by regarding them only as clinical entities. Its cultural authority has been used to medicalize life, draining experience of meaning by redefining it as a series of medical events. Its pervasiveness discourages personal responsibility for individual health by promising a technological resolution for all ailments. In questioning the role and necessity of the hospital, critics have assailed its onerous personal and social costs.[1]

The contemporary critique of the hospital rejects the fundamental principle of modern diagnosis and treatment: that the human organism can best be understood and treated through a medicine that reduces the complexity of life into its simplest component processes. The contemporary hospital, which provides narrowly medical therapeutics to patients of all social classes, is based upon this assumption. In the absence of a medical style that emphasized discreteness and specificity, the spread of hospitalization beyond the socially marginal would have been less likely. Had sickness and health continued to be understood primarily in relation to the individual's interactions with his environment, as they had been in the mid-nineteenth century, hospital medicine—which abstracts the patient from his everyday world—would have remained second-class treatment.

Several factors account for the gradual emergence of the reductionist and mechanistic orientation that grew to characterize medicine during the nineteenth century. Specificity—the identification of diseases as discrete clinical entities with unique causes, courses, and pathologies—narrowed its focus from the organ to the tissue to the cell. New instruments like the stethoscope, ophthalmoscope, laryngoscope, and x-ray made it less necessary for physicians to interact with patients on a human level and encouraged them to understand diseases as narrow dysfunctions. Germ theory likewise shifted the doctor's concern away from the whole person, and sought and found in infection by microorganisms the causes of many of mankind's most troubling ailments. The laboratory translated life processes into quantitative data. Specialization furnished the system that best organized medical care according to these principles and most effectively capitalized on these techniques.[2]

But reductionist medicine is not merely a product of scientific and technical developments. Its widespread acceptance is predicated on the prevalence of "scientific" or modern attitudes. These attitudes are characteristic of an urban and industrial world. Not every culture is equally prepared to give more credence to enzyme analyses than to vital forces in evaluating sickness and health. Causes and consequences are inseparable, however, for modern attitudes are themselves partially the result of a familiarity with science.

Hospital, medicine, and society are similarly intertwined in a web of mutually reinforcing influences. Hospital based physicians most readily assimilated reductionist medicine. They reshaped the institution to fit their needs, emphasizing scientific medicine in place of the charity that had defined the traditional hospital. The hospital, in turn, provided a fitting setting for the medical style that reduced the patient to physiological and biochemical processes. A public increasingly attuned to scientific medicine came to appreciate the curative benefits of this style and to trust the expert authority of the hospital.

Social factors also helped make hospitalization an appropriate recourse in illness and accident. An urban and industrial society that redefined what the individual did for himself, and what families should do for their members, made individuals less capable of caring for themselves in sickness. Physically constricted urban living spaces made traditional home care in illness more difficult. So too did another characteristic of the modern industrial order, the spatial differentiation of work from residence. In sickness, this might mean the separation of a potentially nurturing family member from a weakened invalid. Home and family became less available; at the same time, the hospital grew more attractive. The familiarity of urban and industrial citizens with divisions of labor and specialized settings for different activities heightened their appreciation of the hospital. The segmentalization of urban life was mirrored in the evolution of the hospital. A reductionist modern world view reinforced the reductionist medical practice that made the hospital possible.

Finally, the hospital promoted modern values within the society at large. Hospital practice has reoriented the practice of medicine away from the traditional doctor-patient relationship, helping to create a situation in which physicians treat anonymous patients. The hospital, as an institution of transcendent significance, has helped to abstract birth and death, disease and pain, from the normal range of human experience. Its consequences, like its causes, extend beyond the practice of medicine.

Critics are right to point out the humane failings of the hospital. But in challenging the basic values on which medicine and the hospital are based, they are engaging in a romantic rejection of modern society, a yearning for an edenic past in which people were not only happier but healthier than they are today. It is intellectual preciousness to deny the obvious benefits of the modern hospital, with its impressive array of therapeutic technologies and procedures. The hospital is a feature common to all industrialized nations, capitalist and Marxist alike.

This does not mean that the hospital had to take precisely the form that it did in the United States. America's pluralistic society, for example, is mirrored in its hospital establishment. Rather than a single or nearly unified system of institutions organized according to some master plan, we have a variety of hospitals, often under competing ethnic or religious auspices. These hospitals originated in the needs of parochial constituencies. Some represented the stewardship of the fortunate for those displaced by urbanization and industrialization. Others were defensive acts of group cohesion for immigrants adrift in a hostile environment. Many were marginal. To survive the turn-of-the-century transition from relatively inexpensive charities to costly apotheoses of modern medicine, hospitals had to generate substantial new revenues. In the absence of centralized funding or direction, they pursued individualistic strategies of survival by competing for paying patients. Hospitals secured these admissions by offering affiliations to physicians, who then referred their private patients and treated them within the institution. Comparatively promiscuous hospital affiliations for practitioners reoriented medical practice, leading to much higher rates of hospitalization per capita in the United States than elsewhere.

With this reservation about one of the secondary characteristics in which the American hospital differs from its European counterpart, it is worth remembering Oliver Wendell Holmes's warning: "To write of 'Medicine in Boston' is not unlike writing of the tides in Boston Harbor. Boston is a fraction of the civilized world, as its harbor is part of the ocean."[3] Arguments about American exceptionalism as it applies to the hospital—or the asylum or the prison, for that matter—are suspect. The contemporary hospital has assumed different forms in different places, but it is a product of a modern medicine in a modern society.

# Notes

## Introduction

1. J. M. Toner, "Statistics of Regular Medical Associations and Hospitals of the United States," *Transactions of the American Medical Association* 24 (1873): 314-33. Toner listed 178 hospitals, but included 58 institutions identifiable as insane asylums in his total.

2. U.S., Bureau of the Census, *Historical Statistics of the United States, 1789-1945,* 1949, p. 51.

3. *Bulletin of the Institute of the History of Medicine* 4 (1936): 573-81.

4. E. H. L. Corwin, *The American Hospital* (New York, 1946), pp. 95-96.

5. Ibid., pp. 80-81, 95-96.

6. Charles E. Rosenberg, "The Therapeutic Revolution: Medicine, Meaning and Social Change in Nineteenth Century America," in Morris J. Vogel and Charles E. Rosenberg, eds., *The Therapeutic Revolution: Essays in the Social History of American Medicine* (Philadelphia, 1979), pp. 3-25.

7. Ivan Illich, *Medical Nemesis: The Expropriation of Health* (New York, 1976), passim.

## Chapter 1

1. Thomas Ryan is a pseudonym. Massachusetts General Hospital, West Surgical Records of Male Wards, vol. 144 (1869-70), p. 166, Countway Library, Boston. Attached to this record, an uncommon practice at the time, is the letter from Lawrence stating the facts of the case (Dr. C. N. Chamberlain to Dr. B. S. Shaw, 7 January 1870).

2. Massachusetts General Hospital, West Surgical Records of Male Wards, vol. 144 (1869-70), inside front cover, p. 166. Cabot was married to Hannah Lowell Jackson, daughter of James Jackson's brother, Patrick Tracy Jackson. Coolidge was married to Mary Lowell, granddaughter of James Jackson's sister, Hannah Jackson Lowell.

3. Massachusetts General Hospital, Medical Records, vol. 287 (1869-70). A house pupil was a medical student getting optional hospital experience before he took his degree.

4. In 1870, 858 of 1,302 patients were treated on free beds (Massachusetts General Hospital, *57th Annual Report, 1870,* p. 23).

5. Massachusetts General Hospital, *58th Annual Report, 1871,* pp. 16-17.

6. Lee F. Schnore and Peter R. Knights, "Residence and Social Structure: Boston in the Ante-Bellum Period," in Stephan Thernstrom and Richard Sennett, eds., *Nineteenth Century Cities: Essays in the New Urban History* (New Haven, 1968), p. 249; David Ward, "Nineteenth Century Boston: A Study in the Role of Antecedent and Adjacent Conditions in the Spatial Aspects of Urban Growth," Ph.D. diss., University of Wisconsin, 1963, pp. 49-51, 159.

7. U.S., Bureau of the Census, *U.S. Ninth Census, 1870, Population,* 1872, vol. 1, p. 778; Ward, "Nineteenth Century Boston," pp. 149-50, 165, 348, 361; Massachusetts, Bureau of Statistics of Labor, *Census of Massachusetts, 1875, Population* (Boston, 1876), vol. 1, pp. 551-54.

8. Ward, "Nineteenth Century Boston," pp. 150-51, 187-88, 223, 367; Walter Muir Whitehill, *Boston: A Topographical History* (Cambridge, Mass., 1959), pp. 112-14.

9. Ward, "Nineteenth Century Boston," pp. 117-19, 156, 360; Whitehill, *Boston,* pp. 61-65, 124-31, 156-64; Robert A. Woods, ed., *Americans in Process: A Settlement Study* (Boston, 1903), pp. 56-57; Frederick Cople Jaher, "The Boston Brahmins in the Age of Industrial

Capitalism," in his *The Age of Industrialism in America* (New York, 1968), p. 190; *U.S. Ninth Census, Population*, vol. 1, p. 778.

10. Massachusetts, Bureau of Statistics of Labor, *1st Annual Report, 1869/70*, pp. 213-15, 268-70, 329, 331; *3d Annual Report, 1871/72*, pp. 57, 421-31. The *Boston Evening Transcript* listed work accidents on an almost daily basis in 1870.

11. *U.S. Ninth Census, Vital Statistics*, vol. 2, pp. 96-99 (in the absence of reliable statistics on disease incidence, I have used disease mortality as an indicator of the significance of certain diseases); Ward, "Nineteenth Century Cities," p. 371; Oscar Handlin, *Boston's Immigrants, 1790-1880: A Study in Acculturation*, rev. ed. (New York, 1968) pp.115-17, 254; Massachusetts, Bureau of Statistics of Labor, *5th Annual Report, 1874/75*, pp. 32, 98-101; *Boston Evening Transcript*, 14 March 1888.

12. Tuberculosis was the leading cause for refusing admission to applicants at Massachusetts General Hospital (Massachusetts General Hospital, Annual Reports, 1870-80).

13. *U.S. Ninth Census, Vital Statistics*, vol. 2, pp. 96-99; the *Boston Evening Transcript* carried numerous accounts of transportation accidents in 1870.

14. See, for example, the directions for the home sickroom in Catherine E. Beecher and Harriet Beecher Stowe, *The American Woman's Home: Or, Principles of Domestic Science...* (New York, 1870), pp. 340-43.

15. Boston, *Proceedings at the Dedication of the City Hospital* (Boston, 1865), p. 58.

16. *Boston Evening Transcript*, 10 June 1886.

17. *Boston Evening Transcript*, 14 March 1887.

18. *Boston Evening Transcript*, 14, 17 March 1887; *Boston Medical and Surgical Journal* 116 (1887):268. Another "frightful disaster" with the same general pattern occurred with the wreck of an excursion train on the Old Colony Railroad, 9, 10 October 1878. There was a different pattern after a crash on the Eastern Railroad in Revere. A greater proportion of the injured were hospitalized; on a vacation excursion, many of the survivors were further from home (*Boston Evening Transcript*, 28 August 1871; Massachusetts, Board of Railroad Commissioners, *3d Annual Report, 1871*, pp. xcv-cv).

19. *Boston Medical and Surgical Journal* 85 (1871): 340.

20. *Boston Medical and Surgical Journal* 92 (1875): 521-24.

21. *Boston Evening Transcript*, 11 June 1880.

22. In 1827, servants were moved into the attic so two private rooms could be fitted up in their former quarters (Visiting Commitee Minutes, 16 March 1827, copy in Phillips House File, Massachusetts General Hospital Archives); Massachusetts General Hospital, *60th Annual Report, 1873*, p. 9; *61st Annual Report, 1874*, p. 6; *65th Annual Report, 1878*, p. 29; *66th Annual Report, 1879*, p. 24.

23. *Boston Evening Transcript*, 21 April 1876.

24. Ibid., 24 December 1874, 18 October 1875.

25. *Boston Medical and Surgical Journal* 86 (1872): 81, 82. The North End Diet Kitchen was founded in 1874, the South End Diet Kitchen a short time later (*Boston Evening Transcript*, 20 October 1874, 9 November 1875, 2 December 1878).

26. Boston Lying-in Hospital, *Annual Report for 1881*, quoted in *Boston Medical and Surgical Journal* 106 (1882): 462.

27. Children's Hospital, *Appeal*, 1869, in "Papers and Clippings, 1869-1879," a scrapbook kept by Dr. Francis H. Brown, Countway Library; *Boston Evening Transcript*, 28 October 1876, 1 April 1881, 17 November 1883.

28. Children's Hospital, *Appeal*, 1869, in Papers and Clippings; this kind of literature often specifically mentioned woman and child labor.

29. I have used Stephan Thernstrom's classification system as the basis for my analysis of hospital data (*The Other Bostonians: Poverty and Progress in the American Metropolis, 1880-1970* [Cambridge, Mass., 1973], pp. 50, 51, 289-302). Thernstrom does not classify census data for 1870 into his socioeconomic categories—white collar, skilled blue collar, semi-skilled and service, and unskilled and menial—so hospital figures for both 1870 and 1880 are compared with data for the general population derived from the 1880 census. Since

Thernstrom finds very little change in the city's occupational structure from 1880 to 1920, this is not unreasonable. See also chap. 5, n. 99 below.

30. The category of skilled workers here consists entirely of patients listed by the hospital as "mechanics." This is an ambiguous term and appears to have been applied differently in 1870 and 1880. The number of male patients in this category fell from 291 in 1870 to 219 in 1880. Over the same years there was a large jump in laborers (the whole of my unskilled category) from 187 to 580. This suggests that mechanics were not all skilled workers in 1870 and that their 41.9 percent of the male patient population overrepresents skilled workers among the hospital's patients. At the same time, the figure of 26.9 percent may undercount the proportion of hospital patients who were unskilled in 1870. Massachusetts General admitted 780 males (85 unclassified, all minors) in 1870 and 1,363 (235 unclassified) in 1880 (computed from Massachusetts General Hospital, Annual Reports).

31. Computed from Boston City Hospital, Annual Reports.

32. Computed from Massachusetts General Hospital and Boston City Hospital, Annual Reports.

33. Including only the city's two major hospitals, admissions totaled 746 in 1850 (Massachusetts General Hospital alone), 3,698 in 1870, and 6,541 in 1880. Other institutions founded from the 1860s on increased the total hospital admissions, but not significantly. For example, Children's Hospital admitted 69 patients in 1870 and 178 in 1880; Carney Hospital admitted 453 patients in 1879, and a total of just over 5,000 from 1863 through 1879.

34. Massachusetts General Hospital, "The Report of a [trustees'] Committee on the Financial Condition of the Massachusetts General Hospital, 16 February 1865." The trustees dated their financial difficulties from the change from "the industrious classes of our native population," many of whom had paid something toward their board, to the foreign born, who dramatically increased the numbers treated free. The trustees' committee recommended carefully restricting the number of nonpaying patients (read foreign born) and segregating them in a distinct section of the hospital, so that the hospital could get back to serving "the classes for whose advantage it was established." The trustees rejected that suggestion, apparently because of the urging of the medical staff which feared that decreasing the numbers of the really poor would hurt medical education (Massachusetts General Hospital Trustees, [printed letter], 1 April 1865, both in Countway Library; Nathaniel I. Bowditch, *A History of the Massachusetts General Hospital,* 2d ed. (Boston, 1872), p. 454).

35. Computed from Massachusetts General Hospital, Annual Reports. A sizable proportion of the hospital's population came from Massachusetts outside of Boston. The state-wide percentage of foreign born—24.2—makes the foreign born majority of hospital patients more dramatic (*U.S. Ninth Census, Population,* vol. 1, pp. 299, 386).

36. Computed from Boston City Hospital, Annual Reports.

37. Francis E. Kobrin, "The American Midwife Controversy: A Crisis of Professionalism," *Bulletin of the History of Medicine* 40 (1966): 350-63; Boston, Board of Health, *Annual Report for 1879,* p. 20.

38. New England Hospital for Women and Children, Mss Records, Countway Library; *Boston Evening Transcript,* 17 April 1874; Boston Lying-in Hospital, *Annual Report for 1930,* p. 58; *Boston Medical and Surgical Journal* 92 (1875): 543; 110 (1884): 363, 364.

39. Joseph Edgar Chamberlin, *The Boston Transcript: A History of Its First Hundred Years* (Boston, 1930), p. 165.

40. *Boston Evening Transcript,* 24 February 1888.

41. Ibid.

42. Ibid.

43. E.g., a long feature article, "The Origin of Hospitals," in the *Boston Evening Transcript,* 13 July 1886.

44. *Boston Evening Transcript,* 29 November 1881, 10 July 1885. The insane asylum in this account is McLean's Asylum, a branch of Massachusetts General Hospital. For a more extensive discussion of these hospital stories, see my dissertation, "Boston's Hospitals, 1870-1930: A Social History," University of Chicago, 1974.

45. Odin Anderson, *The Uneasy Equilibrium: Public and Private Financing of Health Services in the United States, 1875-1965* (New Haven, 1968), p. 29; John Green, *City Hospitals* (Boston, 1861), p. 12.

46. Jackson and Warren, 1810 Circular Letter, in Bowditch, *A History*, pp. 3-9; Massachusetts General Hospital, *58th Annual Report, 1871*, p. 7; *Christian Register*, 8 May 1869, in Papers and Clippings; "Fireside," *Boston Evening Transcript*, 22 January 1879.

47. Jaher, "Boston Brahmins," p. 189; Handlin, *Boston's Immigrants*, pp. 221-22.

48. *Boston Evening Transcript*, 28 March 1874.

49. John Collins Warren, *To Work in the Vineyard of Surgery: The Reminiscences of John Collins Warren (1842-1927)*, ed. Edward D. Churchill (Cambridge, Mass., 1958), pp. 186-87.

50. Printed letter on behalf of Children's Hospital, signed F. H. Brown, M.D., dated October 1871, 73 copies issued, in Papers and Clippings. On Ames, see Jaher, "Boston Brahmins," p. 253; Edward Chase Kirkland, *Men, Cities and Transportation: A Study in New England History, 1820-1900* (Cambridge, Mass., 1948), 2:466. Ames was a manager of Children's Hospital from 1885 until his death in 1893; Ames and Thayer were the only trustees shared by the two institutions in the nineteenth century. Ames was a Massachusetts General trustee from 1888 to 1893, but he was on the board as an appointee of the governor. The state charter provided that four of twelve trustees be appointed by the governor. Later, the first Irish Catholic, the first woman, the first Italian, and the first Jew on the Massachusetts General Hospital board would be appointed by the governor.

51. Leonard Eaton, *New England Hospitals 1790-1833* (Ann Arbor, 1957), p. 27.

52. Annie Birnie, pseud., "How Edie Wallace Cured a Little Girl's Broken Leg," *Christian Register*, 8 May 1869, in Papers and Clippings, with initials F. H. B. written in next to Annie Birnie. See also Annie Phillips, pseud., "A Hospital Story," *Christian Register*, 8 May 1869, in Papers and Clippings, with Miss Phipps written in.

53. *Christian Register*, 5 June, 16 October 1869, in Papers and Clippings; *Boston Evening Transcript*, 9 July 1870, 17 April 1874; Children's Hospital, *1st Annual Report, 1869*, p. 19; *5th Annual Report, 1873*, p. 8.

54. Henry J. Bigelow, *Medical Education in America* (Cambridge, Mass., 1871), pp. 5-6; Charles E. Rosenberg, "Social Class and Medical Care in Nineteenth Century America: The Rise and Fall of the Dispensary," *Journal of the History of Medicine and Allied Sciences* 29 (1974): 40.

55. Oliver Wendell Holmes, "Medicine in Boston," in Justin Winsor, ed., *The Memorial History of Boston, including Suffolk County, Massachusetts, 1630-1880*, 4 vols. (Boston, 1880-81), 4:569.

56. For some accounts of medical Bostonians in Europe, see: James Jackson, *Memoir of James Jackson, Jr., M.D.* (Boston, 1835); Warren, *Vineyard of Surgery*, pp. 86-139; E. H. Bradford, "Medical Education Fifty Years Ago," *Boston Medical and Surgical Journal* 189 (1923): 748-61.

57. Bowditch, *A History*, p. 3.

58. Henry J. Bigelow, "Fees in Hospitals," *Boston Medical and Surgical Journal* 120 (1889): 378.

59. Quoted in *Boston Medical and Surgical Journal* 106 (1882):137.

60. "A Statement made by four physicians . . ." (Boston, 1869), in Papers and Clippings; Children's Hospital, *1st Annual Report, 1869; Journal of the Gynecological Society* (1869): 122, in Papers and Clippings; Boston, City Council Proceedings, Board of Aldermen, 18 October 1875; *Boston Medical and Surgical Journal* 93 (1875): 621, 622; *Boston Evening Transcript*, 21 April 1883 (advertisement), 18 October, 5 November 1889, 1 January 1890.

61. *Dictionary of American Biography*, s.v. "Henry Jacob Bigelow"; *Boston Medical and Surgical Journal* 86 (1872): 81, 82; 89 (1873): 437; F. H. Brown, *Medical Register for the Cities of Boston, Cambridge, Charlestown, and Chelsea* (Boston, 1873), unpaginated; F. H. Brown, *Medical Register for the State of Massachusetts* (Boston, 1875), pp. 104-5; John W. Farlow, "The Staniford Street Dispensary," *Boston Medical and Surgical Journal* 192 (1925): 165-71.

62. Farlow, "Staniford Street Dispensary," p. 168-69.

63. Shaw's letter to the editor, *Boston Daily Advertiser*, 19 April 1869, in Papers and

Clippings. This account of opposition to both new hospitals is from the *Journal of the Gynecological Society* (August 1869): 119-23, in Papers and Clippings; Massachusetts General Hospital, *64th Annual Report, 1877*, pp. 6, 7; *68th Annual Report, 1881*, pp. 6, 7; *70th Annual Report, 1883*, p. 7; *71st Annual Report, 1884*, p. 6; Children's Hospital, *13th Annual Report, 1881*, p. 8. These annual reports were directed at donors, suggesting that this competition was for the funds that supported the medical work of the institutions.

64. Clarence J. Blake (President, West End Nursery and Infants' Hospital) to Samuel Eliot (Chairman, Massachusetts General Hospital Trustees), 10 March 1897, C. J. Blake File, Massachusetts General Hospital Archives; same to same, 9 June 1897, ibid.

65. Massachusetts General Hospital Trustees Mss Records, 14, 28 March 1873, 4 February 1874.

66. C. B. Porter and J. Collins Warren to Massachusetts General Hospital Trustees, 18 April 1884, Administration of House Officers File, Massachusetts General Hospital Archives; Report of trustees committee, ibid.; Massachusetts General Hospital Trustees Mss Records, 29 May 1884.

67. *Boston Medical and Surgical Journal* 111 (1884): 164-65.

68. Ibid.

69. John M. T. Finney, *A Surgeon's Life: The Autobiography of J. M. T. Finney* (New York, 1940), p. 61; Richard C. Cabot to Edmund Dwight, incorrectly dated 1886, Richard C. Cabot Papers, Harvard University Archives.

70. The "settlement of old scores" involved Dr. Henry J. Bigelow and the consideration of charging fees of hospital patients (see below, chap. 5, p. 107); Frederick C. Shattuck to Eleanor Whiteside, 18 May 1884, George C. Shattuck Papers, Massachusetts Historical Society; George C. Shattuck To Eleanor Whiteside, 3 February 1886, ibid.; Eleanor Whiteside to George C. Shattuck, 29 January, 1886, ibid.; George C. Shattuck to Eleanor Whiteside, [6 February 1886], [28 February 1886], ibid.; Francis Minot to Thomas Hall, 17 February, 3 March 1886, Frederick C. Shattuck File, Massachusetts General Hospital Archives; Massachusetts General Hospital Trustees Mss Records, 12 March 1886; Massachusetts General Hospital *73d Annual Report, 1886*, p. 3; Henry J. Bigelow to Massachusetts General Hospital Trustees, 24 March 1886, Professional Services: Organization of Surgical Services File, Massachusetts General Hospital Archives; Henry J. Bigelow to William Endicott, 27 December 1888, ibid.; Henry J. Bigelow to Massachusetts General Hospital Trustees (privately printed), 18 February 1886, ibid.; Henry J. Bigelow to Massachusetts General Hospital Trustees, 24 March 1886, ibid.

71. Bowditch, *A History*, p. 415; Carney Hospital, Annual Reports, 1879-89.

72. Boston Dispensary, *Annual Report*, quoted in *Boston Medical and Surgical Journal* 106 (1882): 137; Children's Hospital, *Appeal*, 1869, in Papers and Clippings.

73. *Boston Evening Transcript*, 20 April 1881.

74. Children's Hospital, *Appeal*, 1869; *1st Annual Report, 1869*, p. 11; *Boston Evening Transcript*, 25 February 1875.

75. Children's Hospital, *3d Annual Report, 1871*, p. 8.

76. Charles E. Rosenberg, "The Practice of Medicine in New York a Century Ago," *Bulletin of the History of Medicine* 41 (1967): 224-25, 230-33.

77. Children's Hospital, *3d Annual Report, 1871*, p. 8.

78. Children's Hospital, *1st Annual Report, 1869*, p. 10; *Boston Evening Transcript*, 20 April 1881.

79. Children's Hospital, *1st Annual Report, 1869*, p. 13; *3d Annual Report, 1871*, pp. 8-10; *8th Annual Report, 1876*, p. 8. It is perhaps unfair to draw so sharp a distinction between medicine and charity in this case. Koch's work was yet to come, and there was no hard medical knowledge of the transmission of tuberculosis.

80. *Christian Register*, 5 June 1869, in Papers and Clippings.

81. Children's Hospital, *3d Annual Report, 1871*, pp. 7-8.

82. "The Children's Hospital: What 'Fireside' Thinks about It," *Boston Evening Transcript*, 22 January 1879.

83. *Charlestown Chronicle*, 11 November 1871, in Papers and Clippings; *Boston Post*, 1 March

1872, ibid.; Children's Hospital, *Appeal*, 1869, ibid. Children's Hospital, *1st Annual Report, 1869*; p. 13; *3d Annual Report, 1871*, p. 10; *5th Annual Report, 1873*, p. 9. Young readers of the *Christian Register* were invited to come with their mothers to visit "the dear little occupants" (*Christian Register*, 8 May 1869, in Papers and Clippings).

84. Children's Hospital, *1st Annual Report, 1869*, p. 13, back cover; *15th Annual Report, 1883*, p. 9.

85. *Boston Post*, 1 March 1872, in Papers and Clippings.

86. "Fireside," *Boston Evening Transcript*, 22 Janury 1879.

87. Ibid.

88. *Boston Medical and Surgical Journal*, 83 (1870): 140, 141, editorial (Brown doubled as the editor of the *Journal*).

89. Letter to the Editor, *Boston Sunday Times*, 29 December 1872, in Papers and Clippings; "My Visit to the Children's Hospital, by 'A Lady,'" *Boston Evening Transcript*, 22 February 1875.

90. *Boston Post*, 1 March 1872, in Papers and Clippings; Children's Hospital, *7th Annual Report, 1875*, p. 13.

91. Carney Hospital, *Annual Report, 1884*, pp. 27, 28; *Annual Report, 1885-1886*, pp. 47, 48. Many people were in the almshouse because of blindness—as a cause of debility and almshouse institutionalization it was probably third only to old age and delirium tremens (Long Island Hospital, Mss Papers, 1896-1905, Countway Library).

92. St. Elizabeth's Hospital, *9th Report, 1893-1898*, p. 8; *Boston Evening Transcript*, 11 December 1874.

93. *Boston Evening Transcript*, 1 December 1870. Though it treated adults, New England Hospital more nearly duplicated Children's Hospital than Massachusetts General Hospital (cf. below) in its positive attitude toward uplifting its patients. The fact that these adult patients were women perhaps explains why they were considered, like children, to be amenable to benign influence.

94. Grace W. Myers, *History of the Massachusetts General Hospital: June, 1872, to December, 1900* (Boston, 1929), p. 12; Dr. D. B. St. John Roosa described the visitors lining up at the gate for the twice weekly visiting hour at New York Hospital, and how visitors were searched before entering (*The Old Hospital and Other Papers*, 2d ed. [New York, 1889], p. 12).

95. E.g., Massachusetts General Hospital Trustees Mss Records, 3 August 1877.

96. "Fireside," *Boston Evening Transcript*, 22 January 1879; Massachusetts General Hospital, Annual Reports, 1870-1910.

97. *Boston Evening Transcript*, 20 April 1881.

98. Children's Hospital, *7th Annual Report, 1875*, p. 7; *Boston Evening Transcript*, 22 January 1879.

99. Registrar's Report of the City of Boston, quoted in *Boston Medical and Surgical Journal* 85 (1871): 83-84; *Boston Evening Transcript*, 20 April 1881; Letter to the Editor, *Boston Evening Transcript*, 29 February 1888.

100. McDonald v. Massachusetts General Hospital, 120 Mass. 432, in E. B. Callander, "Torts of Hospitals," *American Law Review* 15 (1881): 640; *Boston Evening Transcript*, 12 July 1875.

101. Stogdale v. Baker, reported in *Boston Evening Transcript*, 21 November 1885, 12 December 1887, 5 January 1888.

## Chapter 2

1. Boston City Hospital, *A History of the Boston City Hospital*, (Boston, 1904), pp. 168-70.

2. Boston, City Document #27, 1880, *Majority and Minority Reports of the Committee on Ordinances on the order requesting the mayor to petition the legislature for an act incorporating the Trustees of the City Hospital*, pp. 20-22.

3. Boston City Hospital, Visiting Staff Mss Minutes, 4 April 1884.

4. Boston, City Document #27, 1880, pp. 27-29, 34-38.

5. Massachusetts General Hospital Trustees Mss Records, 28 December 1883; Massachusetts

General Hospital trustees appointed by the governor included William Sturgis Bigelow (1893-1903) and William Endicott, Jr. (1877-97). Bigelow's father served the hospital as visiting surgeon for forty years, and his grandfather had been visiting physician for twenty. Bigelow himself had been on the surgical staff and remained a member of the hospital corporation until his death in 1926. Endicott served as an appointee of the governor, 1877-83. His son was later a trustee, chairman, and president.

6. Walter Muir Whitehill, *Boston Public Library: A Centennial History* (Cambridge, Mass., 1956), pp. 107-12, 133; Boston, City Document #27, 1880, p. 35; Roger Lane, *Policing the City: Boston, 1822-1885* (Cambridge, Mass., 1967), pp. 180-219.

7. Boston, City Document #27, 1880, pp. 27-28.

8. Thomas C. Amory, Jr. "Address...," *Boston City Hospital Dedication*, p. 56.

9. Boston, City Document #56, 1849; *Boston Medical and Surgical Journal* 40 (1849): 406; 41 (1849): 344, 406.

10. *Boston Medical and Surgical Journal* 143 (1900): 511.

11. Elisha Goodnow Will, quoted in *Boston City Hospital Dedication*, p. 40.

12. *Boston Medical and Surgical Journal* 56 (1857): 305-7.

13. Boston, City Document #67, 1860, pp. 4-6; *Boston Medical and Surgical Journal* 54 (1856): 46-47.

14. *Boston Medical and Surgical Journal* 56 (1857): 45.

15. Quoted in *Boston City Hospital Dedication*, p. 6.

16. Boston, City Document #37, 1857, p. 5.

17. *Boston Medical and Surgical Journal* 65 (1862): 507, 508.

18. *Boston City Hospital Dedication*, p. 41; Boston City Hospital Trustees Mss Records, 19 July 1864, quoted in Boston City Hospital, *A History*, p. 162. I have been unable to locate manuscript records of Boston City Hospital trustees meetings prior to 1880.

19. *Boston City Hospital Dedication*, pp. 34-35, 40-41.

20. Ibid., pp. 49, 57.

21. Ibid., pp. 27, 41, 62; Boston City Hospital Rules, in *1st Annual Report, 1864*, p. 95.

22. Compare the figures given in chap. 1, pp. 11-12, for the nativity and occupations of male patients of the two hospitals.

23. *Boston Medical and Surgical Journal* 56 (1857): 264; Boston City Hospital, *4th Annual Report, 1867*, p. 8; *Boston City Hospital Dedication*, p. 39.

24. *Boston City Hospital Dedication*, p. 58.

25. This was changed to five years in 1878. The settlement law is given fully in Robert W. Kelso, *The History of Public Poor Relief in Massachusetts, 1620-1920* (Boston, 1922), pp. 60-63.

26. *Boston City Hospital Dedication*, pp. 58, 59.

27. Boston City Hospital, *10th Annual Report, 1873/74*, pp. 24-29.

28. Ibid.

29. Boston City Hospital, *6th Annual Report, 1869/70*, p. 65; *10th Annual Report, 1873/74*, p. 10.

30. Boston, City Document #37, 1857, p. 5; Boston City Hospital, *14th Annual Report, 1877/78*, p. 20.

31. Kelso, *Public Poor Relief*, p. 149; Associated Charities of Boston, *Directory of the Charitable and Beneficent Organizations of Boston*, 3d ed. (Boston, 1891), pp. 216-18; *Boston Evening Transcript*, 23 January, 7 March, 10 April 1878, 29 April 1882.

32. Boston City Hospital, *10th Annual Report, 1873/74*, pp. 30, 31; *14th Annual Report, 1877/78*, pp. 18, 19; *Boston Evening Transcript*, 29 April 1882.

33. Boston City Hospital, *14th Annual Report, 1877/78*, p. 20.

34. Nathan Irwin Huggins, *Protestants Against Poverty: Boston's Charities, 1870-1900* (Westport, Conn., 1971), pp. 57-79.

35. Boston City Hospital, Trustees Mss Records, 20 August 1884.

36. Boston City Hospital, *14th Annual Report, 1877/78*, p. 6.

37. Ibid., p. 20; *15th Annual Report, 1878/79*, pp. 19-22.

38. Boston City Hospital, *13th Annual Report, 1876/77,* p. 6; *18th Annual Report, 1881/82,* p. 7.

39. Boston City Hospital, Trustees Mss Records, 21 July 1880, 18 May 1881, 18 August 1882. Though the hospital met with little difficulty in collecting from other towns—only Cambridge refused to pay—the state did not make its first payment until 1885 (Boston City Hospital, *18th Annual Report, 1881/82,* p. 7; Boston City Hospital Trustees Mss Records, 21 September 1881, 22 July 1885).

40. *Boston Evening Transcript,* 29 April 1882. About eighty patients were being admitted each week.

41. Boston City Hospital, *14th Annual Report, 1877/78,* p. 18.

42. Boston City Hospital, *20th Annual Report, 1883/84,* pp. 6, 23, 24; *21st Annual Report, 1884/85,* p. 19.

43. Boston City Hospital, *25th Annual Report, 1888,* p. 30.

44. See, in this regard, accounts by Martin Lomasney, Councilman Joseph Lomasney, and Alderman Keenan, Boston, City Council Proceedings, 21 June 1888, 18 July 1892, 2 January 1904, 6 December 1909. Settlement workers aware that the political boss provided some needed services noted: "He must secure for the sick admission to the hospital" (Woods, ed., *Americans in Process,* p. 174). For requests to excuse payment, see Boston City Hospital, Trustees Mss Records, 27 October 1897.

45. See, for example, "Reform Needed: What Was Shown in Regard to the City Hospital at One of Judge McCafferty's Inquests," *Boston Evening Transcript,* 18 May 1885: "There was evidence that death from the same cause [asphyxiation while unconscious] had occurred on several occasions, and that in such cases as Kelly's the patient would not be received at the City Hospital." Also, *Boston Evening Transcript,* 26 April 1886, 24 September 1889; *Boston Globe,* 21 June 1891.

46. Boston, City Council Proceedings, 21, 24 May 1883.

47. Boston City Hospital, Trustees Mss Records, 18 June 1891.

48. Ibid., 22 March 1893, 21 February, 22 March, 19 December 1894.

49. Ibid., 29 March 1905.

50. Boston, City Council Proceedings, 6 December 1894.

51. Boston City Hospital, *52d Annual Report, 1915/16,* p. 174.

52. *Boston City Hospitals Dedication,* p. 57.

53. Ibid., pp. 14–15.

54. Ibid., pp. 92–96; Boston City Hospital, Visiting Staff Mss Minutes, 12 July 1865.

55. Boston City Hospital, *25th Annual Report, 1888,* pp. 33–34; *33d Annual Report, 1896/97,* pp. 22–23.

56. The need to enforce internal discipline also lessened as the medical nature of the hospital's patient population changed, i.e., as patients were increasingly bedridden (see below, chap. 3, pp. 72–75).

57. *Boston Evening Transcript,* 22 February 1879; Boston, City Document #27, 1880, p. 96; Whitehill, *Boston Public Library,* pp. 98, 166.

58. Boston, City Council Proceedings, 18 November 1880, 9 April 1886, 15 September, 25 October 1902; Boston City Hospital, Trustees Mss Records, 18 November 1885, 22 June 1892, 22 February 1893, 17 April 1895, 29 October, 18 November 1896, 25 May, 29 June 1898, 16 June, 27 August, 17 September, 15, 29 October 1902.

59. Boston City Hospital, Trustees Mss Records, 6 February 1901, 31 August 1904, 26 March 1915, 15 March 1909, 11 March, 22 April, 13, 27 May 1903.

60. *Boston Medical and Surgical Journal,* 148 (1903): 220; Boston, City Council Proceedings, 18 July 1892.

61. Boston City Hospital, Visiting Staff Mss Minutes, 31 March, 9 May 1898; Boston City Hospital Trustees Mss Records, 13 October 1911, 19 March, 8 April 1912.

62. Boston City Hospital, Visiting Staff Mss Minutes, 4 April, 11 July 1884, 30 March, 16 November 1896, 25 May, 2 June 1897, 10 January, 31 March, 9 May 1898.

63. Various Boston newspaper clippings concerning homeopathic teaching, unidentified, are included in the Boston City Hospital Trustees Mss Records, July, August, 1885; Boston City Hospital Trustees Mss Records, 1 October 1886.

64. Dr. William M. Conant to Dr. Richardson, November, 1911, copy in Medical Education File, Massachusetts General Hospital Archives.

65. *Boston Globe*, 20 February 1880.

66. Galvin noted: "It may not be known to the profession that all railroad superintendants make it a point to give light work to those who have been hurt, but are able to go about, without loss of pay" (*Boston Medical and Surgical Journal* 124 [1891]: 134–136).

67. Ibid.

68. Ibid., pp. 138–42.

69. These statistics are taken from the Boston Emergency Hospital, *1st Annual Report, 1892*. Of the 4,192 injuries, 2,329 were listed as miscellaneous wounds.

70. Ibid.; *Boston Evening Transcript*, 16 July 1891. Emergency Hospital requests for a city subsidy, Boston, City Council Proceedings, 14, 28 January 1892; and for annexation, Boston, City Council Proceedings, 15 June 1893.

71. Letter to the editor from a Boston Dispensary district physician complaining that an impoverished woman was charged five dollars for a home visit by an Emergency Hospital surgeon, *Boston Medical and Surgical Journal* 131 (1894): 523, also *Boston Medical and Surgical Journal* 146 (1902): 481–84.

72. Boston, City Council Proceedings, 15 June 1893.

73. Boston Emergency Hospital, *Report, 15 November 1894–15 November 1895*.

74. Ibid., p. 7.

75. Boston City Hospital, Visiting Staff Mss Minutes, 11 February, 3 March 1892; Boston City Hospital Trustees Mss Records, 10 March 1892; Boston City Hospital, *Report of the Trustees of the Boston City Hospital on the Advisability of Establishing Cottage or Branch Hospitals in the Several Wards of the City* (Boston, 1893), p. 35 (hereafter, Boston City Hospital, *Report of the Trustees, 1893*); Boston City Hospital, *31st Annual Report, 1894/95*, p. 39.

76. Of course, Galvin's work may have heightened medical awareness of the concept of a medical emergency. Boston City Hospital, Visiting Staff Mss Minutes, 2, 14 June 1896; *Boston Medical and Surgical Journal* 128 (1893): 24.

77. Boston City Hospital, *Report of the Trustees, 1893*, pp. 24–29, 36; Boston City Hospital Trustees Mss Records, 23 June 1896.

78. Boston City Hospital, *33d Annual Report, 1896/97*, pp. 19–20; *34th Annual Report, 1897/98*, p. 30; *Boston Medical and Surgical Journal* 139 (1898): 419.

79. Wage Earners' Emergency and General Cooperative Hospital Association, *1st Annual Report, for the Year Ending September 20, 1900*, passim; Massachusetts, *Thirteenth Annual Report of the Bureau of Statistics of Labor, 1899*, pp. 177–78; *Boston Medical and Surgical Journal* 141 (1899): 222, 223, 301.

80. Wage Earners' Emergency and General Cooperative Hospital Association, *1st Annual Report, 1900*, passim.

81. *Boston Medical and Surgical Journal* 114 (1886): 285; *Boston Evening Transcript*, 31 October 1887.

82. Boston City Hospital, Visiting Staff Mss Minutes, 9, 19 September 1899.

83. Boston City Hospital, Visiting Staff Mss Minutes, 19 September 1899.

84. Boston City Hospital, Visiting Staff Mss Minutes, 19 September, 23 October 1899; Boston City Hospital Trustees Mss Records, 4, 25 October 1899.

85. E.g., Mayor Nathaniel Shurtleff's inaugural, 1870, quoted in *Boston Evening Transcript*, 3 January 1870. Boston City Hospital, *10th Annual Report, 1873/74*, p. 55; *11th Annual Report, 1874/75*, p. 77; *26th Annual Report, 1889*, p. 9.; *28th Annual Report, 1891/92*, p. 47.

86. Boston City Hospital, *15th Annual Report, 1878/79*, pp. 20–22.

87. Boston City Hospital, *28th Annual Report, 1891/92*, p. 50; *29th Annual Report, 1892/93*, p. 57.

88. Boston, City Council Proceedings, 12 May, 16 June 1881, 28 January 1884, 18 January, 29 March, 1 April, 10 May 1886, 27 December 1888, 12, 16 December 1889. A common council committee had found that East Boston, separated from mainland Boston by a ferry, did not need its own ambulance. In serious cases, an ambulance could reach East Boston forty-five minutes after being called. East Boston's councilman, Don Sweeney, said the measure was voted down only because it was feared that once East Boston got its own ambulance, every section would demand one (Boston, City Council Proceedings, 23 September, 26 November 1880).

89. Amory, in *Boston City Hospital Dedication*, pp. 50, 51.

90. Green, *City Hospitals*, p. 41.

91. Massachusetts General Hospital, on the other side of the city, had been built on tidal lands along the Charles River. Neither institution had been attractively sited, and both had drainage problems for many years.

92. *Boston Evening Transcript*, 3, 6, 14 August, 24 September 1872.

93. Not every member of the council knew what parcel he was voting for (*Boston Evening Transcript*, 11 October 1872).

94. *Boston Evening Transcript*, October 1872–January 1873, passim. During the cholera scare in 1892, the same kinds of neighborhood protests were heard in the city council (Boston, City Council Proceedings, 13 October, 15 November 1892).

95. Boston, City Council Proceedings, 3 April 1876; *Boston Evening Transcript*, 24 March 1876.

96. Boston, City Council Proceedings, 26 July, 1, 29 November, 23 December 1880; *Boston Evening Transcript*, 5, 12 August, 4 November 1880; Boston, City Document #122, 1880.

97. Boston, City Document #203, 1895; Boston, City Document #110, 1896; Boston, City Council Proceedings, 25 November, 16, 23 December 1895; 13 January, 24 February, 2, 10 March, 25 May, 8, 15, 22 June, 7, 27 July, 14 September, 26 October 1896; *Boston Medical and Surgical Journal* 134 (1896): 249; 135 (1896): 48, 50; Sam Bass Warner, Jr., *Streetcar Suburbs: The Process of Growth in Boston, 1870–1900* (New York, 1969), pp. 43, 60. Mayor Quincy vetoed the ordinance (Boston, City Document #146, 1896).

98. Mayor Quincy gave this as his reason for vetoing the ordinance that would have forced the Cullis Home to move (Boston, City Document #146, 1896).

99. Boston, City Council Proceedings, 1876–1909.

100. Wylie, *Hospitals*, pp. 50, 90–93; Green, *City Hospitals*, pp. 10, 12.

101. Boston, City Council Proceedings, 23 November, 10, 28, 30 December 1891.

102. Boston City Hospital, Visiting Staff Mss Minutes, 11 February, 3 March 1892; Boston City Hospital, *Report of the Trustees, 1893*, p. 30, passim.

103. Boston City Hospital, *Report of the Trustees, 1893*, pp. 10, 30, 31.

104. E.g., Boston, City Council Proceedings, 1 December 1892, 5 January, 20 April, 28 September, 28 December 1893, 8, 22 March, 1 June 1894, 10, 24 January, 25 April, 10, 27 June 1895. West End request, Ald. Thomas Keenan, 10 December 1891.

105. Boston City Hospital, *39th Annual Report, 1902/3*, p. 25; *44th Annual Report, 1907/8*, pp. 30, 31; *45th Annual Report, 1908/9*, p. 25.

106. Boston, City Council Proceedings, 24 June 1891.

107. *Boston Evening Transcript*, 24 August 1891.

108. These are treated in chap. 5.

109. David W. Cheever, "A Reminiscence of My Professional Life," *Boston Medical and Surgical Journal* 165 (1911): 435–39, 483–86, 525–28; Boston City Hospital, *A History*, p. 156, note.

## Chapter 3

1. *Boston Medical and Surgical Journal* 118 (1888): 589–93, 613–16.

2. Ibid.

3. Boston City Hospital, *4th Annual Report, 1867*, p. 27.

4. This practice began with the annual report for 1870/71 and continued through the

nineteenth century. Boston City Hospital, *7th Annual Report 1870/71*, p. 18; *8th Annual Report, 1871/72*, p. 18.

5. Warren blamed the conservatism of the older surgeons who completely dominated the profession (*Vineyard of Surgery*, pp. 145-46).

6. Warren, *Vineyard of Surgery*, p. 158; Arthur Tracy Cabot, Untitled Short Autobiography, n.d., p. 1, typescript carbon, Countway Library; Myers, *History of the MGH, 1872-1900*, pp. 52-54; Boston City Hospital, *A History*, p. 123; J. Collins Warren, "Aseptic and Antiseptic Details in Operative Surgery," *Boston Medical and Surgical Journal* 125 (1891): 367-70; H. L. Burrell and G. R. Tucker, "Aseptic Surgery," *Boston Medical and Surgical Journal* 121 (1889): 327-32; Massachusetts General Hospital, *75th Annual Report, 1888*, pp. i, ii, 6; Children's Hospital, *23d Annual Report, 1891*, p. 7.

7. David Cheever, "The New Surgery," *Boston Medical and Surgical Journal* 137 (1897): 1-5; *Boston Medical and Surgical Journal* 148 (1903): 22-24; Massachusetts General Hospital, *90th Annual Report, 1903*, p. 144.

8. Warren, "Aseptic and Antiseptic Details," p. 369.

9. Cabot, Short Autobiography, p. 4.

10. David Cheever, quoted in Hyman Morrison, "The Chapter on Appendicitis in a Biography of Reginald Heber Fitz," *Bulletin of the History of Medicine* 20 (1946): 261; A. J. Ochsner, *A Handbook of Appendicitis*, 2d ed. (Chicago, 1906), p. 9.

11. Howard A. Kelly, *Appendicitis and Other Diseases of the Veriform Appendix* (Philadelphia, 1909), pp. 10, 13; Ochsner, *Appendicitis*, p. 11; Warren, *Vineyard of Surgery*, p. 172; Fitz, quoted in Morrison, "Reginald Heber Fitz," pp. 264, 265.

12. Boston City Hospital, *25th Annual Report, 1888*, p. 36.

13. Charles M. Whitney, "Intubation of the Larynx in Private Practice: Results in 78 Cases," *Boston Medical and Surgical Journal* 129 (1893): 341.

14. Boston City Hospital, *25th Annual Report, 1888*, p. 36; *27th Annual Report, 1890*, p. 52; *33d Annual Report, 1896/97*, p. 30; *Boston Medical and Surgical Journal* 124 (1893): 388.

15. On the difficulty of removing children ill with diphtheria to the hospital before 1894, see Boston, Board of Health, *18th Annual Report, 1889*, p. 33. The antitoxin treatment was dramatic not just statistically, but also in the almost immediate relief of suffering and gasping for breath (Dr. J. H. McCollum, quoted at a dinner of the Boston City Hospital Club, in *Boston Medical and Surgical Journal* 134 [1896]: 178).

16. Boston City Hospital, *33d Annual Report, 1896/97*, p. 30; *35th Annual Report, 1898/99*, p. 24; *36th Annual Report, 1899/1900*, p. 23.

17. Children's Hospital, *1st Annual Report, 1869*, p. 11; *3d Annual Report, 1871*, pp. 9, 10, 14; *10th Annual Report, 1878*, p. 7.

18. Children's Hospital, *6th Annual Report, 1874*, p. 8; *7th Annual Report, 1875*, p. 8.

19. From 1869 through 1882, the hospital admitted 884 patients classified as medical cases and 870 classified as surgical. In 1883, the figures were 102 medical and 178 surgical. From 1883 through 1900, 3,536 patients were admitted on the medical wards and 6,390 for surgical treatment.

20. Children's Hospital, *34th Annual Report, 1902*, pp. 5, 6.

21. Children's Hospital, *20th Annual Report, 1888*, pp. 5-12; *27th Annual Report, 1895*, p. 7.

22. Children's Hospital, *19th Annual Report, 1887*, p. 9; *21st Annual Report, 1889*, p. 7.

23. Children's Hospital, *22d Annual Report, 1890*, p. 7; *23d Annual Report, 1891*, p. 6; *26th Annual Report, 1894*, p. 8; *31st Annual Report, 1899*, p. 9.

24. Children's Hospital, *10th Annual Report, 1878*, p. 9.

25. Association of Hospital Superintendents (hereafter American Hospital Association), *7th Annual Conference, 1905*, pp. 116-32, 135, 141.

26. American Hospital Association, *5th Annual Conference, 1903*, p. 129; *7th Annual Conference, 1905*, p. 187; *9th Annual Conference, 1907*, pp. 189, 190.

27. Massachusetts General Hospital Trustees Mss Records, 19 May, 2 June 1893; Frederick

C. Shattuck to Massachusetts General Hospital Trustees, 23 May 1893, F. C. Shattuck File. This was actually followed by a reduction in the use of oxygen (Massachusetts General Hospital Trustees Mss Records, 16 June 1893).

28. Massachusetts General Hospital Trustees Mss Records, 1 March 1895, 17 January, 10 April 1896; Boston City Hospital Trustees Mss Records, 3 April 1900.

29. Children's Hospital, *21st Annual Report, 1889,* pp. 6, 7; *26th Annual Report, 1894,* p. 10; *27th Annual Report, 1895,* pp. 6, 7.

30. American Hospital Association, *7th Annual Conference, 1905,* pp. 150-51; *10th Annual Conference, 1908,* p. 219.

31. Massachusetts General Hospital, *85th Annual Report, 1898,* p. 7; *87th Annual Report, 1900,* pp. 6, 7; *89th Annual Report, 1902,* pp. 9-10; Massachusetts General Hospital Trustees Mss Records, 14 June 1907.

32. Children's Hospital, *27th Annual Report, 1895,* p. 11; Massachusetts General Hospital, *85th Annual Report, 1898,* pp. 125-28; Boston City Hospital, *40th Annual Report, 1903/4,* p. 26.

33. An analogous situation is analyzed by Charles Perrow, in "Goals and Power Structure: A Historical Case Study," in Eliot Freidson, ed., *The Hospital in Modern Society* (New York, 1963), pp. 112-46. Perrow begins this period in 1929, but the thirty-year difference is due to his studying a Jewish hospital founded in 1885. Its economic marginality probably gave its trustees control for a longer period (because money remained a more significant resource). Aside from Perrow's chronology, his analysis applies to the situation at Boston's major hospitals.

34. There is no adequate work on the standardization movement which grew out of the scientific orientation most marked in the medical and surgical specialities. A good place to begin is with Ernest Amory Codman, a Boston surgeon instrumental in founding the American College of Surgeons. Codman devoted part of his text, *The Shoulder* (Boston, 1934), to an autobiographical statement about his efforts (pp. v-xi; epilogue, pp. 1-29).

35. Boston Dispensary, *78th Annual Report, 1874,* p. 10.

36. Eaton, *New England Hospitals,* pp. 103-5.

37. Massachusetts General Hospital Trustees Mss Records, 7 February 1877; Massachusetts General Hospital, *64th Annual Report, 1877,* p. 17.

38. E.g., Massachusetts General Hospital Trustees Mss Records, 10 January, 14 February, 14, 28 March, 11 April 1873.

39. Report submitted by Dr. James Whittemore, 13 February 1877, OPD File, Massachusetts General Hospital Archives; New England Hospital for Women and Children, Mss Rules, 10 November 1877, Countway Library.

40. Massachusetts General Hospital, *64th Annual Report, 1877,* p. 19; Massachusetts General Hospital Trustees Mss Records, 11 April, 16 May, 10 October 1884, 16 November 1888. In 1900, the trustees thanked the Massachusetts Institute of Technology for a scientific consultation by allowing its corporation "to nominate a student patient to a free bed at the General Hospital at any time during the ensuing five years" (Massachusetts General Hospital Trustees Mss Records, 16 November 1900).

41. Massachusetts General Hospital, *64th Annual Report, 1877,* pp. 5, 6.

42. New England Hospital for Women and Children, Mss Rules, 10 November 1877, 14 October 1878; Benjamin S. Shaw to Trustees, 28 May 1870, OPD File; *Boston City Hospital Dedication,* pp. 89, 93; Boston City Hospital, *2d Annual Report, 1865,* p. 15; Massachusetts General Hospital Trustees Mss Records, 2 May 1873.

43. Boston Dispensary, *78th Annual Report, 1896/97,* p. 177; Boston City Hospital, *34th Annual Report, 1897/98,* p. 192.

44. Boston City Hospital, *33d Annual Report, 1896/97,* p. 177; *34th Annual Report, 1897/98,* p. 192.

45. Massachusetts General Hospital, *82d Annual Report, 1895,* p. 9; Endicott to Howard, 18 November 1897, 28 December 1898, 5 July 1901, William Endicott, Jr., File, Massachusetts General Hospital Archives.

46. F. B. Harrington to admitting physician, 1 July 1905, 22 April 1907, F. B. Harrington File, Massachusetts General Hospital Archives; H. H. A. Beach to Howard, 5 October 1905, Henry H. A. Beach File, Massachusetts General Hospital Archives. There are other such letters in the Beach and Harrington files.

47. Massachusetts General Hospital Trustees Mss Records, 9 July 1920.

48. Richard H. Shryock, *Medicine and Society in America, 1660-1860* (New York, 1960), p. 155; *Boston Medical and Surgical Journal* 97 (1877): 630.

49. Massachusetts General Hospital, Mss Patient Records, vol. 1, p. 1; James Jackson and John Collins Warren to Richard Sullivan and Theodore Lyman, a committee of the trustees, 30 October 1822, VD File, Massachusetts General Hospital Archives; Massachusetts General Hospital, *By-laws, Rules and Regulations. Acts and Resolves* (Boston, 1856), p. 17; Massachusetts General Hospital, Annual Reports.

50. Boston City Hospital, *2d Annual Report, 1865,* p. 17.

51. Boston City Hospital, *29th Annual Report, 1892/93,* p. 55.

52. Boston City Hospital, *3d Annual Report, 1866,* p. 23; *6th Annual Report, 1869/70,* p. 36.

53. Harvard Medical School, Mss Faculty Minutes, 3 November 1877, Harvard Medical School Archives, Countway Library.

54. Jackson and Warren to Sullivan and Lyman, 30 October 1822, VD File.

55. *Boston Medical and Surgical Journal* 94 (1876): 82, 583; Harvard Medical School, Mss Faculty Minutes, 3 November 1877, Harvard Medical School Archives.

56. *Boston Medical and Surgical Journal* 97 (1877): 630.

57. Boston City Hospital, Visiting Staff Mss Minutes, 8 January 1885; C. Irving Fisher, "The Other Infectious Disease: A Plea for a New Hospital," *Proceedings of the National Conference of Charities and Corrections* 16 (1889): 60.

58. Massachusetts General Hospital Trustees Mss Records, 29 May 1890, 4 February 1891; Massachusetts General Hospital, Medical Board, Records, 5 December 1890, 3 February 1891, copies in VD File.

59. Richard H. Shryock notes that "physicians who by 1900 knew well how to diagnose, treat and prevent both syphilis and gonorrhea, found themselves hemmed about with all sorts of restrictions" ("Freedom and Interference in Medicine," *Annals* 200 [1938]: 44). In this instance, though, the Massachusetts General Hospital staff apparently felt their powers did not reach to syphilis. Yet when the trustees reported that the hospital might receive a bequest of $150,000 should it agree to use the fund for treatment of venereal disease only, the visiting staff voted in favor of accepting the bequest (Massachusetts General Hospital Trustees Mss Records, 29 June, 13 July 1894).

60. *Boston Medical and Surgical Journal* 141 (1899): 544; David W. Cheever to Charles Eliot, n.d., Charles Eliot Papers, Harvard University Archives.

61. Simon Flexner to Henry A. Christian, 29 September 1910, Henry A. Christian Papers, Countway Library; Henry F. Dowling, "Comparisons and Contrasts Between the Early Arsphenamine and Early Antibiotic Periods," *Bulletin of the History of Medicine* 47 (1973): 236, 242.

62. Also operating to bring syphilitics into the hospital was the fact that Ehrlich gave salvarsan to a limited number of American hospitals for testing. Flexner, of the Rockefeller Institute, acted as his American agent and offered some to Christian, dean of the Harvard Medical School, for use at Massachusetts General Hospital and Boston City Hospital (Flexner to Christian, 29 September 1910, Henry A. Christian Papers).

63. Massachusetts General Hospital, *100th Annual Report, 1913,* p. 6.

64. Diagnosis was by the Wassermann reaction (see below). Massachusetts General Hospital, *102d Annual Report, 1915B,* p. 37; other recruiting, *104th Annual Report, 1917B,* p. 50, *106th Annual Report, 1919B,* p. 42, *107th Annual Report, 1920,* p. 120.

65. Carney Hospital, *52d Annual Report, 1915,* p. 47.

66. Reporting their results, Massachusetts General Hospital physicians Roger Lee and Wyman Whittemore were enthusiastic ("The Wasserman [*sic*] Reaction in Syphilis and Other Diseases," *Boston Medical and Surgical Journal* 160 [1909]: 410-12). In a later report on the

150    Notes to Pages 72–77

same research, Whittemore concluded that "the reaction should prove of great clinical value" ("The Wasserman Reaction for Syphilis," ibid., pp. 651–52). Massachusetts General Hospital, *96th Annual Report, 1909*, p. 79; *98th Annual Report, 1911*, p. 86; *99th Annual Report, 1912*, p. 113; *100th Annual Report, 1913*, p. 125.

67. Peter Bent Brigham Hospital, *2d Annual Report, 1915*, p. 127.

68. Massachusetts General Hospital, *102d Annual Report, 1915B*, p. 37.

69. Massachusetts General Hospital, *116th Annual Report, 1929*, p. 21; this practice was also medically sanctioned because of a fear of infection.

70. Massachusetts General Hospital, *58th Annual Report, 1871*, pp. 33, 34; Massachusetts General Hospital Trustees Mss records, 24 June 1892; Children's Hospital, *34th Annual Report, 1902*, p. 5.

71. Massachusetts General Hospital, *86th Annual Report, 1899*, p. 7.

72. Massachusetts General Hospital, Annual Reports; Massachusetts General Hospital Trustees Mss Records. Of course the poor may also have stayed longer because they were sicker. They were more prone to the diseases of poverty and less likely to see a physician early on to forestall grave complications.

73. *Boston Medical and Surgical Journal* 81 (1869): 29; Carney Hospital, *Annual Report for 1880–1881*, pp. 5, 13.

74. Carney Hospital *1st Annual Report, 1879*, pp. 10, 19; *Annual Report for 1880–1881*, p. 21; *Annual Report for 1882*, pp. 22–25; Cabot, Short Autobiography.

75. Carney Hospital, *Annual Report for 1883*, pp. 12, 13.

76. Carney Hospital, *Annual Report for 1880–1881*, pp. 9–13; *Annual Report for 1882*, p. 10; *Annual Report for 1883*, p. 17; *Annual Report for 1887–1889*, p. 11.

77. *Boston Medical and Surgical Journal* 126 (1892): 389.

78. Massachusetts General Hospital, *88th Annual Report, 1901*, p. 6.

79. Massachusetts General Hospital, Annual Reports; Massachusetts General Hospital Trustees Mss Records, 18 October 1901.

80. Boston City Hospital, Annual Reports.

81. Boston City Hospital, *19th Annual Report, 1882/83*, p. 21; *22d Annual Report, 1885*, p. 5; *24th Annual Report, 1887*, p. 12; *7th Annual Report, 1870/71*, p. 46.

82. Children's Hospital, *6th Annual Report, 1874*, p. 8; *7th Annual Report, 1875*, p. 9; *8th Annual Report, 1876*, p. 8. It moved to Wellesley soon after.

83. Massachusetts General Hospital, *67th Annual Report, 1880*, pp. 5, 6; Massachusetts General Hospital Trustees Mss Records, 20 February, 5 March 1880.

84. Children's Hospital, *24th Annual Report, 1892*, p. 40; *25th Annual Report, 1893*, p. 41; *26th Annual Report, 1894*, p. 46; *27th Annual Report, 1895*, p. 46; *30th Annual Report, 1898*, p. 37; *31st Annual Report, 1899*, p. 28; *32d Annual Report, 1900*, pp. 29–31; *44th Annual Report, 1912*, p. 21; *45th Annual Report, 1913*, p. 94.

85. Massachusetts General Hospital, *97th Annual Report, 1910*, pp. 9, 43; *93d Annual Report, 1906*, p. 47.

86. Boston City Hospital, *6th Annual Report, 1869/70*, p. 6.

87. Boston City Hospital, *33d Annual Report, 1896/97*, p. 26.

88. William T. Councilman to J. Collins Warren, 21 November 1893, Pathology and Bacteriology File, Massachusetts General Hospital Archives.

89. Peter Bent Brigham Hospital, *1st Annual Report, 1913/14*, pp. 39, 42; *11th Annual Report, 1924*, p. 2.

90. Peter Bent Brigham Hospital, *4th Annual Report, 1917*, p. 48; *9th Annual Report, 1922*, p. 67. The fact that the institution finally felt secure enough to risk the charge of experimentation did not mean, of course, that the charge was not made.

91. Boston Lying-in Hospital, *1923 Annual Report, 91st Year*, pp. 15–16.

92. Massachusetts General Hospital, *84th Annual Report, 1897*, p. 42; *90th Annual Report, 1903*, p. 17. For a catalog of hospital technology, see Malcolm T. MacEachern, *Hospital Organization and Management*, 2d ed. (Chicago, 1946), pp. 21, 22.

93. *Boston Medical and Surgical Journal* 155 (1906): 327.

Chapter 4

1. Maurice Howe Richardson to William Sturgis Bigelow, 26 December 1893, Pathology and Bacteriology File.

2. Richard H. Shryock, *The Unique Influence of the Johns Hopkins University on American Medicine* (Copenhagen, 1953).

3. J. B. Blake, "Administration of Ether at the Boston City Hospital," *Boston Medical and Surgical Journal* 141 (1899): 312-14. Other examples include *Boston Medical and Surgical Journal* 93 (1875): 283-84, 620-21; 103 (1880): 430; 114 (1886): 462; 133 (1895): 454; 137 (1897): 215-16. A full account of the early use of ether is in Bowditch, *A History*, pp. 215-348.

4. Warren, *Vineyard of Surgery*, pp. 152-53.

5. Ibid.; Massachusetts General Hospital Trustees Mss Records, 13, 27 December 1895, 1 May 1896.

6. Charles Eliot to Henry P. Bowditch, 21 June 1900, Henry P. Bowditch Papers, Countway Library.

7. President Eliot's Annual Report for 1888 discussed this difficulty (quoted in Thomas Francis Harrington, *The Harvard Medical School: A History, Narrative and Documentary*, 3 vols. [New York, 1905], 3:1079).

8. Ibid.; Warren, *Vineyard of Surgery*, pp. 193-94.

9. Harvard Medical School, Mss Faculty Minutes, 2 February, 9, 30 March, 18 May, 1 June 1889, 7 November, 6 December 1890, 6 June 1891, Massachusetts General Hospital Trustees Mss Records, 10 January, 14 February, 16 May, 1 August, 17 October 1890; Harvard Medical School, Faculty Committee Reports of 9 March 1889 and [1892] Correspondence on Improved Clinical Facilities, 1889-92, Harvard Medical School Archives; Harvard Medical School Faculty Committee to Samuel Eliot, [1890], copy, ibid.; Samuel Eliot to Harvard Medical School Faculty Committee, 2 May 1890, ibid.; Anonymous to E. W. Hooper, Treasurer, Harvard Corporation, 31 January 1892, ibid.; E. W. Hooper to Frederick C. Shattuck, 8 February 1892, ibid.

10. Warren, *Vineyard of Surgery*, p. 196.

11. Edith Gittings Reid, *The Life and Convictions of William Sydney Thayer, Physician* (New York, 1936), passim.

12. George B. Shattuck to Charles Eliot, 7 December 1889, Eliot Papers; Charles Eliot to David W. Cheever, 18 December 1899, ibid.

13. William S. Thayer to Charles Eliot, 30 December 1899, Eliot Papers; Charles Eliot to Frederick C. Shattuck, 9 June 1900, ibid.

14. R. H. Fitz to Charles Eliot, 20 May 1900, Eliot Papers; Frederick C. Shattuck to Charles Eliot, 8 November, 9, 17 December 1899, ibid.; Charles Eliot to George B. Shattuck, 7 January 1900, ibid.; George B. Shattuck to Charles Eliot, 11 January 1900, ibid.; Charles Eliot to Frederick C. Shattuck, 16 February, 6 June 1900, ibid.

15. R. H. Fitz to Charles Eliot, 20 May, 2 June 1900, Eliot Papers.

16. Henry P. Walcott to Charles Eliot, 26 February 1901, March 1901, Eliot Papers; Henry P. Bowditch to Charles Eliot, 23 June 1900, ibid. William Thayer was appointed clinical professor of medicine at Hopkins in 1905 when Osler left for Oxford. In 1912, when Harvard finally controlled some hospital appointments and also enjoyed a closer relationship with Massachusetts General, Thayer was offered the clinical professorship (F. C. Shattuck's chair) at Harvard but refused it. He did serve Harvard for some years as a member of its board of overseers (Reid, *William Sydney Thayer*, passim).

17. Peter Bent Brigham Hospital, *1st Annual Report, 1913/14*, p. 1; David McCord, *The Fabrick of Man: Fifty Years of the Peter Bent Brigham* (Boston, 1963), pp. 12-14. At Brigham's death the *Transcript* remarked: "Brigham's in the parlance of a future generation of Bostonians will enjoy a very different significance from that which it had with a past generation. It is a poetic justice of the purest kind that the thoughtless gaity and money-scattering in a hostelry like 'Brigham's' should finally go to help the poor, the thriftless, the sick, and the sin and sorrow burdened. Many a lineal heir of the spendthrifts of the past will come by their own again in the Brigham Hospital for the sick poor" (*Boston Evening Transcript*, 30 May 1877).

18. Warren, *Vineyard of Surgery*, pp. 198-99. Public outcry against Harvard's perversion of the will did not arise until 1905, when the arrangement became common knowledge. James Michael Curley, always ready to attack the university, denounced the theft of the Brigham money and tried to have it used instead for the tuberculosis hospital he believed Boston's most pressing health need (Boston, City Council Proceedings, 29 December 1905). The attack on Harvard was continued in 1909 when the Brigham trustees sought a change in their state charter that would enable the institution to hold an increased endowment (Boston, City Council Proceedings, 18 February, 25 March, 15 April 1909; *Boston Medical and Surgical Journal* 160 [1909]: 148, 386, 420). All the arrangements between the school and the hospital had been made several years before, between 1900 and 1902.

19. Charles S. Minot to Charles Eliot, 11 May, 7, 8 June, 13, 22 December 1899, 15 January 1900, Eliot Papers; William L. Richardson (Dean, Harvard Medical School) to Charles Eliot, 6 June 1899, ibid.; Harvard Medical School, Mss Faculty Minutes, 3 February 1900.

20. Warren remembered that a desirable site directly across the Charles River from Harvard Square, in the vicinity of what is now Soldiers Field and the Business School, was not precluded by the will. Prior to the erection of the Charles River Dam in 1908, however, that area flooded in springtime (*Vineyard of Surgery*, pp. 204-5, footnotes by Edward Churchill).

21. At a time when Warren and Bowditch seemed to have given up, Henry Walcott wrote to Eliot: "Warren and Bowditch have had all sorts of schemes for getting a great sum of money out of some millionaire—but they appear now to have more moderate views—and I think we can get down to buildings more adopted to our resources" (5 February 1901, Eliot Papers). When they had succeeded and credit was going to others, Francis Lee Higginson wrote to Eliot: "I want to call your attention to the whole story. Warren and Bowditch started this whole affair, they were laughed at, jeered at, called cranks by other Drs—but they insisted that it could be done" (10 August 1901, ibid.).

22. Warren remembered how auspicious the formation of United States Steel was for approaching J. P. Morgan for money for Harvard: "The winter of 1900 had been one of unusual national prosperity and many large business undertakings had been carried through successfully. The climax seemed to be reached when the great banking house of J. P. Morgan succeeded in uniting the steel industries of the country into one gigantic corporation. Was not this the moment for which we had been waiting so long?" (*Vineyard of Surgery*, pp. 209-10).

23. Charles Eliot to J. P. Morgan, 4 July 1901, Eliot Papers; J. Collins Warren to Charles Eliot, 11 September 1901, ibid.

24. J. Collins Warren to Charles Eliot, 27 September 1901, Eliot Papers.

25. Land purchase memo, dated 6 August 1900, in "Harvard University. Papers concerning the proposed new buildings and endowment for the Medical School," Eliot Papers; Peter Bent Brigham Hospital, *1st Annual Report, 1913/14*, p. 144.

26. Peter Bent Brigham Hospital, Trustees Mss Records, Committee Report, 27 October 1902.

27. Ibid.; Rowe strongly opposed giving medical school faculties power to nominate for hospital staff positions (American Hospital Association, *4th Annual Conference, 1902*, p. 55).

28. H. P. Bowditch, W. L. Richardson, and J. C. Warren to H. P. Walcott and A. T. Cabot, 16 June 1902, copy in Warren Papers, Countway Library; Warren, Vineyard of Surgery, p. 15.

29. Henry P. Walcott, Arthur Tracy Cabot, and Charles Francis Adams 2d to Alexander Cochrane, 27 June 1902, copied into Peter Bent Brigham Hospital Trustees Mss Records, vol. 1, pp. 168-71; Cochrane to Walcott, Cabot, and Adams, 6 November 1902, ibid. Adams to Cochrane, 1 December 1902, ibid.; Peter Bent Brigham Hospital Trustees Mss Records, 11 December 1902. The absence of a formal agreement was to create problems in later years.

30. Henry P. Walcott to Charles Eliot, 29 March 1901, Eliot Papers.

31. William T. Councilman to Charles Eliot, 26 July 1906, Eliot Papers.

32. Warren, *Vineyard of Surgery*, pp. 197-98; Boston City Hospital, Visiting Staff Mss Minutes, 10 July, 3 November 1892; Boston City Hospital Trustees Mss Records, 11 April 1906.

33. E.g., William T. Councilman to Charles Eliot, 26 June 1902, 10 June 1905, 7 May, 26 July 1906, Eliot Papers.

34. Jerome Greene (Eliot's secretary) to Henry P. Walcott, 14 March 1907, Eliot Papers; Walcott to Eliot, 5 September 1907, ibid.; Contract, 1907, between Carney Hospital and Henry A. Christian, Henry A. Christian Papers; *Boston Medical and Surgical Journal* 159 (1908): 589, 590.

35. William T. Councilman to Charles Eliot, 28 July 1907, 20 September 1907, Eliot Papers; Henry Lee Higginson to Charles Eliot, 6 July 1907, ibid.; Eliot to Higginson, 9 July 1907, quoted in Henry James, *Charles W. Eliot: President of Harvard University, 1869-1909,* 2 vols. (Boston, 1930), 2:160-61.

36. Christian to Charles Eliot, [late January, early February, 1908], Henry A. Christian Papers; Peter Bent Brigham Hospital Trustees Mss Records, 8 May, 12, 29 June 1908, 11 April 1910, 15 March 1912.

37. Peter Bent Brigham Hospital Trustees Mss Records, 12, 16 December 1912.

38. Cushing's appointments of his first assistants seemed to belie this change. John Homans and David Cheever were both fourth generation physicians of distinguished Boston medical families. Though both were educated locally, Homans had gone afterwards to Hopkins and worked under Cushing (McCord, *Fabrick of Man,* pp. 44-47).

39. Peter Bent Brigham Hospital, *7th Annual Report, 1920,* p. 63; *9th Annual Report 1922,* p. 53; *11th Annual Report, 1924,* p. 73.

40. Children's Hospital, *44th Annual Report, 1912,* p. 34; *Boston Medical and Surgical Journal* 170 (1914): 554; Harvard Medical School, Mss Faculty Minutes, 6 May 1911; Henry P. Walcott to Charles Eliot, 1 July 1902, Eliot Papers; Charles Eliot to J. P. Morgan, 24 April 1903, ibid.

41. An account of the reorganization appears in Frederic A. Washburn, *The Massachusetts General Hospital: Its Development, 1900-1935* (Boston, 1939), pp. 67-135.

42. Massachusetts General Hospital, *92nd Annual Report, 1905,* p. 9.

43. Boston City Hospital, *27th Annual Report, 1890,* pp. 24-25; Boston City Hospital, Visiting Staff Mss Minutes, 26 January 1890.

44. George Rosen, "Changing Attitudes of the Medical Profession to Specialization," *Bulletin of the History of Medicine* 12 (1942): 343-54; George Rosen, *Fees and Fee Bills: Some Economic Aspects of Medical Practice in Nineteenth Century America,* Supplement to *Bulletin of the History of Medicine,* no. 6 (Baltimore, 1946), p. 71 and passim; F. H. Davenport, "Specialism in Medical Practice; Its Present Status and Tendencies," *Boston Medical and Surgical Journal* 145 (1901): 81-86.

45. James Clarke White, *Sketches from My Life, 1833-1913* (Cambridge, Mass., 1914), pp. 267-71.

46. Boston City Hospital, Visiting Staff Mss Minutes, 14 February 1868, 30 November 1870.

47. Boston City Hospital, *A History,* pp. 364-65; Boston City Hospital, Visiting Staff Mss Minutes, 12 December 1878, 14 May, 12 November 1885, 14 January 1886, 1 January 1891.

48. White, *Sketches from My Life,* pp. 274-75; Massachusetts General Hospital Trustees Mss Records, 12 January 1872.

49. White, *Sketches from My Life,* p. 275.

50. Edward Wiggleworth to F. H. Peabody, 10 January 1881, Special Departments File, Massachusetts General Hospital Archives; Boston City Hospital, Visiting Staff Mss Minutes, 8 January 1885.

51. Massachusetts General Hospital Trustees Mss Records, 16 October 1874, 7 May 1875, 18 February 1876; Dr. Henry H. A. Beach to Trustees, 2 November 1874, OPD File; Trustees Committee Report, ibid.

52. The *Boston Evening Transcript* carried a series of articles in 1879 examining a wide variety of the city's charities. Stories on medical charities included: "A Misunderstood Charity: The Massachusetts Charitable Eye and Ear Infirmary," 22 January 1879; "At Carney Hospital," 10 February 1879; "Childrens Hospital: The Babies' Way of Being Sick," 7 April 1879; "The City Hospital: A Village of Invalids," 22 April 1879; "Quiet but Efficient: The House of the Good Samaritan," 12 May 1879; "The Channing Home: A Place for Consumptives," 28 July

1879: "The Boston Dispensary: The Work of a Private Charity," 11 August 1879; "A Triple
Charity: St. Joseph's Home and St. Elizabeth's Hospital," 13 October 1879; "In the Charity
Building: The Homeopathic Dispensary," 10 November 1879.
    53. *Boston Medical and Surgical Journal* 102 (1880): 233-34.
    54. James H. Whittemore to C. H. Dalton, 14 June 1880, OPD File; Massachusetts General
Hospital Trustees Mss Records, 16 September 1880; James H. Whittemore, "Are Free Dispensaries Abused?" *Boston Medical and Surgical Journal* 104 (1881): 77-79. Whittemore, of
course, did not take into account multiple visits and visits from nonresidents in arriving at his
alarming picture of a city in which almost one-quarter of the population was not paying medical
fees. That there was an increase in free outpatient care cannot be debated, however. In its
editorial remarks, the *Journal* suggested one reason for the growing number of outpatients was
that doctors in private practice were refusing to treat poor patients at no charge; the *Journal*
criticized the attenuation of this once traditional obligation of the profession (*Boston Medical
and Surgical Journal* 104 [1881]: 89). This phenomenon was perhaps indicative of the diminished social cohesiveness of an urban society.
    55. *Boston Medical and Surgical Journal* 103 (1880): 613-15.
    56. Massachusetts General Hospital Trustees Mss Records, 21 January, 2 February 1881;
Henry J. Bigelow and James Warren to Trustees, 20 January 1881, OPD File; Massachusetts
General Hospital Circular, "Out Patient Department," 1 April 1881, ibid.; *Boston Evening
Transcript,* 9 March 1881 (reprint of a letter to the editor from Samuel Eliot, Chairman of the
Trustees, whch appeared in the *Boston Advertiser,* 9 March 1881); *Boston Medical and Surgical
Journal* 104 (1881): 210-11.
    57. James C. White, F. L. Knight, James L. Putnam, and O. F. Wadsworth to Trustees, 23
February 1881, OPD File; Massachusetts General Hospital Trustees Mss Records, 4 March
1881; *Boston Medical and Surgical Journal* 106 (1882): 282-83.
    58. F. I. Knight, J. J. Putnam, J. C. White, O. F. Wadsworth, "To the Trustees of the
Massachusetts General Hospital," Undated Printed Petition, OPD File; Massachusetts General
Hospital Trustees Mss Records, 16 June 1882.
    59. Massachusetts General Hospital Trustees Committee Report, 13 October 1882, OPD File;
Massachusetts General Hospital Trustees Mss Records, 13 October 1882.
    60. Massachusetts General Hospital Trustees Committee Preliminary Report, 1 December
1893, OPD File; Massachusetts General Hospital Trustees Committee Supplementary Report, 2
November 1894, ibid.; Massachusetts General Hospital Trustees Mss Records, 2 November
1894.
    61. Massachusetts General Hospital Trustees Committee Report, [1894], OPD File.
    62. Massachusetts General Hospital, *85th Annual Report, 1898,* p. 7; Nathaniel Faxon, "The
South Surgical Service and the Massachusetts General Hospital," 1962, South Surgical Service
File, Massachusetts General Hospital Archives.
    63. Boston City Hospital, Visiting Staff Mss Records, 10, 15 April 1899.
    64. Maurice Howe Richardson to Massachusetts General Hospital Trustees, 21 November
1893, OPD File; Mt. Sinai Hospital (Boston), *7th Annual Report, 1908,* unpaginated.
    65. Edward A. Tracy, "The Pauperization of Medical Service in Boston" *Boston Medical
and Surgical Journal* 149 (1903): 663-64; Boston Medical Society, "Circular Letter to Superintendents and Trustees of the Various Hospitals of Boston," December 1909, Richard C. Cabot
Papers.
    66. *American Magazine* 81 (April 1916): 7-9, 77-78; 81 (May 1916): 43, 44, 76-81.
    67. Dr. Charles Malone, Letter to the Editor, *Boston Medical and Surgical Journal* 174
(1916): 70-71; Dr. J. W. Courtney, Letter to the Editor, *Boston Medical and Surgical Journal*
174 (1916): 698-700. Other charges and the proceedings, correspondence, and report of the
Committee on Ethics and Discipline, *Boston Medical and Surgical Journal* 174 (1916): 921-23;
also, *Boston Evening Transcript,* 6 June 1916.
    68. Edward A. Tracy, Letter to the Editor, *New England Journal of Medicine* 198 (1928):
317-18.

69. Peter Bent Brigham Hospital, *2d Annual Report, 1915*, pp. 145-46.

70. Massachusetts General Hospital, *102d Annual Report, 1915A*, p. 5-6, 66; *1915B*, pp. 32-33; *103d Annual Report, 1916A*, pp. 6, 142; Massachusetts General Hospital Trustees Mss Records, 11 December 1914, 12, 26 November 1915; *Boston Medical and Surgical Journal* 181 (1919): 755.

71. Children's Hospital, *22d Annual Report, 1890*, p. 7; *27th Annual Report, 1895*, p. 6; *29th Annual Report, 1897*, pp. 5-7; *30th Annual Report, 1898*, pp. 5-6; Richard C. Cabot to Dr. Huddleston, 14 November 1913, Richard C. Cabot Papers.

72. Agnes C. Vietor, "The Abuse of Medical Charity: The Passing of the 'Charity' Hospital and Dispensary," *Boston Medical and Surgical Journal* 140 (1899): 417-22. This sentiment was shared by Mary Richmond of the Philadelphia Charity Organization Society. In addressing the Association of Hospital Superintendents, Richmond noted that the chief advantage of dispensaries over hospitals was that the former preserved family life intact (American Hospital Association, *4th Annual Conference, 1902*, p. 136).

## Chapter 5

1. Circular Letter, 1810, in Bowditch, *A History*, pp. 3-9; *Boston Evening Transcript*, 31 October 1881. The Cambridge Hospital opened in April 1886.

2. Patient records from Boston City Hospital in this period are unavailable. These data are from the published annual reports. They serve only to indicate that roughly one-half or more of the hospital's adult patients were unattached individuals.

Age, civil condition and percentage of unattached adults among patients at Boston City Hospital

| Year | <20 | ≥20 | Single | Widowed | Married | % Net Unatt. Adults[a] | (N) |
|---|---|---|---|---|---|---|---|
| Male | | | | | | | |
| 1865 | 143 | 472 | 369 | 46 | 200 | 57.6 | (615) |
| 1870/71 | 212 | 1207 | 798 | 142 | 479 | 60.2 | (1419) |
| 1875/76 | 497 | 1420 | 739 | 497 | 681 | 52.0 | (1917) |
| 1881/82[b] | 377 | 2196 | 1441 | 245 | 863 | 59.6 | (2573) |
| Female | | | | | | | |
| 1865 | 138 | 313 | 264 | 84 | 103 | 67.1 | (451) |
| 1870/71 | 167 | 810 | 518 | 212 | 247 | 69.5 | (977) |
| 1875/76 | 267 | 996 | 554 | 351 | 358 | 63.1 | (1263) |
| 1881/82[c] | 270 | 1264 | 737 | 298 | 490 | 60.5 | (1534) |

[a] The formula for the percentage of net unattached adults is

$$\frac{(s + w) - (<20)}{\geq 20} \times (100)$$

The formula assumes that everyone under 20 is a child, unmarried, and a member of the family of procreation, and thus not eligible for inclusion among unattached adults. This, no doubt, substantially and significantly reduces the percentage of unattached adults. At the same time, the number of unattached individuals may be overestimated because some of the single and widowed aged 20 and over may have been living within families.

[b] 24 unknown.

[c] 9 unknown.

3. Albert Benedict Wolfe, *The Lodging House Problem in Boston* (Boston, 1906), p. 10.

4. Compiled by Wolfe from the Tenth and Twelfth U.S. Census (*Lodging House Problem*, pp. 38-40; also, pp. 21-25).

5. E.g., *Boston Evening Transcript*, 21 December 1887; *Boston Globe*, 29 September 1901. The latter is a story about homesick girls spending free time at the public library reading hometown newspapers.

6. Wolfe, *Lodging House Problem*, p. 109; *Boston Evening Transcript*, 21 December 1887; figures compiled by Wolfe (*Lodging House Problem*, pp. 42-43).

7. E.g., a letter condemning tipping in restaurants as "An Unrepublican Practice" commented that "the number of persons who depend for their meals on restaurants is constantly increasing, and happily, there is no lack of establishments, great and small, where the demand may be supplied" (*Boston Evening Transcript*, 5 June 1885).

8. Wolfe, *Lodging House Problem*, p. 27.

9. Ibid., pp. 35-36; "The Diet Kitchens: The Good They Do and How They Do It," *Boston Evening Transcript*, 2 December 1878.

10. *Boston Evening Transcript*, 12 September 1885, 1 July 1887, 27 December 1882.

11. State Charities Aid Association of New York, Committee on Hospitals, *New Hospitals Needed in Greater New York*, State Charities Aid Association of New York Publication no. 101 (New York, [1908]), p. 56; Robert H. Bremner, *From the Depths: The Discovery of Poverty in the United States* (New York, 1956), pp. 3-13; Wylie, *Hospitals*, p. 63. Theodore Roosevelt repeated the same argument as Wylie ("Medical Charities," *Proceedings of the National Conference of Charities and Corrections* 4 (1877): 31-38).

12. A regular contributor to the *Transcript* noted: "The straits which people who live in flats have to resort to to get along in half as much room as they have all their lives been accustomed to are often quite pathetic to witness" (*Boston Evening Transcript*, 14 October 1889).

13. State Charities Aid Association, *New Hospitals Needed*, p. 56.

14. Real Estate Matters, *Boston Evening Transcript*, 13 January 1890.

15. *Boston Evening Transcript*, 1 May, 27 August 1890.

16. *Boston Evening Transcript*, 12 October 1883. Examples of newspaper accounts may be found in: *Boston Evening Transcript*, 25 October 1878, 9 August, 13 October 1881, 12 November 1884, 29 May, 24 October 1885, 19, 30 January, 28, 30 September 1886, 21 April, 1 July 1887, 1 September 1888, 14 October 1889, 13 January 1890.

17. Sidney E. Goldstein, "The Social Function of the Hospital," *Charities and the Commons* 18 (1907): 163; William H. Mahoney, "Benevolent Hospitals in Metropolitan Boston," *Journal of the American Statistical Association* 13 (1913): 426. Mahoney was a fellow in the research department of the Boston School for Social Workers.

18. Boston Lying-in Hospital, *1915 Annual Report*, p. 12; "Cambridge Hospital and Cambridge" (Cambridge, Mass., 1927), Countway Library; Paul R. Hawley, "Medicine as a Social Instrument: The Hospital and the Community," *New England Journal of Medicine* 244 (1951): 256-59.

19. American Hospital Association, *14th Annual Conference, 1912*, p. 86.

20. *Boston Evening Transcript*, 25 October 1875; Wolfe, *Lodging House Problem*, p. 112; Hawley, "Medicine as a Social Instrument," pp. 256-57.

21. Boston City Hospital, *24th Annual Report, 1887*, p. 13.

22. "Annals of the American House," *St. Margaret's Quarterly* 1, no. 1 (January 1920): 7-9; 1, no. 2 (April 1920): 6-8; 2, no. 2 (April 1921): 7. The early years of the "Annals" are the personal narrative of Sister Jessie, one of the first group of three to come to Boston.

23. The Church of the Advent moved in 1879 to the corner of Brimmer and Mt. Vernon streets, near that part of the Back Bay that was eclipsing Beacon Hill.

24. "Annals,"*St. Margaret's Quarterly* 3, no. 2 (April 1922): 9-11; 3, no. 3 (August 1922): 6-9; 4, no. 1 (February 1923): 8-11; 8, no. 1 (February 1927): 18-20; Associated Charities, *Directory* (1891), pp. 23-24; *Boston Medical and Surgical Journal* 149 (1903): 391.

25. No residence is given for most patients. Most patients are not listed at all, as there are no

actual hospital records. The diaries of Mother Louisa, Superior of the convent, furnish much information about the hospital, though they are too incomplete to be sampled other than impressionistically. There are sparse notations during the early days. Often names of patients are not given and entries are incomplete, e.g., "Dr. Homans' new patient from Pawtucket came" (27 April 1882); "Dr. Strong operated on his patient upstairs" (15 December 1884); "Mrs. ——— left" (25 June 1885). Further, these records are a diary; during Mother Louisa's summers in Lowell and her visits abroad there are no hospital records (Mss Diaries in possession of St. Margaret's Convent, Louisburg Square, Boston).

26. W. Strother Jones, Jr., to George Cheyne Shattuck, 27 September 1884, written from Young's Hotel, Boston, George C. Shattuck Papers, Massachusetts Historical Society. Also *Boston Evening Transcript*, 17 July 1874, editorial comment on the death of Dr. William F. Basto, an irregular physician assailed in the *Boston Medical and Surgical Journal:* "Our hotels were largely patronized by guests from distant cities who came here and were cured." John Collins Warren, cofounder of Massachusetts General Hospital, performed his first operation under ether in private practice in November 1846, at the Bromfield House, a popular resort of business and professional men (*Vineyard of Surgery*, pp. 33, 34 and note).

27. E.g., Mrs. Phelps from New York in a boarding house on Mt. Vernon Sreet, cited in Maurice Howe Richardson to Theodore Dwight, 21 November 1893, OPD File; and a woman from New England, cited in Haskett Derby, "Of the Abuses Connected with Gratuitous Medical Treatment," *Boston Medical and Surgical Journal* 113 (1885): 462-63.

28. E.g., an advertisement in the classified section under Board Wanted: "A Boston physician (specialist) wishes a place in Boston for one or more patients to board a part of the time, with nursing when necessary" (*Boston Evening Transcript*, 10 September 1887).

29. E.g., an advertisement in the classified section: "Board—To the Faculty. Mrs. Jones having taken a house at no. 42 Dover Street, is thus able to offer invalids, or ladies in confinement, a quiet and retired home. Pleasant and airy rooms, with good nursing" (*Boston Evening Transcript*, 15 September, 15 October 1875). Again, an advertisement facing the title page of the *Medical Register for New England*, Francis H. Brown, comp. (Boston, 1877), announcing to physicians the facilities of Mrs. M. S. Ware for the care of ladies, including confinements.

30. Wolfe, *Lodging House Problem*, p. 63.

31. An account of the inquest and the response of the medical community is in the *Boston Evening Transcript*, 25, 27, 29 July, 1, 3, 17, 19 August 1876. This was the only licensed lying-in in Boston at the time (Boston, City Council Proceedings, 17 July 1876: Boston, Board of Health, *Annual Report for 1876*). The girl was from Canton, Massachusetts, and unmarried. Some elements of the medical community attempted to force the coroner to resign as a result of his handling of the inquest. Other physicians defended him (*Boston Evening Transcript*, 17, 19 August 1876, 21 March 1877).

32. Warren, *Vineyard of Surgery*, p. 255; Mother Louisa, Diary Entries, 3, 19 April, 5 June 1882, 26 April 1885, 22 April 1887, 12, 13 January, 12 May 1891.

33. Mother Louisa, Diary Entries, 14 June 1882, 31 December 1887, 5, 12 January, 24, 27 April 1888.

34. Carney Hospital, *By-laws*, 1891; *Boston Medical and Surgical Journal* 112 (1885): 332; 148 (1903); 191-92; 149 (1903): 391; Cabot, Short Autobiography, pp. 4-5.

35. *Boston Medical and Surgical Journal* 149 (1903): 391; Finney, *A Surgeon's Life*, p. 70.

36. Charles B. Porter to Edmund Dwight, 15 March 1894, Private Ward (1894) Folder, Phillips House File, Massachusetts General Hospital Archives; Frederick C. Shattuck to Edmund Dwight, 16 March 1894, ibid.; Boston Directory, 1892, 1893, 1894, 1895; Edward J. Forster, "A Sketch of the Medical Profession of Suffolk County," *Professional and Industrial History of Suffolk County*, 3 vols. (Boston, 1894), 3:219-20.

37. Dr. [Edward] Reynolds, "Figures Relative to Private Hospitals," typescript carbon, 1911, C. H. W. Foster Folder, Phillips House File.

38. *Boston Medical and Surgical Journal* 150 (1904): 576, 628, 629; Charles B. Porter to

Edmund Dwight, 15 March 1894, Private Ward (1894) Folder, Phillips House File; Henry P. Bowditch, Santa Barbara, Calif., to Selma Bowditch, 25 February, 2 March 1905, Henry P. Bowditch Papers.

39. "Hospital on New Lines," Circular, 22 May 1911, C. H. W. Foster Folder, Phillips House File.

40. David J. Rothman, *The Discovery of the Asylum: Social Order and Disorder in the New Republic* (Boston, 1971), pp. 131–33, 237–40; Gerald N. Grob, *The State and the Mentally Ill: A History of the Worcester State Hospital in Massachusetts, 1830–1920* (Chapel Hill, 1966), pp. 61, 75–79, 203, 229–33.

41. Bowditch, *A History,* p. 98; Eaton, *New England Hospitals,* p. 122; Massachusetts General Hospital, *82d Annual Report, 1895,* pp. 6–7; *88th Annual Report, 1901,* p. 210; *103d Annual Report, 1916A,* p. 86; Massachusetts General Hospital Trustees Mss Records, 30 August, 27 September 1895, 5 April 1901.

42. E.g. an advertisement for the American Sanatorium, *Boston Evening Transcript,* 6 May 1876.

43. See above, n. 26, for Boston's Dr. William Basto, an irregular practitioner who attracted to the city's hotels patients who had been "unsuccessfully treated by the regular profession at home."

44. *Boston Evening Transcript,* 9, 13 November 1875, 25 April 1882; *Boston Globe,* 27 February, 12, 15 March 1889.

45. Stanley H. King, *Perceptions of Illness and Medical Practice* (New York, 1962), p. 129.

46. Richard H. Shryock, *National Tuberculosis Association, 1904–1954: A Study of the Voluntary Health Movement in the United States* (New York, 1957), p. 46; Edward Livingston Trudeau, *An Autobiography* (Garden City, N.Y., 1934), pp. 77, 99, 154, 155; *Boston Evening Transcript,* 28 March 1885.

47. E.g., a large feature article, "Invalids in the South. Some Facts and Some Advice—A Few Words to the Thoughtful who Contemplate Climatic Cure—Some Southern Discomforts and Delights," *Boston Evening Transcript,* 25 March 1878; also *Boston Medical and Surgical Journal* 97 (1877): 286–289, 315–16; "Aiken, South Carolina, as a Health Resort," *Boston Medical and Surgical Journal* 98 (1878): 228–33.

48. These institutions included the Adams Nervine Asylum and the Channing Private Hospital in the Boston area, and Shady Lawn which, caring for both nervous diseases and addiction, was located appropriately on Gothic Street in Northampton. More distant institutions—Sunnyside Medical Retreat in Fort Washington, New York, and Parrish Hall in Brooklyn—advertised in Boston for well-to-do opium addicts. (Brown, *Medical Register for New England* [1880], unpaginated advertising section; *Boston Medical and Surgical Journal* 98 [1878]: 89).

49. Boston, City Document #35, 1868; "Nor shall any officer or servant of the Hospital receive a gift or fee from any patient" (*Boston City Hospital Dedication,* p. 94; this injunction was repeated in subsequent annual reports).

50. For who used private rooms at Boston City Hospital, see Thomas Amory, "Address," *Boston City Hospital Dedication,* p. 60; *Report on Fees for Medical Treatment at the City Hospital,* Boston City Document #35, 1868. For Massachusetts General Hospital, see above, chap. 1, p. 10.

51. John C. Warren to the Trustees, 30 April 1844, Private Patients Folder, Phillips House File; Massachusetts General Hospital Trustees Committee Report, 19 May 1844, ibid.

52. J. H. Whittemore to Samuel Eliot, 19 November 1880, 18 February 1881, Professional Staff: Physicians' and Surgeons' Fees File, Massachusetts General Hospital Archives; Massachusetts General Hospital Trustees Mss Records, 19 November 1880, 18 February, 4, 18, March 1881.

53. George Cheyne Shattuck to Eleanor Shattuck, 12 September 1876, George C. Shattuck Papers, Massachusetts Historical Society, discussing his travel plans to visit patients in New York and New England; other of his letters to Eleanor in the 1870s mention a good deal of traveling to see patients in Worcester, Providence, Hartford, Albany, etc. ibid.; Richard C.

Cabot to Ella Lyman, 8 May 1894, Richard C. Cabot Papers; Dr. G. H. Watson, Bridgewater, Mass., to Frederick C. Shattuck, 26 November 1896, F. C. Shattuck Papers, Countway Library.

54. *Boston Medical and Surgical Journal* 62 (1860): 26. Examples of referrals: James H. Etheridge, Chicago, to F. C. Shattuck, 31 October 1891, F. C. Shattuck Papers, Countway Library; J. W. C. Ely, Providence, to F. C. Shattuck, 28 September 1888, ibid.; W. W. Keen, Providence, to F. C. Shattuck, 18 June 1896, ibid.

55. Boston, City Document #35, 1868, p. 8.

56. *Boston Medical and Surgical Journal* 113 (1885): 462–63. For this same situation from the point of view of an out-of-town physician, see *Boston Medical and Surgical Journal* 132 (1895): 118–19.

57. Maurice Howe Richardson to Edmund Dwight, 21 November 1893, OPD File; Henry J. Bigelow to the Trustees of Massachusetts General Hospital, 24 March 1886, Professional Services: Organization of Surgical Services File.

58. Henry J. Bigelow to the Trustees of Massachusetts General Hospital, Printed Letter, 18 February 1886, Henry J. Bigelow File, Massachusetts General Hospital Archives; Henry J. Bigelow to the Trustees of Massachusetts General Hospital, 24 March 1886, Professional Services: Organization of Surgical Services File; Henry J. Bigelow to William Endicott, 27 December 1888, ibid.; Henry J. Bigelow to Charles Dalton, 27 December 1888, Professional Staff: Physicians' and Surgeons' Fees File; Henry J. Bigelow, "Fees in Hospitals," *Boston Medical and Surgical Journal* 120 (1889): 377–78; Massachusetts General Hospital Trustees Mss Records, 15 January, 3, 12, 26 February, 26 March, 16, 23 April 1886, 11 March 1887, 17 January 1891. In 1896, William Sturgis Bigelow, Henry's son and himself a trustee of Massachusetts General, offered the hospital a bust of his father (Massachusetts General Hospital Trustees Mss Records, 9 October 1896).

59. Circular Letter to the visiting staff from Edmund Dwight, H. P. Walcott, and William Endicott, Jr., a committee of the trustees, March 1894, Private Ward (1894) Folder, Phillips House File.

60. R. H. Fitz to Edmund Dwight, 18 March 1894, Private Ward (1894) Folder, Phillips House File; Maurice Howe Richardson to Edmund Dwight, 22 March 1894, ibid.; John Homans to Edmund Dwight, 15 March 1894, ibid.

61. Frederick C. Shattuck to Edmund Dwight, 16 March 1894, Private Ward (1894) Folder, Phillips House File; R. H. Fitz to Edmund Dwight, 18 March 1894, ibid.; J. Collins Warren to Edmund Dwight, 18 March 1894, ibid.; H. H. A. Beach to Edmund Dwight, 15 March 1894, ibid.; "Trustees' tabulation of staff responses," ibid.

62. Frederick C. Shattuck to Edmund Dwight, 16 March 1894, Private Ward (1894) Folder, Phillips House File; John Homans to Edmund Dwight, 15 March 1894, ibid.; J. Collins Warren to Edmund Dwight, 15 March 1894, ibid., Maurice Howe Richardson to Edmund Dwight, 15 March 1894, ibid.; Charles B. Porter to Edmund Dwight, 15 March 1894, ibid.; Elbridge G. Cutler to Edmund Dwight, 17 March 1894, ibid.

63. To from $28 per week and up, at the discretion of the resident physician (Trustees Committee Report, 29 March 1894, Private Ward [1894] Folder, Phillips House File).

64. *Boston Medical and Surgical Journal* 142 (1900): 522.

65. A. Rittenhouse to John Pratt, 6 March 1894, Private Ward (1894) Folder, Phillips House File; William R. White to John Pratt, 8 March 1894, ibid.; M. E. P. Davis to John Pratt, n.d., ibid.; W. W. Keen to John Collins Warren, 23 February 1894, ibid.; Robert Abbe to J. Collins Warren, 24 February 1894, ibid.; Charles M. Burney to J. Collins Warren, 6 April 1894, ibid.; Louis A. Stimson to J. Collins Warren, 24 February 1894, ibid.; Nicholas Senn to J. Collins Warren, 28 February [1894], forwarded, with message from Warren, to Edmund Dwight, 2 March [1894], ibid.

66. John A. Williams to John Pratt, 7 March 1894, Private Ward (1894) Folder, Phillips House File; George H. M. Rowe to John Pratt, 7 March 1894, ibid.; Boston City Hospital Trustees Mss Records, 12, 26 December 1906.

67. *Boston Medical and Surgical Journal* 152 (1905): 295–314.

68. Ibid., pp. 295-300.

69. In addition to Gay of Boston City Hospital, Haskett Derby of the Massachusetts Charitable Eye and Ear Infirmary, Alfred Worcester of Waltham Hospital, E. W. Cushing of Boston, and Samuel Crowell of Dorchester. Critic J. W. Elliott was a visiting surgeon at Massachusetts General.

70. *Boston Medical and Surgical Journal* 152 (1905): 298, 312.

71. Ibid., pp. 297-300, 306, 308.

72. Dr. George H. M. Rowe's presidential address to the Association of Hospital Superintendents, delivered in Boston in 1905, reaffirmed the same message (*Boston Medical and Surgical Journal* 153 [1905]: 511-15).

73. H. B. Howard to C. H. W. Foster, 30 January, 16 February 1906, C. H. W. Foster Folder, Phillips House File.

74. The "Boston trustee" is discussed at length in Gerald T. White, *A History of the Massachusetts Hospital Life Insurance Company* (Cambridge, Mass., 1955).

75. H. B. Howard to C. H. W. Foster, 30 January, 16 February 1906, C. H. W. Foster Folder, Phillips House File.

76. "Massachusetts General Hospital: Warren Hospital Fund," typescript circular, n.d., C. H. W. Foster Folder, Phillips House File; C. H. W. Foster to Frederick C. Shattuck, 15 April 1911, ibid.; Massachusetts General Hospital, *97th Annual Report, 1910,* p. 9.

77. Physicians: Arthur T. Cabot*, W. T. Councilman, R. H. Fitz*, J. L. Goodale*, F. B. Harrington*, Henry Jackson, Robert Lovett, John L. Morse, Edward Reynolds, Maurice Howe Richardson*, F. C. Shattuck*, E. W. Taylor*, Paul Thorndike.
*denotes Massachusetts General Hospital staff members. Of the others, Jackson had been a Massachusetts General Hospital house officer.
Lay Directors: Charles F. Adams 2d, Arthur H. Brooks, C. Minot Weld, C. H. W. Foster, Charles A. Coolidge, F. L. Higginson, Augustus Hemenway, G. M. Lane, Neal Rantoul, John E. Thayer.

78. "Proposed Private Hospital," Circular, 1 May 1911, C. H. W. Foster Folder, Phillips House File; *Boston Evening Transcript,* 22 May 1911, reprinted as circular, "Hospital on New Lines," ibid.; for other public service corporations, see White, *Massachusetts Hospital Life Insurance Company,* pp. 7-22; David Culver, "Tenement House Reform in Boston, 1846-1898," Ph.D. diss., Boston University, 1972, p. 145.

79. Minutes, Meeting of Directors, 17 November 1911, C. H. W. Foster Folder, Phillips House File.

80. R. H. Fitz to C. H. W. Foster, 12 May 1911, C. H. W. Foster Folder, Phillips House File.

81. Charles Foster, Untitled Memorandum on background of Phillips House, typescript, 1948, C. H. W. Foster Folder, Phillips House File; Massachusetts General Hospital Trustees Mss Records, 20 March, 1, 15 May 1908, 24 June 1910; Administrator's Report, Massachusetts General Hospital, *98th Annual Report, 1911,* p. 43; Massachusetts General Hospital, *99th Annual Report, 1912,* p. 104.

82. Massachusetts General Hospital Trustees Mss Records, 26 December 1913; C. H. W. Foster to Frederick C. Shattuck, 15 April 1911, C. H. W. Foster Folder, Phillip House File; Massachusetts General Hospital, *103d Annual Report, 1916A,* p. 7; *104th Annual Report, 1917A,* p. 10.

83. Massachusetts General Hospital refused the same offer. Barnes and Yale accepted along with Hopkins.

84. Massachusetts General Hospital, *100th Annual Report, 1913,* p. 7.

85. Massachusetts General Hospital, *97th Annual Report, 1910,* p. 44; *104th Annual Report, 1917A,* p. 86; Massachusetts General Hospital, Private Ward Executive Committee (PWEC) Mss Records, 9 January 1919.

86. Warren, *Vineyard of Surgery,* p. 255.

87. Massachusetts General Hospital, *104th Annual Report, 1917A,* pp. 85, 138.

88. Massachusetts General Hospital, PWEC Mss Records, 10 January 1918, 14 February

1919; R. H. Fitz to C. H. W. Foster, 12 May 1911, C. H. W. Foster Folder, Phillips House File.

89. Paul Dudley White, *My Life and Medicine: An Autobiographical Memoir* (Boston, 1971), pp. 13, 14; Massachusetts General Hospital, PWEC Mss Records, 20 July, 9, 19 November 1917; Massachusetts General Hospital, *104th Annual Report, 1917A,* pp. 6, 85; *105th Annual Report, 1918A,* p. 84.

90. Massachusetts General Hospital, *104th Annual Report, 1917A,* p. 6; "Proposed Private Hospital," Circular, 1 May 1911; Massachusetts General Hospital Trustees Mss Records, 25 January 1918, 11 July 1924.

91. Massachusetts General Hospital, PWEC Mss Records, 29 May, 13 September 1917; Massachusetts General Hospital, *104th Annual Report, 1917A,* pp. 6, 7, 85, 86; Boston Lying-in Hospital, *1915 Annual Report,* p. 24.

92. Francis E. Kobrin, "The American Midwife Controversy," pp. 362-63.

93. Boston Lying-in Hospital, *1903 Annual Report,* pp. 9, 13; *1907 Annual Report,* p. 14; *1915 Annual Report,* p. 12.

94. Computed from statistics in Boston Lying-in Hospital, *1930 Annual Report,* pp. 58-69.

95. Foreign born patients at Boston Lying-in: 1873-79, 54 percent; 1880-89, 58 percent; 1890-99, 56 percent; 1900-1909, 54 percent; 1910-19, 55 percent. Computed from ibid. U.S. census data for Boston show the following foreign born percentages: 1870, 35.1 percent; 1880, 31.6 percent; 1890, 35.3 percent; 1900, 35.1 percent; 1910, 36.3 percent; 1920, 31.9 percent; 1930, 29.4 percent. Figures for 1920 and 1930 are for foreign born whites. Calculated from data in Boston Lying-in Hospital, *1930 Annual Report,* pp. 62, 63.

96. All figures for Massachusetts General Hospital are computed from data in its annual reports. For the 1880s, the percentage of patients who were residents of Boston was 42 percent; in the 1890s, 35 percent; 32 percent, 1900-1909; and 21 percent, 1910-19.

97. Calculated from data in Boston Lying-in Hospital, *1930 Annual Report,* p. 66.

98. Boston City Hospital published no data on patient residence. All percentages are calculated from data in Boston City Hospital, Annual Reports. Cf. above, n. 95, for comparison with city-wide population figures.

99. Stephan Thernstrom's socio-economic classifications were generally adhered to in this analysis, except in the cases where occupations listed in hospital records do not appear in *The Other Bostonians.* These occupations I have assigned as best I could. Because of the difficulty of classifying occupations according to socioeconomic status and the added difficulty deriving from the changing meaning of an occupational description over time, this method is not completely satisfactory. Yet the results thus derived are supportive of the changing picture of hospital use that emerges from the qualitative data.

I use four basic categories: white collar, skilled blue collar, semiskilled and service, and unskilled and menial. White collar includes professionals (doctors, lawyers, clergy, etc.) and managers, officials and proprietors of varying status, as well as clerk-salesmen and semiprofessionals (actors, newspapermen, nurses, etc.). For some comparisons, this group is divided into two categories: professionals and other white collar. Skilled workers include carpenters, gasfitters, tinsmiths, and the like, while semiskilled and service include butchers, most factory operatives, and teamsters. Unskilled laborers and menial service workers—clearly including laborers and more arbitrarily perhaps including bootblacks, gardeners, lumbermen, and the like—are in the last category. Fortunately, "laborers" are always the overwhelming majority in this latter category. Those remaining unclassified include patients described as children, students, unemployed, discharged soldiers, and "not classified." These were subtracted from the patient population before the percentages in the classified groups were calculated. Finally, since works such as Thernstrom's regrettably deal only with male occupations, female occupations, though they are often excruciatingly detailed in the published hospital reports, are skipped over because of the lack of a suitable comparative base (Thernstrom, *The Other Bostonians,* pp. 50, 289-302).

100. Of these, 90.3 percent were described as "laborers" in the city hospital report for 1870/71, as were 89.5 percent in 1880/81 and 81.4 percent in 1900/1901. The occupational

levels of the general population are Thernstrom's calculations from the U.S. census (*The Other Bostonians,* p. 50).

101. Until 1902, employed males were divided into twelve or fewer categories and blue collar occupational definitions fluctuated wildly. Laborers, for example, went from 26.9 percent of the male patients in 1870, to 51.4 percent in 1880, to 24.4 percent in 1890, and to an improbable 72.8 percent in 1900, with skilled workers accounting for only 5.0 percent in that latest year. Still, the gross differences between white and blue collar are usable for these years. In the twentieth century, occupations were broken down in much greater detail; there are over a hundred fifty male categories in 1910. From 1915 through 1919, the labor force was divided and subdivided by industry and category; helpers, craftsmen, and operatives were separated by the nature of the tasks each performed and the setting in which each worked. Further, professions were listed under that heading, making it clear, for example, that a masseur was considered a semiprofessional (white collar) and not a personal service worker (blue collar, semiskilled).

102. Comparisons for 1919 may be matched against those for 1880. In 1880, the census showed three percent professional, the hospital records 1.5 percent; thirty percent other white collar versus 16.6 percent; thirty percent skilled versus 51.4 percent. The occupational levels of the general population are Thernstrom's calculations from the U.S. census. (*The Other Bostonians,* p. 50); data for Massachusetts General Hospital are calculated from the hospital's annual reports.

## Chapter 6

1. Massachusetts General Hospital Trustees Mss Records, 9 July 1920, 9 December 1921, 10 November, 8 December 1922, 27 July 1923, 4, 18 April, 2 May 1924; Boston City Hospital Trustees Mss Records, 17 December 1919, 3, 14 May 1926.

2. Massachusetts General Hospital, *91st Annual Report, 1904,* p. 11; Massachusetts General Hospital, Trustees Mss Records, 13 May, 16 September 1904, 14 June 1907.

3. See, for example, "Health Societies," *Boston Evening Transcript,* 22 November 1878, reprinted from the *St. Louis Post.* This described a scheme in which families contributed only while healthy, that is, while medical care was effective, and received treatment without charge in illness. Also, James L. Schwartz, "Early History of Prepaid Medical Care Plans," *Bulletin of the History of Medicine* 39 (1965): 450-75.

4. Cabot noted that under Galvin the hospital "had always been managed upon a partially cooperative basis," though the plan had been "faulty in execution." It was the idea of James Mumford, Cabot's medical and religious (in the Emmanuel Movement) colleague to purchase the hospital. Mumford was to be chief surgeon, Cabot chief physician (Richard C. Cabot, "James Gregory Mumford, M.D.," *Boston Medical and Surgical Journal* 172 (1915): 472.

5. Chapter 751, Resolves of 1911, quoted in Francis D. Donoghue, "The History and Operation of the Massachusetts Workingmen's Compensation Law," *Boston Medical and Surgical Journal* 175 (1916): 898.

6. Roy Lubove, *The Struggle for Social Security 1900-1935* (Cambridge, Mass., 1968), pp. 58-61. Originally, the law provided for only two weeks of medical care and compensation for time lost at a rate of 50 percent of the worker's wage. Such compensation began after a two-week waiting period. Coverage, however, was large scale. In the first year of operation, 81 percent of the injured workers in Massachusetts were insured. Though employers could elect whether to pay for the insurance, the statute had an effective compulsory feature. It suspended the fellow servant rule of the common law. This meant that an employer could no longer defend a suit for damages brought by an injured worker by claiming that the accident was even slightly due to the negligence of the worker or a fellow employee. Under the act a worker could sue and collect from an uninsured employer even if the employer were only partially responsible for the accident (*Boston Medical and Surgical Journal* 175 [1916]: 888, 898).

7. *Boston Medical and Surgical Journal* 173 (1915): 580; 175 (1916): 401, 461, 462; 176 (1917): 236-37.

8. *Boston Medical and Surgical Journal* 175 (1916): 903.

9. Boston City Hospital Trustees Mss Records, 21 August, 22 November 1912, 3 January

1913; Massachusetts General Hospital Trustees Mss Records, 15 November, 13 December 1912.

10. Boston City Hospital Trustees Mss Records, 12 August 1912, 14 May 1915, 27 April 1917; *Boston Medical and Surgical Journal* 169 (1913): 414; *New England Journal of Medicine* 198 (1928): 256-57.

11. Massachusetts General Hospital Trustees Mss Records, 15 November, 13 December 1912; *Boston Medical and Surgical Journal* 173 (1915): 581; 180 (1919): 137-38; Massachusetts General Hospital, *104th Annual Report, 1917A*, p. 137.

12. Boston City Hospital Trustees Mss Records, 10 January 1913, 11 June 1915, 11, 18 April 1918, 17 December 1919; *Boston Medical and Surgical Journal* 172 (1915): 870-71; 183 (1920): 59-60; 188 (1923): 416-17.

13. *Boston Medical and Surgical Journal* 168 (1913): 285, 371-72; 175 (1916): 401, 470-71; 176 (1917): 76, 397-401; 178 (1918): 595, 598.

14. *Boston Medical and Surgical Journal* 169 (1913): 411, 417; 170 (1914): 12; 173 (1915): 581; 175 (1916): 470-71, 893; 180 (1919): 664; 184 (1921): 652.

15. *Boston Medical and Surgical Journal* 173 (1915): 581; 175 (1916): 470-71; 180 (1919): 665; *New England Journal of Medicine* 198 (1928): 255, 423, 831; Massachusetts General Hospital, *102d Annual Report, 1915A*, p. 65; *104th Annual Report, 1917A*, pp. 10, 11; Massachusetts General Hospital, General Executive Committee Records, 21 April 1920, 5 January 1921.

16. For example, "The directors of the West End Street Railway have voted to engage free beds at the Massachusetts General Hospital, City Hospital, and Cambridge Hospital, commencing with January 1, 1890, and that the general manager be authorized in his discretion to send employees to such hospitals" (*Boston Medical and Surgical Journal* 121 [1889]: 617).

17. Massachusetts General Hospital Trustees Mss Records, 23 December 1892, 7 March 1902, 24 January 1908, 13 December 1912.

18. Massachusetts General Hospital, *75th Annual Report, 1888*, p. 5; Massachusetts General Hospital Trustees Mss Records, 10 April 1891; Peter Bent Brigham Hospital, *8th Annual Report, 1921*, p. 5; *9th Annual Report, 1922*, p. 3.

19. Massachusetts General Hospital Trustees Mss Records, 14 October 1898; Massachusetts General Hospital, *100th Annual Report, 1913*, pp. 6, 109; *103d Annual Report, 1916A*, p. 16; *1916B*, p. 49; *104th Annual Report, 1917A*, p. 30; *106th Annual Report, 1919B*, pp. 50-51; *107th Annual Report, 1920*, p. 20; *108th Annual Report, 1921*, p. 23.

20. Massachusetts General Hospital Trustees Mss Records, 29 April 1904, 3 October 1904; Massachusetts General Hospital, *91st Annual Report, 1904*, pp. 11, 12; *94th Annual Report, 1907*, pp. 10, 11.

21. Massachusetts General Hospital Trustees Mss Records, 18 May 1923, 13 June 1924; Massachusetts General Hospital, *110th Annual Report, 1923*, p. 5; *111th Annual Report, 1924*, pp. 11-27, 254; *Boston Medical and Surgical Journal* 190 (1924): 1047.

22. Massachusetts General Hospital Trustees Mss Records, 1 May, 24 December 1925, 9 July 1926; Massachusetts General Hospital, *112th Annual Report, 1925*, pp. 6-7, 239-41; Massachusetts General Hospital, "The MGH—one of the great medical centers of the world—is your hospital" ([Boston], [1926]). This sort of campaign led to strains within the medical profession. The committee on ethics and discipline of the state medical society was forced to reexamine the matter of advertising. Professional fund raisers tried to attract support for hospitals by publicizing institutional achievements, and this meant the activities of staff physicians. The ethics committee decided that this was a transgression of medical ethics, because a nonhospital doctor would clearly be charged with such a violation if he permitted the "glorification" of his own work in the public press (*Boston Medical and Surgical Journal* 198 [1928]: 975).

23. Massachusetts General Hospital, *113th Annual Report, 1926*, pp. 16-71; *114th Annual Report, 1927*, pp. 5-6.

24. Massachusetts General Hospital Trustees Mss Records, 17 April 1914; Massachusetts General Hospital, *106th Annual Report, 1919A*, p. 24; *107th Annual Report, 1920*, pp. 8-9, 20; *108th Annual Report, 1921*, pp. 14-16, 24; *113th Annual Report, 1926*, pp. 10-14.

25. *Boston Medical and Surgical Journal* 135 (1896): 614.

26. *St. Elizabeth's Hospital, Brighton, Mass., with an account of the Great Ten Day $200,000 Campaign successfully conducted in its behalf* ([Boston], [1914]), p. 65; St. Elizabeth's Hospital, *Eighth Triennial Report, 1890-1893*, p. 5; Carney Hospital, *Annual Report for 1880-1881*, p. 5; *Boston Medical and Surgical Journal* 149 (1903): 608; *Boston Globe*, 5 August 1902.

27. William A. Glaser, *Social Settings and Medical Organization: A Cross-National Study of the Hospital* (New York, 1970), pp. 32-35.

28. *Boston Evening Transcript*, 10 September 1883, 21 July 1888; Woods, ed., *Americans in Process*, pp. 337, 348-49.

29. *Boston Evening Transcript*, 10 December 1874; Robert H. Lord, John E. Sexton, and Edward T. Harrington, *History of the Archdiocese of Boston*, 3 vols. (New York, 1944), 3:380.

30. St. Elizabeth's Hospital, *Great Ten Day Campaign*, pp. 14-16; Donna Merwick, *Boston Priests, 1848-1910: A Study of Social and Intellectual Change* (Cambridge, Mass., 1973), pp. 3, 159-69; *Boston Medical and Surgical Journal* 187 (1922): 460; 162 (1910): 692-93.

31. Carney Hospital, *Annual Report for 1894*, pp. 9-10; *Annual Report for 1897*, p. 38; *Annual Report for 1916*, p. 81; *Boston Medical and Surgical Journal* 163 (1910): 812.

32. *Boston Medical and Surgical Journal* 165 (1911): 535; Boston City Hospital Trustees Mss Records, 27 October 1911, 1 April 1912.

33. *Boston Globe*, 5 August 1902; Mt. Sinai Hospital, *10th Annual Report, 1911*, unpaginated.

34. Hyman Morrison, "A Study of Fifty-one Cases of Debility in Jewish Patients: From the Out-Patient Department, Massachusetts General Hospital," *Boston Medical and Surgical Journal* 157 (1907): 816-19.

35. *Boston Medical and Surgical Journal* 145 (1901): 503; Mt. Sinai Hospital, *7th Annual Report, 1908*, unpaginated; *10th Annual Report, 1911*, unpaginated; *Annual Report for 1912*, pp. 8-9; *Annual Report for 1913*, pp. 10-11; *Annual Report for 1914*, p. 8; Herman Dana, *The Early Days of the Beth Israel Hospital, 1911-1920* (n.p., 1950), pp. 6-7; Charles F. Wilinsky, "Beth Israel Hospital: Symbol of Service," in *Fifty Years of Jewish Philanthropy in Greater Boston, 1895-1945* (Boston, 1945), p. 33.

36. Dana, *Early Days*, pp. 6-8, 11, 13; Barbara Miller Solomon, *Pioneers in Service: The History of the Associated Jewish Philanthropies of Boston* (Boston, 1956), pp. 84-85; *Boston Medical and Surgical Journal* 173 (1915): 630; 176 (1917): 329; Albert Ehrenfried, *A Chronicle of Boston Jewry from Colonial Settlement to 1900* (n.p., [1963]), pp. 753-54; Mt. Sinai Hospital, *7th Annual Report, 1908*, unpaginated; Beth Israel Hospital, Directors Typescript Minutes, 28 December 1921.

37. Interviews with Mrs. Nehemiah H. Whitman, 24 May 1971, Brookline, Mass.; Dr. Jacob Fine, 25 May 1971, Boston; Mrs. Abraham E. Pinanski, 3 June 1971, Brookline; Beth Israel Hospital, Directors Typescript Minutes, 10 May, 14 June, 12 December 1920, 10, 21, January 1921, 28 January, 9 April, 11 June, 12 November, 12 December 1923; Beth Israel Hospital, Report of the Committee on Scope and Plans, Directors Typescript Minutes, 30 March 1922; Ben Rosen, *The Trend of Jewish Population in Boston* (Boston, 1921), p. 11.

38. Interviews with Whitman, Pinanski, and Dr. Herman Blumgart (2 June 1971, Boston); Herman Blumgart, "Address to Beth Israel Alumni Meeting, November 1969," draft at Beth Israel Hospital, Boston.

39. St. Elizabeth's Hospital, *Great Ten Day Campaign*, p. 65.

## Epilogue

1. Renée C. Fox, "The Medicalization and Demedicalization of American Society," *Doing Better and Feeling Worse: Health in the United States, Daedalus* 106, no. 1 (Winter 1977): 9-22; John H. Knowles, "The Responsibility of the Individual," ibid., pp. 57-80; Ivan Illich, *Medical Nemesis*.

2. Edmund D. Pellegrino, "The Sociocultural Impact of Twentieth Century Therapeutics," in Vogel and Rosenberg, eds., *The Therapeutic Revolution*, pp. 245-66; Charles E. Rosenberg,

"The Therapeutic Revolution," pp. 3-25; Stanley Joel Reiser, *Medicine and the Reign of Technology* (Cambridge, 1978), pp. 23-68, 122-57.

3. Oliver Wendell Holmes, "Medicine in Boston," 4:549.

# Index

Abbot, Samuel, 33, 35
Abortion, 102
Accidents, 47; industrial, 5, 7-8; railroad and street railway, 9-10, 43, 138 n.18; street, 9
Alcohol, patients and, 34, 40, 43-44, 70
Ambulance, 9, 52, 146 n.88
American Hospital Association, 65, 100
Ames, F. L., 16
Amory, Thomas C., Jr., 9, 29, 35-37
Anaesthesia, 79-80
Antisepsis, 2, 60-61, 66
Apartment houses, 99-101
Appendicitis, 61-62
Appleton, Nathan, 5
Asepsis, 2, 60-61, 65
Associated Charities, Boston, 40, 90, 98
Association of Hospital Superintendents. See American Hospital Association
Autopsies, 76, 94

Baby farms, 12-13
Bachelor apartments, 98
Back Bay, 7, 42, 100, 103, 113
Baker, William H., 19
Balboni, Gerrado, 126
Beach, Henry H. A., 69, 108
Beacon Hill, 7, 101, 103
Beth Israel Hospital, 130-31
Bigelow, Henry J., 17-19, 107
Bigelow, William Sturgis, 78
Boardinghouses, 98, 102, 113
Boothby Surgical Hospital, 103
Boston, Board of Health, 8
Boston, central district, 7, 47-49, 57
Boston Almshouse, 18
Boston and Maine Railroad, 124
Boston City Hospital: admissions to, 9, 35, 36, 118-19; charges for workmen's compensation cases by, 121-22; city politics and, 30-32, 42-46, 57-58, 120, 127; control of admissions at, 68-69; dedication of, 9, 35; discipline in, 44-45; exclusion of patients from, 38, 41-43; founding of, 32-35, 52; incorporation of, 29-31; Jewish

patients at, 129; length of patients' stays at, 74; patients' records at, available to employers, 42-43; private patients at, 106, 109-10; specialty services at, 40, 88-89, 92; staff appointments at, 30, 46, 81-82, 86
Boston Dispensary, 18; consultation clinic at, 95; control of admissions at, 67-68; syphilis clinic at, 70
Boston Lying-in, 52; admissions to, 11, 13, 116-17; deaths at, 76-77; Richardson House, 116-17
Boston Manufacturing Company, 6
Boston Medical Association, fee table of, 70, 106
Boston Medical Society, 93
Boston Public Library, 31
Bowditch, Henry P., 82-84, 104
Bradley, John T., 29
Brahmins, 5-6, 7, 15-17, 30, 125
Branch hospitals, 56-57
Brigham, Peter Bent, 81, 82. See also Peter Bent Brigham Hospital
"Brigham Hospital of Harvard University," 85
Brookline, 57, 103, 104
Brophy, Thomas C., 30-31
Brown, Francis H., 16, 19, 25

Cabot, Arthur Tracy, 48
Cabot, Richard C., 22, 93-95, 121
Cabot, Samuel, 5, 9, 22; family of, 124
Cabot Case Records, 94
Caesarian section, 116-17
Cambridge, 97, 103
Cambridge Hospital, 97
Carney Hospital, 25, 61, 86, 103, 127-29; medical care at, 73-74; staff appointments at, 22, 128
Central Labor Union, Boston, 45, 50
*Charities and the Commons*, 100
Charity abuse, 89-92, 95, 110-111
Charlestown, 7, 52
Cheever, David, 29-30, 49, 57-58, 127; lectures on syphilis by, 71